INTERNATIONAL PUBLIC DEBATE
IPDA TEXTBOOK

EDITOR: PATRICK G. RICHEY

**Previous Co-Editor of this Edition:
Web Drake, PhD**

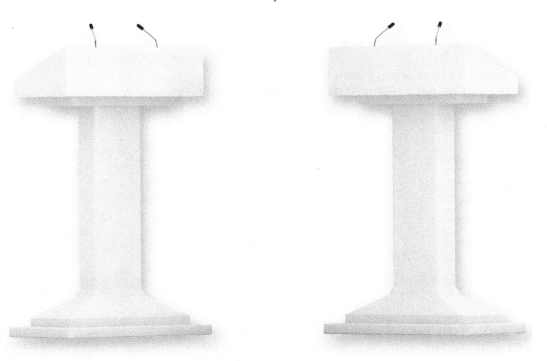

Podium cover image © Shutterstock.com
IPDA logo: Reprinted by permission of the International Public Debate Association.

Kendall Hunt
publishing company

www.kendallhunt.com
Send all inquiries to:
4050 Westmark Drive
Dubuque, IA 52004-1840

Copyright © 2016 by Kendall Hunt Publishing Company

ISBN 978-1-5249-0302-2

All rights reserved. No part of this publication may be reproduced,
stored in a retrieval system, or transmitted, in any form or by any means,
electronic, mechanical, photocopying, recording, or otherwise,
without the prior written permission of the copyright owner.

Printed in the United States of America
10 9 8 7 6 5 4 3 2 1

Contents

Foreword v

Acknowledgments ix

PART 1   Theoretical Underpinnings...1

Chapter 1   The International Public Debate Association: A Brief History - Alan Cirlin...3

Debate in Society (Beyond the Borders) - Shane Puckett............................13

Chapter 2   IPDA and Academic Debate: Honing Necessary Life Skills -
Bennett Strange and Cole Franklin 17

Chapter 3   Ethics and IPDA - Patrick Richey..27

Ethics Sidebar - Lauren Raynor 38

PART 2   Persuasion 39

Chapter 4   Modern Persuasion Theories and Debate - Merle Ziegler 41

Modern Persuasion Sidebar - Shane Puckett 50

Chapter 5   Ethos: The Strongest Proof of All - Cole Franklin 55

Chapter 6   Pathos: Emotional Appeals in IPDA Debate - Michael Ingram..................59

Pathos Sidebar - Lauren Raynor 69

Chapter 7   Logos in IPDA Debate - Keith Milstead 71

PART 3   Public Debate 83

Chapter 8   Striking in IPDA Debate - Dale Sikkema and Patrick Richey...................85

Chapter 9   Evidence in IPDA Debate - Jeffery Dale Hobbs, Jodee Hobbs,
and Piengpen Na Pattalung 93

Chapter 10   Audience Analysis - Adam Key 103

Chapter 11   The Affirmative Case - Robert Alexander 121

Chapter 12   The Negative Case - Christopher Duerringer 141

Preparing for Battle: Negative Sidebar - Anthony McMullen 148

Chapter 13   Cross-Examination - Robert Alexander...151

Whose Cross-Examination Is This Anyway? - Anthony McMullen.............164

iii

Foreword

This foreword has been provided by IPDA President Keith Milstead and Executive Secretary Web Drake in an effort to synthesize and define the true spirit of the International Public Debate Association and to provide this text with a vision for what the organization was, is, and should be.

First, thank you for taking the opportunity to utilize this text in your classroom or for instruction of your competitive program. It has always been the desire for our organization and its competition to provide an open forum where students and the community as a whole can partake in a real exchange of ideas and to allow public debate to flourish on our campuses. In order for this vision to remain and endure, two ideals help IPDA to distinguish itself from other brands of debate.

At the core of IPDA is the use and inclusivity of the "lay" judge. This is perhaps the most aggravating for debate purists who witness our competitions after being exposed to other formats and norms. Yet, nearly all of those very formats were intended to provide a similar atmosphere whereby persuasion, oratory, and understandability were at a premium. What caused the evolution of those formats was essentially the ballot. When trained judges and coaches are the predominant decision makers for winning and losing, those traits often become a lost art. This is not to say that scholars are unworthy to decide rounds; on the contrary, they simply come to expect a style, delivery, and vocabulary that few outside of a debate community can appreciate. If we want public debate to remain public and based on rhetoric and persuasion, geared toward a "real world" audience, and if we are charged with preparing our students to succeed in any field, we must continue to adhere to the principle that debaters must be judged by lay judges.

Secondly, the use of evidence within competitive rounds has provided an equally contentious concern among some debate scholars. It is strictly forbidden to produce printed evidence in a debate round as per IPDA rules. This means that debaters may refer to their handwritten notes and cite sources for support of argumentation, but may not physically have the article or evidence in a round. The purpose of this rule was, at its foundation, to make the debate predominantly about the exchange of ideas and argumentation rather than simply a reading of evidence in the debate. It is our hope that IPDA debate continues to utilize supporting materials as just that, supporting materials. Good persuaders will, at times, need evidentiary substantiation in order to make their claims. However, it is imperative that evidence not be the sole deciding factor in our debates. This is what keeps our format unique and retains the persuasive priority on ideas, rhetoric, and delivery.

It is the very combination of these two principles that provide the pillars for IPDA. So long as our debaters are trained in the art of persuasion and the importance is placed on the very tenets of Aristotle's proofs, this format can and will be true to its roots. We can continue to provide an environment that excels in career readiness for our students, as well as a training ground for real oratory and critical thinking.

Contributed by Keith Milstead and Web Drake. Copyright © Kendall Hunt Publishing Company.

In addition to these principles, which have guided IPDA since its inception, the following excerpt was taken from "A Call to Statesmanship" by Dr. Web Drake, Executive Secretary of IPDA to help establish a vision for its future:

The format of the International Public Debate Association teaches its competitors to be good. It teaches them clarity, critical thinking, and persuasion. I could go as far as to say that it teaches them manners, presentation, and hygiene.

But the argument that I find myself unable to make, the argument that I most desire to make, is that IPDA teaches statesmanship, that it teaches true rhetoric. That it enables our students to learn and to practice public address at its highest level. The level reached so rarely in "real" life, but the level reached for by all who would demand an audience. The level reached by Lincoln, by Roosevelt, and by Reagan. The level missed so famously by both Bushes, by Clinton, by Nixon. The level of the Gettysburg Address, the Challenger Address, the Day of Infamy Address.

And, of course, this problem is far from unique to IPDA. Public speaking teachers, corporate consultants, professional speech-writers, and every debate organization ever formed have all, at least at some level, grappled with this very issue. How is IPDA to be any different? Are we to teach the wind-up oratory of collegiate individual events? Are we to succumb to the logic-only oratory of Parliamentary and Cross-Examination debate? Or are we to continue to be appeased at the stumble-bum, ho-hum rhetoric of most of our own competitors?

I say we can do more! I say we can raise the level of statesmanship expected and practiced in our classrooms and at our tournaments. I say we can and should aim higher! In certain circles, Public Debate is derided as value debate dedicated to the inane, concerned more with the frosting than the cake. I say IPDA is in the perfect position—historically, culturally, and institutionally—to practice and to teach more than "college forensics." I say IPDA can and should be a vehicle to produce true rhetors, statesmen (for lack of a more gender-neutral term) able to move mountains with the sound of their voice, to inspire action in the masses, to change the very course of history with the force of their logic.

Which all sounds wonderful in the abstract, but how do we do it? How do we succeed where others have failed so dramatically? How do we achieve what our textbooks never even dare to dream? How do we systematize that which many would argue is fleeting? How do we dare to expect that which is an exception to the rule?

We do so like true scholars. By identifying it, by analyzing it, and by synthesizing it. In my experience, true rhetoric, true statesmanship, address that inspires and moves, speeches that transcend time and place, have five common characteristics: content that matters, logic that works, passion that moves, values that transcend, and a rhetor who cares. Anything short of that dishonors the memories of great orators from Demosthenes to Barbara Jordan and Edmund Burke to William Jennings Bryan. It also fails to realize the dreams of Alan Cirlin and Jack Rogers. And perhaps most importantly, it sells shorts the potential of those yet-unnamed students who are to pass through our teams, our rounds, and our lives in the years to come.

There is no weapon more dangerous, no tool more useful, no force more powerful than the spoken word. We must teach it with care and yield it with precision. The challenge is ours for the taking. The world awaits.

Many great orators have partaken in an IPDA event, and many more have learned invaluable skills that have translated into their careers. It is up to us as educators, students, and competitors to embrace public debate for what it is, and more importantly for what it can be: a difference-maker on our campuses and in our communities. May this text aid in your endeavor to make that difference one argument at a time.

Acknowledgments

The second edition has been a work in progress for many years and could never have been published without the steadfast loyalty of IPDA and its members. Thank you to each contributor for your patience and for writing your respective chapters. A special thank you to the IPDA executive committee: Web Drake, Mary Jarzabeck, and Keith Milstead, as well as the IPDA governing board. Thank you to assistant editor Web Drake for getting the ball rolling on the second edition. Finally, but not least, thank you to the founders of IPDA—Alan Cirlin and Jack Rodgers. Without your vision, IPDA would never have happened.

Patrick G. Richey, PhD – Editor

May 2016

PART 1
Theoretical Underpinnings

Chapter 1	The International Public Debate Association: A Brief History - Alan Cirlin	1
	Debate in Society (Beyond the Borders) - Shane Puckett	13
Chapter 2	IPDA and Academic Debate: Honing Necessary Life Skills - Bennett Strange & Cole Franklin	17
Chapter 3	Ethics and IPDA - Patrick Richey	27
	Ethics Sidebar - Lauren Raynor	38

Chapter 1

The International Public Debate Association: A Brief History

Alan Cirlin, PhD
St. Mary's University

You readers who have come to these pages are almost certainly supporters of the public debate (PD) format and of the International Public Debate Association. As supporters, you very likely wish the format well and hope it will maintain its integrity. And it would just as likely grieve you to see public debate degenerate into yet another high-speed, motor-mouthing, jargon-riddled, non-rhetorical exercise. Which is to say, you would hate to see IPDA follow the same path and reach the same end as CEDA.

In 1971, when Jack Howe assembled his elite group of like-thinking coaches and launched the Cross Examination Debate Association (CEDA), I'm sure they all had high hopes and aspirations for the new association. And why shouldn't they? In theory, everything looked rosy. They had started with a common philosophy: to create an extracurricular activity which would promote an audience-friendly, rhetorical style of debate. They had a clear list of reasons why they did not like the National Debate Tournament (NDT)-style debate. And they had an equally clear vision of what they wanted CEDA-style debate to look like.

These coaches also had a number of innovations which they believed would ensure that CEDA would live up to their stylistic expectations. These innovations included:

Adding cross-examination to the format—to help ensure a direct clash of ideas and to theoretically limit the number of issues which would be raised in a debate
Using value topics, rather than policy, topics—to eliminate policy arguments which would theoretically cut the number of issues raised in a debate in half
Announcing the new topic late in the summer—to reduce the advantage of big, resource-rich programs that could spend all summer gathering evidence

Contributed by Alan Cirlin. Copyright © Kendall Hunt Publishing Company

Changing debate topics mid-season—to discourage the compilation of huge evidence files and to provide a more level playing field for smaller programs

Emphasizing the CEDA philosophy and its use in training and coaching—to encourage quality communication and discourage excesses of speed, jargon, rudeness, etc.

In theory, at least, these coaches started out with lots of advantages. But what I believe these coaches lacked was a sufficient understanding of the factors and forces which had created the NDT debate style. And they especially lacked an appreciation of the importance of governance in the ability of their new association to 'stay the course' with their innovative ideas.

The result was that within a very few years of the founding of CEDA, numerous cracks began to appear in the foundation of the association. By the 15th year, these cracks had become so large and troublesome that Dr. Howe wrote his famous piece, "CEDA's Objectives: Lest We Forget."[i] And by the 25th year, the 1996-97 season, the experiment imploded. CEDA agreed to share one joint, season-long topic with NDT. At this point, CEDA-style debate, for all intents and purposes, ceased to exist and CEDA had effectively reintegrated with NDT.

What had happened to CEDA? What had gone wrong? More importantly, is IPDA in danger of following the same path? If so, can this be prevented? And, if so, how can it be prevented?

Let me first provide, in a very basic, simplified form, the answers to these questions. Then I'll provide the background behind and my justification for those answers. Next, I'll present an abridged example of what I mean by debate research. And finally, I will offer some practical advice on how IPDA can maintain its integrity and avoid being gradually morphed into an NDT-like activity.

It seemed like a good idea at the time.

Vin Tanner (Steve McQueen) in "The Magnificent Seven"

Explaining why a man suddenly took all his clothes off and jumped into a mess of cactus

What happened to CEDA? I was able to answer this in detail in some of my convention papers and publications.[ii] So I won't repeat all that analysis here. Let me just say that the problem was not that the founders of CEDA forgot their objectives. The problem was that they lost control of their own association and could no longer maintain those objectives. In some ways they were victims of their own success. NDT programs jumped ship and joined CEDA in ever increasing numbers. They gradually took over the association. And then, just as gradually, they voted in a whole set of changes (improvements in the minds of the newcomers). The result was an NDT look-alike activity.

What went wrong? CEDA was popular and grew. At first it only attracted programs that agreed with the CEDA philosophy. But this cut down on the number of programs still entering NDT tournaments. Smaller, more marginal, NDT tournaments folded. That meant less cannon-fodder for the big boys and fewer NDT tournaments. All of which accelerated the exodus. It wasn't long before some of the smaller NDT programs started doing CEDA debate even though they disagreed with the CEDA philosophy. They came because of simple economics—they couldn't afford to attend enough NDT tournaments to make a decent season. So they trickled in and then flooded into CEDA bringing their debate philosophy, judges, and NDT-trained debaters with them. They suggested NDT-like rule changes to improve things. At first these changes were voted down. But the number of NDT-like coaches kept going up and soon they could outvote the CEDA philosophy coaches. As CEDA became more NDT-like, even more NDT programs jumped ship, or they at least started adding CEDA tournaments to their schedule. These NDT-like coaches in CEDA were eventually able to vote themselves into positions of leadership. This was a classic, true-life example of a slippery slope. Within 15 years, Jack Howe clearly saw the end approaching. He may have had an idea of what needed to be done to stop it, but he no longer had the power. Ten years later, CEDA was dead.

Is IPDA in danger of following the same path? Unfortunately, yes. IPDA was designed with the conscious intention of NOT being subject to the vulnerabilities of CEDA. I had conducted a good deal of research in the 1980s trying to identify those vulnerabilities and found they mostly involved governance.[iii] The PD format guaranteed a high-quality style of debate, as long as the rules and procedures remained intact. The rules and procedures remained intact as long as proposed changes were carefully vetted and pretested to ensure that only those with a high probability of having a positive influence got through. The positive vetting process remained intact as long as the top dogs subscribed to the basic IPDA philosophy AND they had the power to block questionable changes. It will remain intact if the small (3-person), self-perpetuating executive committee, who can serve indefinitely and choose their own successors, do the following: (1) stay true to their mission, (2) refuse to allow themselves to be pressured, guilted, double-talked, confused, etc. into letting questionable changes modify the system, and (3) be scrupulously careful in selecting their successors. The danger to IPDA will come from unwise or even random changes in the rules and/or a breakdown in the governance system.

Can the deterioration of IPDA be prevented? Of course. Ask yourself, would CEDA be better off today if there had NEVER been any rule changes at all? Some changes may have been very helpful or even necessary. But you supporters of the original CEDA philosophy out there: would you prefer to have a small, marginally popular, heavily criticized debate association which was true to its original mission, or the large and impressive CEDA-NDT structure as it exists today?

How can the deterioration of IPDA be prevented? Keep up the pressure on the officers of IPDA NOT to give in to pressure and not to value the popularity or size of the association over the quality and integrity of the activity. Remember that no change is far preferable to negative change. And if there is any credible doubt about the wisdom of a proposed 'improvement,' just say no. Demand that suggestions be pretested and empirical proof provided to show that proposals really work, before they are seriously discussed. Be sure to always place an emphasis on research and proof over intuition and what may, at the time, seem to be an obvious truth. Remember that at various points in history, the ideas that the Earth was the unmoving center of the universe, the Earth was flat, diseases could be cured by bloodletting, humans could never travel at more than 35 miles per hour, humans could never fly, humans could never go to the moon, etc. were all considered obvious truths. Just because an idea sounds reasonable and lots of folks believe it, don't make it necessarily so.

You can't reach old age by another man's road.

Mark Twain

We are all unique. Everyone has something in common with you, but no one has everything in common with you. Your path through life may start out being set by others, the adults who raised you, the culture in which you grew up, your friends, and your aggregate life experiences. Following that path, you accumulate a wealth of information which becomes a cognitive amalgam that serves as the bedrock of your beliefs, attitudes, values, and aspirations. But the aspirations you develop can take on a life of their own and often alter your path through life. Not every aspiration will do so, but some of them will for sure.

My decision to earn a PhD may have been inspired by other individuals, but once it became a personal goal, my life was set on a radically different path from where it had been going. The brief history which follows traces the intellectual path in my life that led to the creation of IPDA. And this is the heart of this chapter.

This history is important to our discussion because it documents the way in which public debate was created. It was intentionally researched and engineered to virtually require debaters adopt an audience-friendly, high ethos, and rhetorical speaking style in order to win. Public debate is, to the best of my knowledge, the only debate format in history which was purposefully designed, the design based on extensive research. It was intentionally engineered with specific rhetorical goals in mind. And many variations of the format were extensively pretested to discover which specific format worked best.

All of this helped me to understand the stylistic effects of format changes and to have confidence in the final version of the activity. And let me stress that given my path through life, my initial goal was merely to discover a debate format that would lead to an oratorical style of debate. The goal of launching a debate association to promote and protect such a new format didn't even enter my mind until years later.

The history of IPDA has been detailed elsewhere.[iv] So I'll try not to simply repeat that history here, but rather to annotate it showing how debate research crept into the equation and eventually underpinned and shaped the whole IPDA experiment.

Let me also stress that while I spent years informally accumulating experiences, materials, and ideas, I did not, at first, study debating styles in any systematic way. High school debate, in southern California, in the late 1960s, was a kind of junior, junior version of NDT. It was subject to all of the stylistic abuses of NDT, but in a relatively minor form. And like most students, I emulated whatever seemed to be winning without thinking critically about what I was doing.

In the fall of 1971, I started Junior college, at almost the same time that CEDA was being launched. And even though I lived in the heart of CEDA country, I didn't hear of it until I entered graduate school years later. Two years of junior college debate. Two years of Lincoln-Douglas debate at UCLA. Two years of working. Then in the fall of 1976, back to graduate school as an assistant coach. I was at CSUN which, at the time, was a major CEDA power. Having come from an NDT tradition, I was very skeptical when I first heard of CEDA. But I soon became an ardent supporter. It seemed to be a quantum improvement over the NDT style of debate.

I still wasn't researching debate in any systematic way, but I had developed some intellectual curiosity in NDT versus CEDA. My biggest aspiration when I began working on my M.A. was to become a Junior College debate coach. But my exposure to CEDA got me wondering. What made NDT so bad stylistically? And why was CEDA so much better? I felt like I'd need to know the answer when I became a coach. So as I followed this path, I gathered and kept better track of the materials and ideas which came my way. I had lengthy discussions with competitors, judges, coaches, etc. on the subject. I did a lot of reading of journal and convention articles which various folks brought to my attention. By the time

I left CSUN, I had a large, but rather random, collection of ideas and information and a shaky set of poorly supported opinions on the subject. When I eventually became better informed I ended up rejecting most of those opinions.

During my second and final year at CSUN, I was talked into applying to a few PhD programs by my mentor, William Freeman. Earning a PhD had never been an aspiration of mine, but I thought, 'Why not put in some applications? What have I got to lose?' I ended up at the University of Iowa for three years where I volunteered as an assistant debate coach for the Director of Forensic (DOF), Bob Kemp. His was a quintessential NDT program. I don't remember anyone ever even talking about CEDA. And at that time, I was far too busy working on my degree to worry about style and format in debate. But I did learn about parliamentary debate as practiced by the Canadian and East Coast student-run leagues.

The parliamentary debate leagues allowed graduate student entries. So as a reward for almost three years of volunteering, Dr. Kemp sent a freshman debater and me to participate in a Chicago tournament. It was a wonderful, mind-expanding experience. Stylistically, parliamentary debate was far better even than CEDA. The topics were impromptu. The ambiance was light. Their funding was tight, so most of the rounds were judged by debaters who weren't participating at that tournament. Debaters would often trade-off, participating at some tournaments and judging at others. Many of my ideas concerning format, lay judges, impromptu topics, and allowing completely open entries would grow out of this experience.

In the fall of 1981, degree in hand, I began my first teaching/coaching job at the University of Richmond. CEDA was beginning its 11th season and was just gaining ground on the East Coast at that time. There seemed to be sufficient tournaments to sustain our program so UR became a CEDA school. There were also a handful of parliamentary debate tournaments within striking distance, so we did a bit of parliamentary debate on the side both for fun and for training in effective communication.

If you think education is expensive, try ignorance.

Most commonly attributed to Derek Bok

1981 was also the year I discovered that an assistant professor was expected to do research and publish. So this was the year when I began to study a few select topics including the NDT versus CEDA question. And this was the season when I finally began to study it in a systematic way. It took a year before I could formulate my research objectives clearly enough that even I could understand them.

During my time at UR, I began to conceive of a debate format that might combine the best elements of CEDA, parliamentary debate, and Toastmasters International[v]—a format that would promote serious debate but which could also be fun; a format that would be as open to participation as Toastmasters, as opposed to only allowing undergraduate students to play. I had no clue at the time what the rules of this format might be, but I had a hazy vision and some new aspirations. So more by trial and error, than by design, I began to experiment with a very primitive version of what would eventually become the public debate format. I combined elements of CEDA, parliamentary debate, impromptu, and extemporaneous speaking and a hodge-podge of other sources and used this as a classroom activity. I later introduced it as an experimental tournament event. I would eventually become very systematic at varying elements of this format and pretesting them using a variety of volunteers.

I've presented this brief history not to show how smart I was at the time, but rather how dumb. I had a head full of miscellaneous facts and quotations, and I was developing a vague set of research questions and goals, but I was still lacking even a basic understanding of the dynamics of a debate format. How did a format work to influence debating style? How would altering the format affect the outcome? Most importantly, I had very anemic understanding of the relationships among coaching, judging, and debating styles. And even worse, I was totally ignorant of the critical importance of governance in holding everything else together.

So for three years at UR, I spent a great deal of scholarly effort researching debate formats and debating style. But I didn't feel ready or competent to publish anything about it for a long time. During these three years, I presented two convention papers and had three publications but none of them involved academic debate.

1985 was the year Jack Howe published "CEDA's Objectives: Lest We Forget." By now I knew something was seriously wrong with CEDA and I began to suspect this had as much to do with the way the association had been governed than with some fatal flaws in the format. I was now at an Indiana University satellite campus. There was no debate program so I had a lot more time and energy to research and publish. I was there for four seasons (1984–88). In those four years, I had seven publications and presented ten professional papers at conferences and conventions. Of these, four publications and three to five of the papers (depending on how you count) were about debate.

When I became DOF at St. Mary's University in 1988, I almost immediately started working on my pet debate format project. Within a year, I was experimenting with formats using my students as guinea pigs. Within two years, I got my summer debate institute students involved and added what I called at the time parliamentary debate, but which grew to become known as public debate.[vi]

There were several years of continued study, experimentation, research, and tinkering. The event became hugely successful as an experimental event at St. Mary's big tournament in the fall. And then there was IPDA. Trey Gibson should get the credit for that. In the fall of 1996, Jack Rogers was hosting a development conference as part of UT-Tyler's fall tournament. I was presenting a paper on the status of the PD experimental format. It was Trey who got all excited about my report and suddenly, HIS hand went up and he proposed we form a new debate association around the new format.

As I recall Jack and I looked at each other almost immediately and shot each other expressions which basically said, "no way." And that might have been that. But Trey wouldn't let it go. He got the audience (consisting mostly of coaches, grad students, and top flight debaters) all fired up about the idea. Many of them had participated in, or at least seen, the format at a St. Mary's tournament. By the end of that evening, everyone was acting like this was a done deal and the next year 1997-98 would be season one of the "Public Debate Association." Everyone left smiling. And the next morning, Jack and I looked at each other like two drunkards who just woke up in a gutter. We discussed it. "What have we done?" "What have we committed ourselves to?" "Are we really going to do this thing?" "Does the world really need another debate association?"

But Trey's ardor had not diminished one bit and he had several other coaches chomping at the bit. So Jack and I said, "OK, we'll give it a shot," but we privately agreed we were going to bail as soon as things got too dicey—no bad feelings, no recriminations, just drop the whole project and exit stage left.

I spent that spring pulling everything I thought I knew about debate styles, the evolution of NDT, and devolution of CEDA, debate formats, and the interconnection of all these elements, and pulled them together into the outline of a new debate association. I produced all of the draft documents we would need including a new ballot, a lay judge's instruction sheet, a governance structure, etc.

That summer Jack and I called for a "development conference" and sent out invitations to all interested individuals. Jack and I were the only ones who showed up. We ended up holding our development conference in his hotel room overlooking the Alamo. That was quite symbolic actually. Were we setting up our own massacre?

Jack talked me into a few changes and I talked him into accepting a few of my innovations which he found troubling. Most notably I recall we spent a lot of time going back and forth over the "self-perpetuating" executive board. But this was one element I knew would be critical to the long-term success of the new association. I felt the PDA wouldn't thrive or even survive without it. I pulled out my research on governance and CEDA. I cajoled, persuaded, pleaded. Eventually, I think perhaps mostly to shut me up, Jack agreed to at least give it a try.[vii]

And the rest is history.

So the public debate format is solidly grounded in actual research. All of the elements of public debate, including the rules, procedures, and forms are interactive. They are also synergistic. It is together that they make public debate what it has become. Changes should not, therefore, be made lightly. Changes should be properly tested and evidence that the change will work as intended without unhappy side effects gathered BEFORE any changes are approved. And changes should be beta-tested, if possible, to assess their impact before they are implemented throughout the whole system.

CASCADING CHANGES

The road to hell is paved with good intentions.

Ancient Aphorism attributed, in different forms, to a number of early religious figures

Perhaps the most critical lesson I learned in my years of studying debate is that, quite literally, all of the elements in a debate association are interconnected. Format, time limits, prep time, judging philosophies, debate ballots, topics, geography, budget, and of course governance. All these elements eventually come into a dynamic equilibrium. Once they do, the system becomes, to a degree, self-correcting. But change anything and you can get a cascading series of other changes.

Here's a real-world example from the first season of IPDA. This illustrates not only the interconnectedness of debate elements, but also the problem of un-researched changes which seemed like a good idea at the time.

It was the championship tournament, season one. We were holding one of the first official meetings of the new debate association. The constitution had been approved. Jack had been confirmed as President and I as Executive Secretary. The foundation had been laid to create a nine-member governing board (advisory committee).

Everything looked great!

And then an enthusiastic hand, connected to a familiar and very sincere face, was raised. The voice which came from that face proposed we change the time limits in the rebuttal

10 • *IPDA Textbook*

speeches from 4-2-6-2 - 3-4-3 to 4-2-6-2 - 4-4-2. Why? To allow the affirmative sufficient time to cover all of the negative arguments in the first rebuttal. This may have sounded as reasonable to the IPDA members in that room, as hearing the earth is flat had once sounded to a medieval audience.

The problem was that the gentleman who offered the proposal had no supporting evidence. It just seemed to him, off the top of his head, to be a good idea.[viii]

I, on the other hand, cringed because we had specifically experimented with rebuttal time limits two years before. We had tried 4-4-2 a number of times and found it wanting. In fact, we tried 3-4-3 as a deliberate fix for the problems associated with 4-4-2. And what were those problems?

The 4-4-2 format left First Affirmatives Rebuttals (1ARs) feeling that they could cover the negative constructive point by point. So they speeded up and became more CEDA/NDT like in style. This caused the negative rebuttal to speed up in kind. And the final affirmative rebuttal was often a mess as a result. (Note: These were the tendencies—the effect 'on average.' The actual effects varied by debater, topic, and round.) But we didn't like the effect, so we tried to engineer a fix.

The 3-4-3 variation was intentionally designed to make 1ARs feel they could NOT cover a good negative constructive point by point and they therefore had to synthesize and simplify arguments. Knowing they would have a three-minute final rebuttal to respond to the four-minute negative rebuttal gave them confidence in presenting and supporting their first rebuttal positions.

We pretested these and other variations many times and, in practice rounds, were able to interview many of the participants afterwards. In this way, we were able to verify what they were thinking.

In addition to these immediate changes in speaker style, there were a set of cascading effects as well. One effect was that the most experienced speakers who were using the point-by-point refutation started pressing even harder for 'more qualified' judges who could and would follow their point-by-point analyses. I hope you can see where this road eventually leads. From here all kinds of problems are possible. The call for judge training; a change in the economics of participating in IPDA if a program had to pay for "qualified" judges; a change in how teams spent practice time. Would speed drills come back for rebuttal speeches? Motor-mouthing? Clump and Dump arguments?

Going from 3-4-3 to 4-4-2 in rebuttals may not guarantee such serious problems, but it certainly pushed everything in that direction.

I've only been able to follow IPDA sporadically over the past decade, but I'm told that stylistically while the format is holding its own, it is also slowly creeping toward a more CEDA/NDT style. And this at almost the same rate at which the 'quality' of judges is improving (in the opinion of the top competitors). You can now better understand the interconnections.

I do not believe that the public debate format and all of the IPDA rules, procedures, and guidelines which surround that format are perfect, ideal, and should not be questioned or subject to change. I am confident that improvements are possible. BUT, I also do not believe that desirable changes are likely to be found 'off the top' of various heads, no matter how well intentioned they may be.

He who asserts must prove. Let that be the IPDA watchword. Does someone have what they believe is a great idea? Wonderful. But they should test it first. They should generate some data to make their case. And you guardians who will consider and/or vote on and/or approve of any changes, be sure you're convinced before you implement. It's far easier to change than it is to "unchange." You can alter almost any complex system. But it's virtually impossible to restore that system to exactly what it was before the change.

If all this makes sense to you, ask yourself: Do you think the CEDA format was better or worse at its inception or 20 years later? Do you think CEDA might have been better off making zero changes from its starting point? Surely it would not have grown as fast and would not have become so 'popular' so quickly. But from a pedagogical perspective, would it have been a better or a worse activity in its original form, or as it was in, say, 1992?

IPDA's 20th anniversary is only four years off. We aren't falling apart nearly as fast as CEDA did. But, on balance, are the format and the association really improving over time? Is the sum total of the changes that have been adopted causing us to merely drift randomly? Or worse, are these changes causing us to creep ever closer to some CEDA/NDT-like slippery slope?

CONCLUSION

We have met the enemy and they are us.

Pogo (Paraphrased)[ix] – Walt Kelly

The major threat to IPDA is not attack from without, but rather a slow, virtually imperceptible, rot from within. It's very unlikely that IPDA will be subverted from the outside by those who mean it harm; It is far more likely to be undone from within by a whole set of quiet "improvements" that gradually undermine the activity. And the authors of IPDA's destruction will not be hostile enemies determined to destroy an interloper; If IPDA goes the way of CEDA the death march will begin because of the well-meaning, but naïve, 'contributions' of some of its most loyal and active supporters.

That, I believe, is and will continue to be the major threat to IPDA. Well-meaning, unsupported, untested, and very reasonable sounding calls for minor changes to "improve the quality of judging," "bring more consistency to the activity," "raise the profile of the organization," "increase membership," "make the appointment of leaders more democratic," "improve the quality of the education IPDA provides," etc., etc., etc...

So what are my recommendations?

First and foremost, be very skeptical of proposals for change—the burden of proof should always be heavily on those who bring such proposals.

Be especially skeptical of proposals which are offered unexpectedly during an IPDA meeting discussion—a hand connected to a sincere, familiar face suddenly goes up.

Never vote on a proposal at the same meeting where it is proposed—insist on having time to think, study, research, and talk about the idea first.

Demand proof supporting any proposal before a vote, or even a full discussion, is allowed.

Keep in mind that all of the elements of IPDA are tremendously interactive—change anything and a lot of unexpected cascading changes are likely to follow.

Consider having a committee study all of the changes which have been approved over the years—and, if possible, undo any which are not working or causing trouble.

If an idea looks really good, then, if possible, try beta-testing it on a small scale before adopting it wholesale.

Strive for goodness and high quality—do not strive for popularity or size.

Be gentle and polite with one another—try to keep your egos out of it.

And always remember that 'no change' is better than 'a bad change.'

Well, I've said my bit. Now the rest is up to you. Good luck IPDA. May you prosper and faithfully fulfill your mission for years to come.

Chapter 1 Sidebar

Debate in Society
(Beyond the Borders)

Shane Puckett
Louisiana Tech University

When I start to think of **where** I see debate in society, it's amazing all the places that I see it. I remember my first debate coach making me practice a debate skill drill which involved this very idea. My coach at the time thought I needed work on my "flowing" or note-taking ability, so he made me watch the nightly news stories and "flow" them as if I were flowing a debate round. At first I thought this was silly; news anchors do not follow the debate methodology of an affirmative construction, and even if they did, they definitely would not be giving all the parts of the argument needed to "flow" it. But I was wrong. The more I listened to the news, and more specifically to people in general, I began to understand that we speak and craft argument the same way; whether inside or outside an academic competitive debate round.

The debate community might have its special debate speak (jargon), but the arguments are the same. The methods of approaching arguments are the same. If you really listen to what people are saying, you can hear the stock issues, procedural arguments, and even many critiques/kritiks. Let me demonstrate with a current event that's been in the news lately.

As we look to the stock issues within a debate round, we see the affirmative using these arguments to build a case. Stock issues are nothing more than arguments explaining the need for a plan and why it will work. As a model, let's use the Buffett Rule. In 2011, President Obama proposed a tax plan would apply a minimum tax rate of 30 percent on individuals making more than a million dollars a year. This was called the Buffett Rule. The Buffett Rule is named after American investor, Warren Buffett, who publicly stated in early 2011 that he disagreed with rich people, like himself, paying less in federal taxes, as a portion of income, than the middle class, and voiced support for increased income taxes on the wealthy. Both Buffett and Obama argued that the need was to generate more money through taxes for the government to maintain its programs and to balance the budget. Obama spoke of the significance of this change in how it would solve these problems. Proponents of the Buffet Rule were quick to explain the woes of the current system, and justify the change through the results.

This is the standard stock issue paradigm, howbeit quickly glossed over. The opponents of the Buffett Rule used traditional debate attempts to thwart its passing. First there was an attack at the "inherency" level. Essentially, there's no need for the policy, because there's no barrier to prevent this specific action. Simply put, the opponents argued that if Warren Buffett or any other millionaire/billionaire wanted to pay more taxes, then they are free

Contributed by Shane Puckett. Copyright © Kendall Hunt Publishing Company to do so. There is no law that prevents or denies people from paying more taxes to the government if they choose to do so. As for the harms of the status quo that Obama listed (lack of money for government programing and an unbalanced budget), opponents tried to "turn" them. By "turning" them, I mean that the opponents claimed the Buffett Rule would only create more woes for government programing and the budget. They did this by arguing that the massive increase in taxes from this portion of our population, the "job creators," would prevent them from creating more jobs. This in turn would prevent the taxes from being created from the new jobs, as well as the increase in business/economy which could be taxed. The Buffett Rule would stifle growth which would hurt the US more. With the economy doing better, there is more tax revenue and less need for government programing which helps balance the budget.

Opponents also used arguments that looked like "solvency take-outs" and procedural arguments like "topicality." A "solvency take-out" simply says that the proponents do not solve the problems that they are trying to solve with the plan that they are proposing. A "topicality" argument basically explains that the argument or plan that was given doesn't address the real concerns discussed. Opponents of the rule argued that the problem in government is its spending, not its revenue collection. This argument functions on both levels previously explained. The "solvency take-out" is used by explaining that the lack of money for programing and the unbalanced budget is caused by capricious and frivolous spending. Because the problem stems from the spending and not the collection of revenue, the problems would never be solved. On the "topicality" level, this argument tries to shift the discussion toward spending, and away from tax collection. This "preferred focus" argument claims that we shouldn't be talking about methods and policies of tax collection, because that's not the REAL problem. The discussion should be on the spending practices level because this is what needs to be solved.

While rarely do we use "critiques/kritiks" in IPDA, their use in everyday arguments are all around us. A "kritik" argument is an argument of mindset. It claims that the mindset of the policy has greater implications and effects than the solvency of the policy. Simply put, the policy might fix the immediate problem, but it causes more or bigger problems by its implementation. Let's take the above example of the Buffett Rule. While proponents were claiming that the tax increase would help government programing and help balance the budget, the opposition was claiming that the implementation of the tax increase is "class warfare." This isn't an argument that says that the plan won't work, but it says that the mindset of such policies (like the Buffett Rule) is problematic and bad, and due to its very nature creates worse problems.

Whether cliché or rare, all the arguments we use in a debate round are borrowed from the "real world." Debate is an interesting and important activity which affords us the ability to sharpen our edges so that we can see the completeness of arguments and their direction in society. Argument is all around us. If we can't see it, then our effectiveness as communicators and participants in society dwindles. Remember that debate doesn't shape the way we argue, but helps us understand the shape of argument.

Chapter 1: The International Public Debate Association: A Brief History • 15

[i] *Contributions on the Philosophy and Practice of CEDA* [In what was to become the first CEDA Yearbook], D. Brownlee, Ed., 1981, 1–3.

[ii] "*Improving* the Quality of CEDA Debate Through Judging and Evaluation," 1984; "Comments on Ballots: What are We Saying and What are We Really Saying," 1986; "Judging, Evaluation, and the Quality of CEDA Debate," 1986; "Confessions of a Co-Dependent Coach," 1997; "A Public Debate Manifesto," 1998; "A History of the International Public Debate Association," 1999; "Public Debate," 2000; "The International Public Debate Association," (Written with Jack Rogers) 2001; "In Defense of Lay Judges," 2001; and "A Sociological Approach to Improving Style in Academic Debate," 1997.

[iii] Having *finished* the main body of my research on governance in the 1980s, I used a good deal of that material in other research reports (See endnote 2 above). But I did not get around to writing a paper devoted to the subject until the late 1990s: "Serendipity, Synergy, and the Governance of Public Debate," a paper presented at the Public Debate Association National Convention, Tyler, Texas, in 1998. I also presented a follow-up report concerning the strengths and weaknesses of the 'self-perpetuating board' in actual practice: "The Self-Perpetuating Board: A Report and an Assessment," a paper presented at the International Public Debate Association Convention, Ruston, Louisiana, in 2003.

[iv] "A History of the International Public Debate Association," posted on the IPDA web site, <http://IPDA.anadas.com/History>, 1999. [This site no longer exists, but copies are still available from the author.] See also, "The International Public Debate Association: Background and Philosophy," (written with Jack Rogers), a paper presented at the Tahoe Conference on Academic Debate. Lake Tahoe, California, in 2001.

[v] I had been a long-time member of Toastmasters International and had participated in many of their speaking contests. TI was a real-world public speaking organization which allowed entry to virtually anyone. I began to wonder why academic debate couldn't be like that. Why restrict debate to just students? Wouldn't that make the stylistic result rather inbred and disengaged from real-world audiences? Weren't we preparing our students to enter the real world of politics, business, and law? And wouldn't a completely open division of academic debate get the community involved, serve as a recruiting tool, and encourage some of the best debaters to hang around after graduation to support the program and serve as examples and role models? Apparently not, since I got more flak for and resistance to this idea than almost any other aspect of IPDA.

[vi] It's funny now, but I didn't know what to call my experimental format. I had been calling it parliamentary debate for a long time, since that is what it most closely resembled. But it wasn't really parliamentary and when NPDA was formed the distinction between the two formats became even clearer. So I was in a quandary. I asked everyone I could think of what they thought. I spent almost a full year agonizing over it and finally settled on 'public debate.' Overall, I think it was a really good choice. One of the marks of a really good decision is that over time, it grows on you. Your regrets and concerns fade away and your sense of satisfaction grows stronger. I'd say that describes the selection of 'public debate' for this format extremely well.

[vii] At the end of that first season, Jack told me that the self-perpetuating board had turned out to be really great idea in the final analysis, at least for our debate association.

[viii] I wanted to squash this proposal from the get-go. But Jack persuaded me to let it go. He thought that we shouldn't be too heavy-handed and that this would be a kind of peace offering to those who wanted everything decided by majority vote. Another 'off the cuff' proposal which got voted in at that meeting was to change the name of the association from "The Public Debate Association,"

to "The International Public Debate Association." Why? Because we had a dozen or so international members, mostly professional colleagues of mine who were interested in the public debate experiment. Here again, Jack told me to just let it go. And to this day I don't know whether or not he was right. What would have happened if I had argued strongly against one or both of these proposals? If I'd forced the issue to a crisis would IPDA even exist today? Who knows? I certainly don't.

[ix] This is an oft-repeated quotation from the comic strip, Pogo, by the cartoonist, Walt Kelly. The original wording was "We have met the enemy and he is us."

Chapter 2

IPDA and Academic Debate: Honing Necessary Life Skills

Bennett Strange
Louisiana College
Cole Franklin
East Texas Baptist University

What do the following people have in common: Theodore Roosevelt, Franklin Roosevelt, Lyndon Johnson, John F. Kennedy, Bill and Hillary Clinton, and Oprah Winfrey? They all were competitive debaters while in school. In fact, there are a multitude of political officials, industry leaders, athletes, and entertainers who have debated at either the high school or collegiate level. Debate is certainly so essential to success that John F. Kennedy once said, "Without debate, without criticism, no administration and no country can succeed. And no republic can survive." The point made is participation in forensics can develop those traits which will equip the debaters for leadership, since each of these positions has been filled by former college debaters.

It would seem there would be no argument about the educational aspects of forensics for three reasons. First, educational institutions sponsor it. Second, it is the oldest of the disciplines to be found in the university (Simonson and Strange 1960), and, third, this is a textbook. But that assumption would not be totally accurate and thus begs for defense.

In 2003, Burnett, Brand, and Meister authored an article in *The National Forensic Journal*, which concluded, "the notion of forensics as education is a myth; the reality is that forensics is a game or competition" (20). However, the thesis of this article was also based on a myth that the 11 National Individual Events Association (NIEA) events are forensic events and their case was built against pieces presented in events such as programmed oral interpretation, dramatic interpretation, poetry, etc. This is a misunderstanding of the word *forensic*.

Aristotle identified three different types of speaking: deliberative (legislative speaking), epideictic (ceremonial speaking), and forensic (speaking in the court of law). Since forensic is a legal term, a good field definition is found in Black's Law Dictionary, "Belonging to courts of law" (Garner 1979, 583). Thus, this chapter discusses debate as the true forensic event. As such, it can improve several skills, eight of which we will discuss later in this chapter.

Contributed by Bennet Strange's Estate and Cole Franklin. Copyright © Kendall Hunt Publishing Company

Debate is preparation for all aspects of later life. According to H.C. Lawson-Tancred, "the ability to persuade, convince, cajole, or win the round is one of the most useful skills in human life. It is a capacity that shows its importance equally easily in the market, the court, the council chamber, and the bedroom" (1991, 1). Additionally, as Barten and Frank point out, "Debate is an important career skill. Studies on the subject are consistent. Employers are looking for people who are able to articulate ideas both orally and in writing, create arguments that employ sound reason and evidence, and refute opposing posits that are logically deficient" (1994, 9).

Politicians, presidents, political scientists, journalists, attorneys, and broadcasters, among many, have credited their debate experience as being the catalyst in their careers. In addition to those mentioned above, persons ranging from President Richard M. Nixon to broadcaster Rush Limbaugh have forensic experience in their background (Simonson and Strange 1960). Former Louisiana governor and U.S. Senator Huey P. Long credited his high school debate training as the secret of his success (Strange 1960).

However, it is also true the debater needs to know what he hopes to achieve if he is to become successful in gaining proficiency. Murphy and Ericson made the point, "But you can spend four, or even eight, school years in debating and come out with little benefit unless you know what it is you are trying to do, and what it is you are trying to learn" (1961, 12).

Dr. Waldo Braden, at the 1958 Pi Kappa Delta convention, posited six attributes that contribute to academic debate's popularity. These attributes, proposed over 50 years ago, still hold true today however, regardless of the debate format. The attributes noted by Braden are: 1) superior intelligence, 2) an intense interest in public affairs, 3) a great desire to improve, 4) competition with other bright students, 5) teaching the student how to analyze, to think critically, and to listen, and 6) developing the ability to extemporize, to express thoughts clearly and fluently under pressure.

Through the years, fads and styles in debating come and go, but there are certain skills which have stood the test of time and form the framework for the essence of debate regardless of the organization sponsoring a specific tournament. These are the eight skills alluded to above and which will be discussed below. Competition in academic debate can help a student to hone these necessary skills which will benefit the student, not only in the debate round, but in life itself.

PUBLIC SPEAKING

First, and most obvious, debate is training in public speaking. It has been argued that this is not only the foremost point but also illustrates an essential skill (Murphy and Ericson 1961). It has been observed that in some debate formats, tournament delivery is not a good example of training in public speaking. In fact, the IPDA was developed, in part, to focus more on effective public speaking skills as many other formats of debate had moved away from the basics of public speaking and rather, focused on speed with little thought given to delivery or audience analysis.

This begs the argument that if the student's aim is to gain better public speaking skills, then he or she must practice these skills, not the least of which is delivery. According to Aristotle, delivery should not make a difference. However, in truth, delivery "*does* make a difference, and therefore we must study it" (McCroskey 2006, 269). Good delivery makes a difference because it influences attitude change, comprehension of content, and speaker ethos (McCroskey 2006). One precept upon which parliamentary debate is formatted is that each speech should be delivered in a style which is comprehensible to untrained listeners. Before the formation of parliamentary debate as a competitive format, Sanders (1983) noted, "The entirety of academic debate, as taught today, should have an application in the real world. Since delivery is a part of academic debate, it should have a real world application" (138).

No matter what else one might want to say about debating, it all reverts to a simple fact: Debate is a form of public speaking. If we ignore this understanding, we are abandoning the skill that has been so important in furthering this activity.

Sanders' (1983) idea that we should have a "real world application" for forensics is not a new one. According to Joseph W. Wenzel, "Debating societies developed in this country to fill a gap in the curriculum, to meet the need for better training in rhetoric, to help young men and women cope with the demands of real-life public speaking" (Stepp 1990, 80).

A list of various public speaking skills would include items such as eye contact, gestures, body movement, rate, volume, and organization. Since our purpose here is not to instruct in these skills but to suggest that the academic debater would be best served for this competitive activity if the student would set a goal of mastering these traits by practicing them in the competitive arena, we will not attempt Public Speaking 101 here. However, as the standard IPDA ballot awards points for "delivery", "appropriate tone", and "courtesy", all of which are related to good public speaking skills, the competitive debater must remember that debate is indeed a type of public speaking.

It might be contended this skill could be honed through some prepared speaking contest such as oratory, persuasive speaking, or even after dinner speaking. However, prepared speeches fail to refine all public speaking in two ways: they are the same each time delivered and do not need to be adapted, plus they might not be the product of that student's creation. (Burnett et. al 2003).

CRITICAL THINKING

It follows that the second skill to be honed is critical thinking, but not all agree. Hill (1993) contested that assertion saying, "Developing critical thinking ability has long been assumed to be one of the primary education outcomes a student might receive by participating in competitive debate. While that outcome is presumptively important, the debate community has not generated sufficient research to demonstrate that participating in competitive debate promotes development of critical thinking ability to any significant degree" (18).

Colbert (1995) responded to Hill saying, "The research exploring the debate-critical thinking relationship is not complete. It does, however, establish a relationship. Like other social sciences, debate-critical thinking research operates on the basis of probability not a deterministic model asserting causation" (52). Smith (1994) concurred by noting, "Debate offers individuals a chance to engage in an activity which they perceive as involving critical thinking skills which cannot be found through other avenues" (73).

Through debate, the student learns to seek answers to nine significant questions when analyzing arguments presented by an opponent, the first of which is: "Are the speaker's claims supported by facts and figures, testimony, examples or narratives?" If the assertion is not supported by this evidence and the speaker is not a recognized expert in the field, then the argument is no more than opinion and should be recognized as such.

The second question examines the evidence: "Are supporting materials relevant, representative, recent, and reliable?" Frequently, a speaker will use a label that has no relevance to the argument at hand. Obviously, if there is no clear link to the argument, there is no relevance either. If the purported fact is not reproducible, that is, under similar circumstances we can expect the same results, then we must conclude it is suspect.

Our analysis asks a third question: "Are the sources of information cited credible?" In brief, do we have cause to believe the veracity of the source? A negative answer should be reason to doubt the claim.

As the speaker continues, our fourth question is: "Does the speaker distinguish between facts, inferences, and opinions?" The critical thinker seeks to base decisions of importance on facts and should learn to accept the other two for what they are, attractive additives and of little importance. While inferences are generally based in fact and one's opinion may indeed be factual as well, the competent debater must be able to recognize the differences between the three approaches.

Our fifth question concerns the language and style used by the speaker: "Is the language clear and concrete, or does it seem purposely vague and incomprehensible?" If the speaker manufactures words that can mean anything he wishes them to mean, the critical thinker should recognize this attempt at camouflage.

The opposite of an appeal to logic is an appeal to emotion, which leads to question six: "Does the message ask the listener to ignore reason and does it appeal mainly to emotions and attitudes?" We can indict stereotypes with this charge. Frequently these appeals are also based on too few examples or the fallacy of generalities.

As the speaker draws to a close, the question we ask is: "Does the conclusion follow logically from the information that precedes them?" A syllogistic argument that has a true major premise and an equally true minor premise should result in a true conclusion. If the result of the equation does not follow directly from the preceding variables, then we must conclude that it is unproven if not false. The effective debater must be able to follow the logical progression of the argument and point out any logical inconsistencies.

Many a bottle of snake oil has been sold to unsuspecting listeners because the speaker made appealing suggestions of pleasant results, which begs us to ask: "Does the speaker make outlandish promises or claims?" The old adage of "If it sounds too good to be true, it probably is" holds true, but that has hardly ever deterred the foolish from following demigods.

Finally, the critical thinker must rely somewhat upon his own intelligence and ask: "Does the message fit what he or she already knows about the topic?" The inquisitive mind continues the search for knowledge but must measure what is being offered by the rule of what is already known and verified. This is the ultimate gauge of critical thinking and is enhanced by the debate experience.

LISTENING

Another term for "critical thinking" is "critical listening" which means that another skill to be enhanced by debate is listening. This obvious conclusion was endorsed by Hill and Leeman (1997), "Good listening is necessary for understanding, evaluating your opponents' arguments, and developing appropriate responses to them. Debaters use their listening skills during every phase of the debate process: listening is important before, during, and after the debate" (326).

There is no guarantee all debaters become better listeners; however, it is incumbent upon the debater to seek improvement in this skill just as the better basketball player practices shooting in order to improve.

Hearing is a faculty. It is biological in nature where the sound waves enter the auditory canal of the outer ear and strike the tympanic membrane, causing it to vibrate at the same frequency as the impinging air waves. This is traduced to the auditory centers of the brain. Hearing is entirely a function of physiology. There is nothing about debate that improves the debater's hearing so what about the claim of becoming a better listener?

Listening is a skill, which means it can be taught and improved upon with practice. It is a mental or psychological function rather than being physiological in nature. Therefore, a focus on practicing listening can eventuate in better listening skills.

There are four true stages of listening. Many believe that if one can hear and comprehend the message, then listening has taken place. In truth, this is only half of the process. In order to truly listen, one must engage in four steps: attention, understanding, remembering, and evaluating.

First, the listener must pay attention to what is being said. In order to fully pay attention, one should look at the speaker, be mentally prepared to listen, and eliminate any external distractions. With so many external stimuli competing for one's attention, this becomes a difficult task. However, without paying full attention to what is being said, the listener will likely miss important information. In a debate round, this can be a devastating blow to one's case, resulting in failure to refute the opponent's arguments because of a failure to pay adequate attention.

Second, one must understand. Obviously, you must know the language being used but even within your native language there is room for improvement. Through reading, conversation, and debating you improve your vocabulary. Knowing the meaning of the words being used can lead you to be a better listener. Understanding also can be improved by listening for the speaker's organizational pattern being employed, paraphrasing what has been said to clarify it, and paying close attention to the nonverbal elements being used by the speaker. Often, volume, rate, facial expressions, and gestures more effectively communicate what the speaker thinks or feels than do the words spoken. Another technique that can enhance the listening is questioning. Debaters should utilize the cross-examination period to effectively question their opponent and clarify unclear points to improve their understanding of the arguments.

The third step in the listening process is remembering. Most people forget half of what they hear within an hour, with most forgetting a fourth to a third more within the next eight hours. One must be able to retain what has been said for a period of time. If one immediately forgets an argument made in a constructive speech, how can he or she effectively refute it? Debaters must improve their ability to remember key elements of the debate in order to address those issues in the round. One key to improving memory is to take notes or flow during the debate round. The method used to take notes is an individualized process with each debater using a style that benefits him or her. Regardless of the style used, taking notes is an important process for the debater to use to enhance the ability to remember arguments.

The final step in listening is evaluating the message. This is the critical analysis of what has been heard. One must make a judgment about what a speaker has said and assess its value. The process of evaluation has been covered above in the discussion of critical thinking.

RESEARCH SKILLS

One advantage of IPDA over other forms of debate is the fact that competitors will argue, minimally, six different topics or resolutions during a debate tournament. These issues will vary from quotations, to international affairs, to domestic policy, to sports, to entertainment. While the well-informed debater may know something about the topics available at the topic draw, research will be necessary to develop an effective argument and a successful case. IPDA allows competitors to use any resource available within the 30 minutes of prep time to research the case. This minimal time forces the debater to develop effective and efficient research skills. Many times, a debater must research to develop a cursory understanding of the topic at hand first and then develop the case around the knowledge gathered. Competitive debate assists the student in developing good research skills that can be carried into any other forum outside the realm of debate.

ARGUMENTATION SKILLS

Academic debate would be a foolish expenditure of time if competition was the only goal attained. One of the "real world" attributes is development of skills which can be used outside of the debate round. It matters not if the debater enters the law, the business world, broadcasting, theology, or any other career field; the basic elements of argumentation will be a valuable lifelong skill to learn.

There is a fundamental ingredient of the human nature and that is, in the absence of proof to the contrary, we accept the current situation, i.e. the status quo. If we are to overcome this predilection, then we need to develop our proficiency in argumentation. In the law it is said that the accused is innocent until proven guilty; in sales, we must attempt to part the customer from his money; in theology, we show the sinful nature of man and the need for redemption.

Aristotle said that of the means of persuasion available there are three, which are: putting the audience in the proper emotional frame of mind, the credibility of the speaker as perceived by the audience, and the logical strength of the arguments (pathos, logos, and ethos). The debate experience provides a laboratory to develop the skill of using all three of these means.

ANALYSIS AND INVESTIGATION OF PUBLIC ISSUES

Academic debate, regardless of format, calls upon the successful debater to be knowledgeable of the world in which we live. The debater should be sufficiently informed to discuss in a meaningful manner the events and policies which shape our lives. The debater begins this investigation by reading daily newspapers, current news magazines, or websites, watching news reports and public affairs programs on television, and reading both classical and current popular literature.

It is this practice which leads to the ability to construct valid and persuasive arguments which is the basis of arguments (Winebrenner 1995). Since the rules of both the National

Parliamentary Debate Association and the International Public Debate Association prohibit bringing printed evidence into the debate round, this places a premium upon a good storehouse of knowledge in order to construct effective cases. Factually, the IPDA debate rules state, "Evidence must be memorized or paraphrased for use during debates" (http:// ipdadebate.info).

Even more than being familiar with policy decisions, successful debaters learn to critique the underlying values of these decisions. Gehrke (1998) concluded, "In academic debate, it is critical that the training and experience of the students. . .include the consideration and evaluation of competing value claims. Value conflicts are increasingly central to politics in the United States" (36).

Being able to interpret actions and their underlying values with future implications is a notable skill and grants a lifetime advantage in analyzing events that face each of us in education, business, politics, and, most important, social interaction.

INFLUENCING OTHERS

When a debater learns to construct effective arguments, that student has developed a lifetime skill. ". . .learning how to make cases increases your ability to influence others. People usually want to do the right thing. To show them what to do, you must prove the right reasons" (Fryar, Thomas and Goodnight 1989, 4–5).

There are obvious advantages to be gained here. Lawyers need to influence judges and juries; marketing executives desire to influence audiences to purchase products; preachers want to affect the behavior and/or attitudes of their congregations; teachers expect students to accept theorems or be able to defend them; corporate executives must deal with boards of directors; politicians want to win votes before the election and pass legislation afterwards; and the list could go on of the application of this skill.

The debating chamber is the practical laboratory for this skill because what the advocate is seeking is that the adjudicator cast the ballot for his or her position. It is granted that this is not the only such opportunity, since student government organizations, social groups, and college organizations present such occasions, but they are not as numerous as a debate tournament where there are at least six preliminary rounds, and, for the successful debater, even more rounds for exercise. It can be empirically argued that forensic participation is inherently a better laboratory experience for this skill (Aden 1991-92).

INDEPENDENT THOUGHT

Independent thought might be defined as self-determination of values, concepts, actions, and procedures based on research, observation, and experience. It is in fact the sum of the all of the contributors discussed above. As Wilbanks and Church (1991) noted, "We view learning argumentation and participating in debates. . .as extremely valuable. . .The usefulness of developing abilities such as analysis, problems solving, critical thinking, organization proficiency, research prowess, and confidence in presentations are enduring. Long after the course is over, the student will continue to benefit from these skills" (vii).

When a student gains the ability to look at any situation, to determine a course of action, and to ethically persuade others to agree, there is value enough to participate in forensics. There is an old adage that education is the beginning of learning, and not the completion of it.

In examining these eight skills, it is evident that competitive academic debate can certainly hone each in the debater. These skills are not only necessary in debate, but in life. Regardless of the career field chosen, these skills will benefit the student in every facet of life. In sum, the final word goes to Roger Aden (1991-92) who said:

"While it is rewarding to earn the tangible awards of forensics—trophies—these awards sit on shelves and gather dust. What they represent, however, is that there are people scattered thought the country who possess the intangible ingredients of character, thinking, citizenship and speaking ability. If students have internalized their forensic education—and we can assume most do if it is taught well—we can rest assured that they are spreading these intangibles as well, if only by example. A forensic education, then, is truly a gift that keeps on giving" (17).

REFERENCES

Roger C. Aden (1991/1992). The Goals of a Forensics Education, *The Forensic Educator, 6,* 15–18.

Barten, M., and D. Frank. 1994. *Nonpolicy Debate* (2nd ed.). Scottsdale, AZ: Gorsuch Scarisbrick, Publishers.

Burnett, A., Brand, J., and M. Meister. 2003. "Winning Is Everything: Education as a Myth in Forensics." *The National Forensic Journal.* Vol. 21, No. 1, Spring 2003, pp. 12–23.

Colbert, K. 1995. "Enhancing Critical Thinking Ability through Academic Debate." *Contemporary Argumentation and Debate.* 16 pp. 52–72

Fryar, M., Thomas, D., and L. Goodnight. 1989. *Basic Debate.* Lincolnwood, IL: National Textbook Co.

Garner, B. A. (Ed.). 1979. *Black's Law Dictionary* (5th ed). West Publishing Company, Eagon MN

Gehrke, P.J. (1998). Critique Arguments as Policy Analysis: Policy Debate Beyond the Rationalist Perspective. Contemporary Argumentation and Debate,19, 18–39.

Hill, B. 1993. "The Value of Competitive Debate as a Vehicle for Promoting Development of Critical Thinking Ability." *CEDA Yearbook,* 14.

Hill, B., and R. Leeman. 1997. *The Art and Practice of Argumentation and Debate.* New York: McGraw-Hill.

Lawson-Tancred, H.C. (Ed.). 1991. *Aristotle: The Art of Rhetoric.* New York: Penguin Books.

McCroskey, J. 2006. *An Introduction to Rhetorical Communication: A Western Rhetorical Perspective.* Boston: Pearson Education, Inc.

Murphy, J. J., and J. M. Ericson. 1961. *The Debater's Guide.* Indianapolis, IN: The Bobbs-Merrill Co.

Sanders, G. H. 1983. *Introduction to Contemporary Academic Debate* (2nd ed.). Prospect Heights, IL: Waveland Press.

Simonson, W., and B. Strange. 1960. *Techniques of Debate.* Hattiesburg, MS: Geiger Publishing.

Smith, K. 1994. "Cerebral gymnastics 101: Why do debaters debate?" *CEDA Yearbook,* 15.

Stepp, P. 1990. "Taking EDA Debaters out of the Normal Tournament Setting." *CEDA Yearbook,* 11.

Strange, B. 1960. "High School Debating in the Training of Huey P. Long as a Speaker." *The Rostrum.* May.

Strange, B. 1991. "The Danger Within." *The Forensic Educator,* Volume 6, 2.

Winebrenner, T.C. "Authority as Argument in Academic Debate." Contemporary Argumentation and Debate l6 (1995): 14–29.

Wilbanks, C., and R. Church. 1991. *Values and Policies in Controversy: An Introduction to Argumentation and Debate* (2nd ed.). Dubuque, IA: Kendall/Hunt Publishing Co.

CLASS ACTIVITY

Have the class compile a list of local business leaders, civic leaders, political office holders, religious leaders, and educators, other than those involved in academic debate, who have forensic training. Let each student select one to interview about their experience and their evaluation of it in preparing for their current occupation. Each student should report to the class the interviewee's impression. It might be useful to use only those who have participated at your university.

Assignments

1. Construct a list of occupations in which the skills learned in forensics can be useful. By each occupation, list the specific skills.
2. Analyze your most recent debate either in class or tournament. In which skills were you judged to be best? Do you agree and why? In which skills were you least effective? Determine goals that will allow you to improve.
3. Keep a daily journal for two weeks where you observe teachers, campus leaders, administrators, or professional persons with whom you come into contact. Note the forensic skills they demonstrate and evaluate them.

Chapter 3

Ethics and IPDA

Patrick Richey
Middle Tennessee State University

Every art and every inquiry, and similarly every action and pursuit, is thought to aim at some good.

Aristotle (McKeon 1941, 935)

There is no pancake so flat as to have only one side.

Bennett Strange

Debate is a tool in the pursuit of knowledge. Like any tool, debate can be used for good or for evil. When we look back at some of the best speakers and persuaders of history, names like Roosevelt and Martin Luther King Jr. come to mind. Yet some of the most notorious figures from history were excellent speakers and excellent in persuading the masses. Adolf Hitler is probably the most well-known infamous figure. He was able to sway millions of Germans to follow him without question. Hitler was able to turn neighbor against neighbor because he could speak to an audience. He nearly wiped out an entire race using the power of words.

In the nonacademic world, there are limitations to what one can say, and falsifications can lead to legal problems, severe punitive damages or incarceration. This applies to lawyers, doctors, advertisers, salespeople, and most occupations (Ewbank and Auer 1951). This leads to an important question: Is argumentation always good? If not, what is good and how can we stop from straying into the darkness? What does this mean for the debater, specifically the IPDA debater?

The answer to these questions is ethics. In this chapter, we will explore what ethics are, and more specifically, what role they play in IPDA debate. We will examine many facets of this integral piece of debate, including varying definitions of ethics, their historical background, modern implications, ethics and IPDA, hate speech, fallacies, and finally tips for debating ethically in IPDA.

Contributed by Patrick Gerhardt Richey. Copyright © Kendall Hunt Publishing Company

DEFINED

The exact definition of **ethics** is difficult to pin down. In Jim Hanson's (1991) *NTC's Dictionary of Debate*, ethics is the practice of being ethical, which leads to this definition: "The scholarliness, morality, and legality of someone's actions. Debaters who are courteous and use good research practices are considered ethical." Austin Freeley and David Steinberg (2005, 16) claim that being ethical is "being in accordance with the accepted principles of right and wrong that govern the conduct of a profession or community." In this case, IPDA is the community in question.

FOUNDATIONS AND ARISTOTLE

With Freeley and Steinberg's baseline definition of ethics, it is important to understand the historical context in which ethics has developed. The study of ethics is nearly as old as recorded history. Scholars have found the use of ethics in early religious texts of both eastern and western cultures. Some of the first and most influential treatises written on ethics came from ancient Greece. This is not surprising since many consider this also the birthplace of the study of rhetoric. From the first classes taught by Protagoras of Abdera (481–411 B.C.) through Corax and Tisias (Freeley and Steinberg 2005, 19), Socrates, Plato, and finally Aristotle, ethics evolved. It was Aristotle who first wrote a long treatise on ethics in response to some of the teachings of his professor, Plato, creating the theoretical foundation of today's ethical study.

Aristotle differed from both the Sophists and Plato. The Sophists believed that ethics were "doomed to subjectivity and relativity" (Jones 1980). They thought that there was not a consistent definition of ethics and therefore people ought not to worry about them. Plato, however, believed that ethics should not be based in opinion, but rather in knowledge, and that this could only accomplished through dialect. **Dialect** (dialectic) is the "rigorous interaction between two ideas to determine truth" (Borchers 2006), thus a debate. Aristotle believed that the problem with this form of thinking was that the dialectic was designed to find knowledge or singular truth. He believed that ethics could not be definitive or conclusive (Jones 1980, 260–261). Aristotle chose the middle ground between his mentor and the Sophists. While ethics was opinion-based and created difficulty in finding a singular truth, it can still be useful in structuring thought. Therefore, ethics should not be abandoned.

In fact, Aristotle went further. He believed ethics was also different from science (knowledge) in that it should not be value-free. Scientists do not interfere with experiments in order to prove their hypotheses; they merely observe the outcome. Aristotle believed that there should also be change or manipulation rather than simple observance. One should not only watch but should also do or change. In reality, there are multiple choices and ethics deals with choosing the correct one. Aristotle calls it the *good*. As Jones (1980, 260–261) states, "He (Aristotle) not only questions, 'what is good' but also 'how can it be good?'" Jones (1980, 261) adds:

Aristotle discusses three important points about ethics (specifically in psychology but this applies to argumentation as well). (1) Ethics grows out of the need for choosing among the multiple courses of behavior that the human soul perceives as options at any given time. (2) The good, whatever it is, is the good for man and therefore can be ascertained only by discovering what man is. (3) The study of psychology is valuable in pedagogy and especially in the learning of good behavior and attitudes.

Aristotle believed that ethics were not only a study by humans but also an actual study about humans. He believed that humans had settled patterns over a long course of time, their habits, which he called character (Jones 1980, 276). This could be either good or not, but humans should strive for good. Aristotle moved on to other subjects, but discussed ethics once again when he dealt with rhetoric.

Aristotle defined **rhetoric** as, "the faculty of observing in any given case the available means of persuasion," (McKeon 1941, 1329). He believed that there were three things needed in order for an address and addressor to be persuasive: **pathos, logos,** and **ethos**. Scholars roughly translate pathos as emotional appeal (Lucas 2007, 456). When one watches commercials seeking donations for the starving children throughout the world, the pictures of those children pull at the heartstrings. This is an emotional appeal. Scholars roughly translate logos as logic (Lucas 2007, 444). Logic can go as follows. Patrick Richey is a man. All men are mortal. Therefore, Patrick Richey is mortal. Of course, logic can be much more complex than this. However complex, Aristotle believed it an important part of speaking well. The final component was ethos. Ethos is credibility with an audience (Lucas 2007, 435). Aristotle once again goes back to his definition of character:

> Persuasion is achieved by the speaker's personal character when the speech is so spoken as to make us think him credible. We believe good men more fully and more readily than others; this is true generally whatever the question is, and absolutely true where exact certainty is impossible and opinions are divided. . .his character may almost be called the most effective means of persuasion he possesses (McKeon 1941, 1329).

Aristotle rightly believed that in order for a speaker to successfully convey a message, the speaker had to have the audience perceive him or her as being of good character. People do not buy cars from unreliable used car dealerships where they know other customers were taken advantage of. Advertisers, corporations, stars, and politicians spend millions a year on public relations campaigns. They are essentially building ethos with their respective bases. Once a speaker's ethos is damaged, it is quite difficult for a speaker to restore himself or herself. A whole field of communication deals with apologetics (apologia) and their persuasiveness. Aristotle was on to something but he was not by a long shot the last to speak or write on the subject.

MODERN ETHICS

It would be impossible to even try to cover all those who spoke or wrote on ethics since the time of ancient Greece and Rome. Not much changed during the dark and middle ages. However, thought began to evolve during the Renaissance and really began to shift during the Enlightenment. Two well-known theories on ethics originated from this period. These were Immanuel Kant's **categorical imperative** and Jeremy Bentham's **utilitarianism**.

Immanuel Kant is considered by many as one of the most influential German philosophers. Kant wrote during the waning days of serfdom and monarchy and the American

Revolution. He wanted to develop a system of ethics that would apply to all and called it categorical imperative. He believed that one should only do things that anyone could replicate. If it was allowable for one person to take a cookie without paying for it, it should become a universal law that everyone should be able to take a cookie without paying for it. Once it became a universal law, it became a duty. One must always do their duty according to the categorical imperative regardless of the consequences of the results (Neher and Sandin 2007, 39).

Jeremy Bentham next tackled the subject. He believed that ethical people should do what benefits the *total happiness* of the world; this is utilitarianism. His student, John Stuart Mills, expanded this idea. Bentham and Mills understood that universal laws were not realistic for all, but they liked the idea of maximizing equality and good. Mills theorized that one's actions should be weighed out. Of the options available, the one that benefits the most people ought to be chosen. The concept of the "greatest good for the greatest number" was born (Neher and Sandin 2007, 61–63). This philosophy had a major impact on democracy and its effects are even evident in IPDA. For example, in out-rounds a panel judges competitors and the competitor with the greatest number of ballots wins the round.

POST-MODERN ETHICS

From the Enlightenment, ethics further evolved. Some of the most significant interpretations occurred in the last hundred years. With the rapid advancement of technology, philosophies on humans and what it is to be human have changed drastically. This shift is often called postmodernism. Many scholars have written on ethics, but three important ones come to mind. These are the conflicting theories of Joseph Fletcher's **situational ethics**, Ayn Rand's **ethical egoism**, and Jürgen Habermas's **discourse ethics**.

Joseph Fletcher was a theologian who transcended religious studies and developed a system of ethics applicable for all called situational ethics. He believed that no set of rules or laws (including religious) could be obtainable in all situations. He believed that instead of laws, people should use principles that he called **principle relativism** (Fletcher 1966). Simply stated, he believed that the situation dictated the course of action. Agape (Christ-like) love was the center point of his theory. One should view the situation in a manner that is selfless and sacrifice for the good of others (Neher and Sandin 2007, 47–48). A classic example of situational ethics is that of Miep Gies who hid the Franks (Anne Frank) in the attic to keep them from being sent to the Nazi death camps. She had an ethical dilemma. If she told the Nazis the truth (lying is a sin), then they would take the Franks to the death camps and she would be an accomplice to their deaths (murder is also a sin). Fletcher would say that she should weigh out the options regardless of self and choose the one that has the greatest benefit. Gies chose to lie (large risk to self) to protect their lives (large gain to them).

Ayn Rand believed that Fletcher's self-sacrifice was unnecessary. Her ethical egoism is based upon individualism and self-reliance that she called **objectivism**. It should be noted that Rand defected from the Soviet Union before World War II and detested communism as practiced in the Soviet Union. She believed that every person is an end unto themselves. There is no need for subjugation to the state or others. Rand argued that this does not mean one should indulge oneself. Her **rational self-interest** claimed that one must do what is best and not necessarily, what one wants (Neher and Sandin 2007, 68). A child may want to eat all the cookies in a box at one time, but that is not the best solution for the child. It is unhealthy and there will not be any cookies for later.

Finally, we come to Jürgen Habermas. Habermas grew up in Germany during the Nazi era and has spent his life trying to understand blind nationalism and fascism. He wants to find techniques to ensure it never happens again. He is a member of a group of scholars known as the Frankfurt School. Habermas's study of Kant is clear because of the similarities to Kant's categorical imperative. The distinguishable factor between the two is that Habermas believes that the community, not the individual, should develop laws. Neher and Sandin (2007, 52–54) state that Habermas believes there are four key factors to this process.

1. Nobody who could make a relevant contribution should be excluded.
2. All participants are granted an equal opportunity to make contributions.
3. The participants must mean what they say.
4. Communication must be freed from external and internal coercion so that yes and no stances that participants adopt on criticizable validity claims are motivated solely by the rational force of the better reasons.

Most critics of Habermas see him as over-idealistic and his visions as being unascertainable (Foss, Foss, and Trapp 1991). Only time can tell.

Though this discussion of the history of ethics has only been the tip of the proverbial iceberg, it is necessary to have a basic understanding of the foundations of ethical theory in order to move forward in the discussion of ethical debate. These will be important not only for use in preparing and researching an IPDA round, but also in how a debater ought to conduct oneself in an IPDA round.

IMPORTANCE OF ETHICS IN IPDA

IPDA, though similar to other formats of debate, has several traits that make it unique when compared to other forms of debate. These differences make IPDA accessible to almost anyone; however, this comes with a heavy ethical burden for all involved. This section of the chapter deals specifically with IPDA and ethics.

One of the starkest (and most redeeming) differences is the IPDA's use of **lay judge(s)**. Anyone with reasonable intelligence is allowed to judge an IPDA round (IPDA Constitution, Bylaws B 2008). Lay judges help limit speed and technical jargon in the round. Lay judges tend to not understand what is happening if the debater speaks too fast or uses words that are not familiar to a layperson. Lay judges validate a core principle of IPDA: in order for debate to be truly effective, it must be accessible to all and not just a select, highly educated, sectarian few. IPDA creates and promotes real-world skills (Cirlin 2007) such as critical thinking and public speaking. The real world does not work on link-brink analysis at three hundred words a second. Try that at the next board meeting and see what happens. Not only would a boss not understand you, but he or she would probably also not understand your jargon.

The use of lay judges leads to an ethical dilemma and what some would argue (though false) is a weakness in IPDA. Since judges are not trained as in other formats of debate, it is easier to "fool" them. It becomes the ethical responsibility of the debaters not to lie or misinterpret material in a fashion to purposefully confuse or confound the judge. If caught doing so, the consequences are usually not favorable for the violating party. They will almost certainly lose the round and word of their misdeeds will spread. As noted earlier in regards to Aristotle, a debater's credibility will be damaged and this will follow him or her for quite some time.

Another ethical dilemma faced by debaters in IPDA is that it is inclusive to anyone who wishes to participate. The IPDA constitution (2007) defines inclusiveness as:

> All interested individuals are encouraged to participate regardless of educational background, prior experience, or any other demographics. However, in order to compete, a person must be at the 7th grade level, and in order to judge, a person must be at the 9th grade level.

This leaves some ground for ethical decision making. It allows in the open division for lawyers, graduate students, professors, professionals, and even coaches to compete. The ethical question here lies in the debater's ability verses that of their opponent. If a coach is debating a novice debater who has been placed in open to fill out the division, then it becomes the coach's ethical obligation to compete at a level fair to all involved. If the coach crushes their opponent, nothing of value is gained other than shallow pride and a cheap plastic trophy. This leads directly into the next ethical concern.

IPDA is no different from other formats of debate in that the goal and purpose is the pursuit of knowledge. Some have claimed debate is a form of gaming. To some it may be, but this perspective devalues why most participate in the activity. At the end of a game of monopoly, there is very little value in the information, or knowledge gained. Debate should not be this way. It is the ethical responsibility of debaters, judges, and coaches to ensure that some knowledge is transferred in the round. Whatever be the outcome (whether a win or loss) there should be a feeling of increased knowledge for all those who participated. If there is one thing that most ethicists agree upon, it is that knowledge is important. It becomes the debater's obligation to be the truthful conveyer of this knowledge and they should expound and expand upon it. **Critical thinking skills** (the ability to create knowledge) are becoming a rare commodity in a world of standardized tests and shortening attention spans. It is the debater's ethical obligation to develop notions of critical thought.

There are those within the IPDA community that believe that argumentation is a form of statesmanship, the very heart of the principles of democracy. These proponents believe that rounds should further the causes of significant importance to informed citizens. Even when topics seem a bit trite, debaters ought to look for a higher realm of argumentation that has some social value (Drake 2008).

IPDA does not differ from other formats of debate in its stance towards inclusivity of all minority groups. With this comes a heavy ethical burden. Some scholars believe that **hate speech** (bigoted speech attacking or disparaging a social or ethnic group or a member of such a group) ought to be allowed since it progresses discourse while others believe it ought to be strictly banned because of its attacks on the person rather than an actual topic (Neher and Sandin 2007, 172–174). On one hand, it is important to discuss minority issues fairly because we can only come to true understanding through discourse. On the other hand, the issues often slide into personal and racial attacks rather than true discourse. As a debater, ethical questions not only arise when preparing arguments, but also when confronted by them.

In order to do justice to ethics within the realm of IPDA, it is important to discuss some of the most common ethical abuses in rounds. Often these are known as logical fallacies.

Fallacies

There are many kinds of fallacies. Here, only the most common are presented (Spradley 2006; Lucas 2007, 446, 452–455; Inch and Warnick 2002; Larson 2001).

Hasty generalization: A hasty generalization is when a conclusion is drawn on insufficient or inconclusive information. Example: I saw a light in the sky last night; therefore, it must be an alien spacecraft. The observer probably did not investigate what he or she saw and assumed it was an alien when there are many possibilities.

Red Herring: The legend behind this fallacy is that in Britain in the past it was a common sport of the wealthy to hunt foxes on horseback through the countryside. This obviously upset the farmers because the intrusion would ruin their crops. To deter the dogs, farmers would catch small fish in the streams called red herrings and drag them around their fields. Once the dogs picked up the scent of the fish they would follow it around the field instead of the fox scent through the field. The idea is to mislead someone with irrelevant material. Example: A politician gets in trouble for accepting tainted donations from a large lobbyist, so he or she creates legislation granting all Americans a thousand-dollar tax credit, thus averting attention from the real problem of corruption and focusing it on something else.

Ad Hominem: This is a personal attack on someone rather than an issue. Example: We ought not to vote for candidate John Doe because he is short and short people have power complexes. A person's height does not affect the ability to lead and thus the attack was made on the person. This is a common trick in mudslinging in elections.

Either-or: This fallacy leaves an audience or judicator with two options. Either you agree with one side or this will happen. Example: If we do not stop Iraq's weapons of mass destruction program, we will be faced with a nuclear winter. The question that should be asked on these types of arguments is if there are any other viable alternatives. Pointing these out usually disarms this poor logic.

Slippery Slope: This argument is based upon the notion that if we do not adopt the advocated position, a series of negative things will happen. This is similar to the either-or argument, but much more evolved. Example: If we do not adopt the Kyoto Protocol then it will upset Japan. Since Japan and China are allies, this will upset China. China is threatened by the US nuclear arsenal and feels that a first strike policy is the only way to defend itself. Therefore, we risk the possibility of nuclear winter. These arguments are popular within some circles of debate as to see who can stretch this poor logic to its furthest.

Bandwagon: This fallacy is based on the principle that since it is accepted by the group, one ought to do it as well. Example: Since everyone else has bought this car, so should you. This is a common technique in sales and advertising that relies on peer pressure. If all the other Germans were telling the Nazis where the Jews were hiding, should you?

34 • IPDA Textbook

Straw Man: This is a strategy of portraying your opponent's argument as being a weaker argument than it actually is usually by hyperbole or exaggeration. Example: We should cut the cost of military spending to reduce the deficit. Attack: If we get rid of our military, what will defend us from foreign invaders? What about all the veterans who sacrificed many things for this country? The proposition never mentioned eradication of the military, only downsizing, but the opposition chose to take it out of context and exaggerate it in order to sway an audience or judicator. Good debaters listen for these shifts and call attention to the judge about this technique.

Post Hoc: A false relationship that states that what came first caused what happened later. Example: Because President Smith refused to sign the welfare act into law, we have seen unprecedented levels of welfare applicants. There may be a spurious correlation here since the speaker did not attempt to prove the link between the bill and the levels of applicants.

Ad Verecundiam: This is appeal to an authority who is not truly an authority. It is also called an appeal to reverence. Example: Our forefathers believed that it is our duty to protect countries in the Western Hemisphere from foreign interference. Therefore, we should send troops to El Salvador to stop the spread of Soviet Communism. Are people who have been dead for 200 years experts on modern international politics?

False Cause: The fallacy works under the auspices that there is a single cause to a complex problem: Example: Saddam Hussein is the roadblock to democracy in Iraq. Unfortunately, global issues are not as simple as removing one tyrant. There are much deeper issues and debaters need to be on guard for cases that sound too good to be true.

False Analogy: The idea of comparing two issues that in reality are not similar. Example: A common comparison used is that we should lower the drinking age in the United States because it is lower in Europe and there are less alcohol-related incidents there. A shrewd debater will question this; they will look at cultural and family differences.

Fallacies can be problematic when encountered as a debater. As debaters gain experience, these types of arguments become easier to recognize. They are also too easy to use as strategies against your opponent. Good debaters refrain from such arguments because they are so easily identifiable. It also becomes a badge of honor for an experienced debater to use arguments that are more refined. Now that fallacies have been explored, it is time to move on to the final section of this chapter. With all the knowledge gained thus far on ethics, here are some tips that may help debaters deal with or be more ethical in a round.

TIPS FOR ETHICAL DEBATING IN IPDA

1. When choosing a topic, choose one that has enough room for both sides to debate. Remember that debate is about the progression of knowledge and not a pursuit for cheap plastic trophies.

Chapter 3: Ethics and IPDA • **35**

2. Do not purposefully spend unnecessary amounts of time choosing a topic; it is a time-suck technique to waste your opponent's preparation time.

3. Never "**squirrel**" a topic (take a topic out of context, i.e., Africa = nuclear proliferation). IPDA stands in such stark contrast to many other forms of debate because it focuses on actual issues, focuses on the actual issues of the resolution, and focuses on cases instead of procedurals.

4. Use the simplest, most common definitions for the words you define.

5. Do not structure your case in a way that purposely confuses your opponent or judge.

6. Use realistic values and do not structure your case with parameters that are impossible to refute or argue. Example: You cannot make your opponent prove that murdering kittens is the only way they can win.

7. Do not structure your case as to be so vague that it becomes a moving target and impossible to refute.

8. Do not make up definitions.

9. If you think there could be any favoritism from the judge on your behalf, tell the tab room.

10. Avoid the use of logical fallacies.

11. Always be courteous to your opponent. There is no way to lose a round faster than being rude in a round. Control your competitive nature. If you feel like you are losing, throwing a temper tantrum like a three-year-old probably will not help!

12. Do not challenge information that you know to be true to muddle the round.

13. During Cross examination (CX) , be succinct in answers and questions to not steal the other person's time.

14. While you may not bring in printed material to the round, be sure to source information and do so correctly and within context.

15. Do not "schmooze" with the judge (although genuine friendly banter is fine).

16. Never walk out of a round and/or verbally attack your opponent after the round to try to sway a judge.

17. Never discus the round with a competitor or judge after the round until the ballot is signed and turned in.

18. The golden rule: Do not do anything in debate that you would not like happen to you!

These are some guidelines that may help a debater become more ethical. I have found that as debaters gain experience and become more ethical, they tend to win more rounds. Debaters who are thought of as being ethical are remembered long after the rounds are over and even after their debate careers are over. They were and are the ones who truly progress knowledge. Debate has existed nearly as long as humans have and probably will until the last two humans argue over the last morsel of food. As long as debate continues, it is the obligation of those who participate to be ethical.

ACTIVITIES

1. Print a copy of the most recent State of the Union Address and assign it to students in groups of three to five. Give them 20 minutes to read and prepare notes about which fallacies were used. Then have a class discussion about the findings. Make sure to ask questions; students should be able to verify and validate why they believe certain aspects are fallacious.

2. Have students list the top ten most notorious figures from history to current times. Have them write two sentences why they believe so. Have a class discussion as to who was chosen and why. Pay specific attention to ethical concerns of the infamous persons.

KEY TERMS

Ad Hominem
Aristotle
Categorical Imperative
Dialectic
Either-or
Ethical Relativism
False Analogy
Good
Lay Judges
Objectivism
Principle Relativism
Rational Self-Interest
Rhetoric
Slippery Slope
Straw Man

Ad Verecundiam
Bandwagon
Critical Thinking Skills
Discourse Ethics
Ethics
Ethos
False Cause
Hasty Generalization
Logos
Pathos
Post Hoc
Red Herring
Situation Ethics
Squirrel
Utilitarianism

REFERENCES

Borchers, T. 2006. *Rhetorical Theory: An Introduction*. Belmont, CA: Thomson Wadsworth. 41.

Cirlin, A. 2007. "Academic Debate v. Advocacy in the Real World: A Comparative Analysis." *Journal of the International Public Debate Association* 1 (1): 3–18.

Drake, W. 2008. "A Call to Statesmanship." *Journal of the International Public Debate Association* 2 (1): 3–6.

Ewbank, H. L., and J. J. Auer. 1951. *Discussion and Debate* (2nd ed.). New York: Appleton-Century-Crofts, Inc. 257.

Fletcher, J. 1966. *Situational Ethics: The New Morality*. Louisville, KY: Westminster John Knox Press. 31.

Freeley, A. J., and D. J. Steinberg. 2005. *Argumentation and Debate: Critical Thinking for Reasoned Decision Making* (11th ed.). Belmont, CA: Thomson Wadsworth. 16, 19.

Foss, S. K., Foss, K. A., and R. Trapp. 1991. *Contemporary Perspectives on Rhetoric* (2nd ed.). Prospect Heights, IL: Waveland Press Inc. 266–269.

Hanson, J. 1991. *NTC's Dictionary of Debate*. Lincolnwood, IL: National Textbook Company. 60.

Inch, E.S., and B. Warnick. 2002. *Critical Thinking and Communication: The Use of Reason in Argument* (4th ed.). Boston, MA: Allyn and Bacon.

International Public Debate Association Constitution. (2003, April 29). Retrieved August 23, 2008, from Stephen F Austin State University, website: http://www.ipdadebate.org

Jones, W. T. 1980. *The Classical Mind* (2nd ed.). Fort Worth, TX: Harcourt Brace Jovanovich College Publishers. 260–261, 276.

Larson, C. U. 2001. *Persuasion: Reception and Responsibility* (9th ed.). Belmont, CA: Thomson Wadsworth.

Lucas, S. E. 2007. *The Art of Public Speaking* (9th ed.). Boston, MA: McGraw Hill. 435, 444, 456.

McKeon, R. 1941. *The Basic Works of Aristotle* (14th ed.). New York: Random House. 935, 1329.

Neher, W. W., and P.J. Sandin. 2007. *Communicating Ethically: Character, Duty, Consequences, and Relationships*. Boston, MA: Pearson. 39, 47–48, 52–58, 61–63, 68, 172–174.

Spradley, E. 2006. "Ethics in Public Debate." In S. Jeffcoat and K. Peterson (Eds.), *Public Debate: A Guidebook to IPDA* (pp. 55–61). Mason, OH: Thomson South-Western.

Chapter 3 Sidebar

Ethics Sidebar

Lauren Raynor

University of Arkansas-Monticello

1. A person's reputation is what defines them within an organization, profession, and among peers. American motivational speaker Zig Ziglar said, "The most important persuasion tool you have in your entire arsenal is integrity." No matter what profession a person enters into, ethics and integrity define that person. When presenting an oral argument, the speaker is representing the "client" that she is speaking for, as well as, herself.

2. Never make up a source. As a speaker progresses in IPDA debate rounds, the speaker will reuse information from past debate rounds. This is perfectly fine as long as the information and citation is valid. However, falsifying a citation can permanently damage a speaker's reputation.

3. How speakers act toward their opponents and audience is also an important part of ethical behavior in public speaking. Speakers often become defensive when their opponents negate their arguments. However, that is the point of debating. It is best to follow the golden rule: "Do unto others, as you would have them do unto you." Thus, treat opponents and audiences with the respect and dignity that any speaker would expect.

4. Always tell the entire story. Use an entire quotation when using the citation. Even if part of the quotation harms the point that the speaker is advocating, it will be even more harmful if the opponent has the same quotation and uses all of it to show that the speaker did not choose to finish the quotation. This relays to the judge and audience that the speaker was not telling the entire truth, therefore, harming the speaker's reputation.

38 Contributed by Lauren Raynor. Copyright © Kendall Hunt Publishing Company

PART 2
Persuasion

Chapter 4   Modern Persuasion Theories and Debate - Merle Ziegler 41

                    Modern Persuasion Sidebar - Shane Puckett................................50

Chapter 5   Ethos: The Strongest Proof of All - Cole Franklin.............................55

Chapter 6   Pathos: Emotional Appeals in IPDA Debate - Michael Ingram...................59

                    Pathos Sidebar - Lauren Raynor 69

Chapter 7   Logos in IPDA Debate - Keith Milstead.......................................71

Chapter 4

Modern Persuasion Theories and Debate

Merle Ziegler
Mississippi College

As debaters and debate coaches, we overemphasize the argumentation part of debate and don't emphasize the communication part enough. Unfortunately, you don't always win when you have the best arguments; you win when you are able to persuade the judge or judges that you win. While this doesn't seem equitable, it is, nonetheless, a fact of life. This makes one wonder why we place all the stress in debates solely on logic and rational argumentation.

In this chapter we will examine three modern-day theories of persuasion to see how they can inform us how to become better debaters. Typically, when the word theory is mentioned our eyes glass over and we assume that what is about to be presented is esoteric and of little practical value. However, I would suggest theories do have practical value in that they are simply an individual's way of interpreting what they see occurring in the world around them. If we can pick up on the theorist's understanding and thus broaden our perspective, we will be better for having made the effort. As a result of our efforts here, we will better understand how the receiver of communication processes persuasive messages, thereby giving insight into what we need to consider before we even put the pen to the page or the voice to the microphone.

The first persuasion theories we will examine are the processing theories. Primarily our discussion will focus on the elaboration likelihood model (ELM) as developed by Richard Petty and John Cacioppo (1986). However, within that discussion we will also include the heuristic systematic model (HSM) as developed by Chaiken, Giner-Sorolla, and Chen (1996). Our discussion of these two theories will be blended together since they are very similar in their treatment of the persuasion process.

The theoretical concepts incorporated into these theories fit very well with debate in that the authors themselves were dealing with issues in their research, which resemble very closely what we do in International Public Debate Association (IPDA). For example, Richard Petty (no, not the stock car driver from North Carolina but the researcher from Ohio

Contributed by Merle Wm. Ziegler. Copyright © Kendall Hunt Publishing Company

42 • IPDA Textbook

State University) was interested in studying the effects of source credibility on influencing persuasion around the topic of teenage driving. It sounds like there is an IPDA resolution in there somewhere. What Petty found was the persuasive influence varied depending on the processing route employed by the receiver of the message. Likewise, John Cacioppo of the University of Chicago became interested in finding out how the persuader could best activate each route. The concerns and interests of at least these two theorists closely parallel the concerns and interests of the typical academic debater. He or she is interested in knowing how much effort the persuadee, in this case the judge, is likely to make in processing the effort and then based on this knowledge select arguments which will activate this route of processing.

A third theory of persuasion, which merits consideration, is Walter Fisher's narrative theory. He suggests another view of "logos" from that of Aristotle. Fisher suggests the story or narrative as an effective logical framework from which to structure effective persuasive messages. Fisher feels telling a "convincing story" is as effective in persuasion as piling up the evidence or constructing tightly reasoned arguments. When we think of a story, what often comes to mind is a novel or movie rather than a persuasive speech, but Fisher sees all forms of communication as fitting into what he termed the "narrative paradigm." When a story, or in the case of a debate, the persuasive speech, is told effectively, it has a powerful persuasive effect.

ELABORATION LIKELIHOOD AND HEURISTIC-SYSTEMATIC MODELS

As was mentioned, the ELM model suggests receivers of persuasive messages process them either centrally or peripherally. The "central route" is the one in which the message is carefully scrutinized to see whether or not the ideas presented carry any weight and are therefore worth accepting; thus the term elaborated. Petty and Cacioppo would say elaboration is "the extent to which a person carefully thinks about issue-relevant arguments contained in a persuasive communication" (Petty and Cacioppo 1986, 7). It would be proper to assume this elaboration takes considerable mental effort. Most of us quickly recognize we are not always willing to put in the mental effort necessary and we often look for shorter, simpler ways to make up our mind about the merits of a persuasive message. In these circumstances our theorists suggest we are using the "peripheral route." This route provides shortcuts to reaching our conclusions. The peripheral route allows us to accept or reject a message "without any active thinking about the attributes of the issue or object of consideration" (Petty and Cacioppo 1981, 256). These two methods of processing persuasive messages may be seen as poles on the opposite ends of a continuum. It would seem then that we could employ both the central and peripheral route simultaneously. The ELM model suggests we switch back and forth between them while the HSM model suggests we may use both routes simultaneously. Indeed, it may be that we process part of the persuasive message using the central route, while using the shortcut method, the peripheral route, for parts of the message by which we are less motivated or simply unable to process centrally. The theorists of both the ELM and HSM model emphasize that the central and peripheral routes are on a continuum of degree of mental effort. The ELM model suggests most messages are processed in a "middle ground" between the poles of high mental effort versus low mental effort. However, as the receiver makes greater mental effort to process

Chapter 4: Modern Persuasion Theories and Debate • **43**

information, the less he or she will process the message peripherally. Therefore, there is a trade-off in how a message is processed. If we process a message peripherally, we tend not to be motivated to think critically. When we lack motivation to put in the mental effort, then we rely on "shortcuts" to making our decision about the message. This leads to a very important question for a debater preparing for a debate round, "Will the judge in the round be motivated to carefully consider the persuasive arguments presented in the round?" With this, let's consider the motivation of a receiver of persuasive messages.

VARIABLES AFFECTING CENTRAL PROCESSING

Typically, it should be assumed a person would like to hold and maintain a reasonable position. Ideally, all of us want to carefully consider and mull over any and all arguments that come our way. The reality of the situation is we simple can't do it. We can only process a limited number of ideas to which we are exposed, and we process so many persuasive messages, especially during a debate tournament, that we experience information overload. One of the key characteristics about a message, which will encourage the receiver to centrally process, is the level of personal relevance the topic has for the receiver. The more we see the arguments being presented as personally important, the more likely it is we will pay close attention to the argument being brought forth. Therefore, if you want the judge in a debate round to carefully process your arguments, you must first demonstrate how the topic is of high personal relevance to the judge. Outside of being able to do this you may want to focus your persuasive efforts on the peripheral cues.

A second factor influencing processing, is the receiver's ability to think in a competent way about the message. The ability to think rationally about a message takes intelligence about the subject and the ability to concentrate. It goes without saying that the more information you have on a topic the more you will be able to intelligently process information related to this topic. Thus when considering the topic selection before a round, the wise debater will consider which of the topics lends itself to be processed centrally. It is also important to consider the ability to concentrate. Distractions impact the ability to elaborate, so the more distractions during a debate round, the more difficult it will be for the judge to apply themselves to the elaboration process. Many things occur during the course of a debate round, and the tournament as a whole, which may serve as distractions to the judge in the round. Cell phones, noises from outside the room, and even inadvertent behaviors by yourself or your opposition may serve to distract the judge from processing your arguments effectively. So, if distractions are sufficiently present they may cause the judge to switch from central processing to the peripheral route.

A third factor influencing elaboration is the personal preferences of the judge in the debate round. Petty and Cacioppo (1996) developed what they termed the "Need for Cognition Scale" in recognition of the fact that some of us find it stimulating to engage in deliberating about issues of the day and enjoy processing and solving mental puzzles. Most likely all academic debaters fit this category; however, many judges in debate rounds are not debaters or debate coaches and therefore may not fit this category. Given this scenario, it may be wise to focus on peripheral cues of persuasion in the preliminary rounds of a debate tournament when you have judges who may have a lower need for cognition. Judges in these early rounds are often "volunteers" whose commitment to the activity may be low and therefore given the circumstances have a lower need for cognition. However, in the out rounds where typically debaters and coaches do the judging, you are more likely to be presented with an individual with a higher need for cognition and therefore more motivated to centrally process your arguments in the round. Admittedly, this is a stereotypic judgment but one worth considering.

A fourth factor influencing the elaboration process is the quality of your arguments. Arguments may vary from strong to weak; however, it is not clear what Petty and Cacioppo consider to be a strong argument versus a weak argument. They simply indicate a strong argument is one that leads to favorable thoughts and therefore leads the receiver to adopt the position advocated by the rhetor. Such arguments result in a positive persuasive impact. Concern comes when the arguments are neutral or weak. Petty and Cacioppo point out the neutral argument which leads to elaboration will result in strengthening the position already held by the target which may or may not be the position being advocated. When a target of the persuasion processes a mediocre argument, the resultant ambivalent reaction to the argument will simply strengthen already-held positions on the issue. Worse yet is the weak argument. Weak arguments tend to offend the target rather than enlist them to your cause, resulting in a boomerang effect. For example, in a debate round related to the proposition that "the U.S. Congress has turned a deaf ear to its constituency" the affirmative argued that currently 76 percent of the public disapproved of the current decisions made by Congress. The affirmative then followed this conclusion with specific examples on the escalation of general spending on the part of Congress and in particular, spending related to healthcare. Negative responded with the reply that the electorate had voted these men and women into Congress and therefore also approved of their decisions, no evidence being provided to support the connection between a past vote and the current state of affairs. A weak argument such as this, which only states the obvious and does not directly respond to the contentions made by the affirmative, is likely to result in a "boomerang" reaction by the judge in the round.

As debaters who focus on making sound arguments, we often assume the best argument will win out over the weaker argument. However, according to ELM theory this may not be the case. To the theorists it all depends on the receiver's objectivity when elaborating. Petty and Cacioppo (1986b) contend that biased elaboration, or top-down thinking as they called it, would suggest the receiver would not process the information in an objective manner. If the judge in a debate round comes into the round with a predetermined conclusion on the issue being debated, their elaboration on that issue will more than likely simply bolster those conclusions. What all rational debaters hope for is a "bottom-up" type of judge. Such a judge lets the facts speak for themselves. While it is hoped this type of judge is the most prevalent, we must admit at times it seems they are a rare find.

VARIABLES IN PERIPHERAL PROCESSING

As noted earlier, debaters and debate coaches pride themselves on strong, logical reasoning as the focus of their argumentation. However, most persuasive messages are processed peripherally. Peripheral cues encourage the receiver to process the message in opposition to the persuader's point of view without engaging in elaboration. The most obvious cues which encourage this peripheral processing are tangible rewards linked to the argument, things we typically associate with Maslow's basic or lower order needs such as food, pleasure, money, and so forth. One of the key sources of peripheral processing is source credibility.

An interesting study by Penner and Fritzsche (1993) demonstrated the key role of source credibility—after Magic Johnson announced he had tested HIV positive it resulted in an increase in the rise of male volunteers to help with HIV patients. Penner and Fritzsche indicated the volunteers didn't spend the time reasoning through the need for, or the consequences to, such volunteer work, but rather used the peripheral cue of source credibility to influence their action. This demonstrates that individuals who are likeable experts, on a question or an issue, can have a persuasive impact regardless of their arguments. As an advocate, one can use source credibility through invoking the name of such likeable experts. However, keep in mind Petty and Cacioppo say that only fragile change can be expected through peripheral routes.

As competitive academic debaters, relying on peripheral cues such as source credibility may be fine if we are the final speech of the round and we are not concerned about long-term persuasive effects. However, should we be giving the first speech of a debate round relying solely on such peripheral cues, we will most likely be sorely disappointed.

Finally, it is impossible to construct an exhaustive list of cues that are strictly peripheral (Petty and Wegener 1999). However, models of ELM typically list variables such as reaction to others, external rewards, and speaker credibility. One interesting conclusion made by Booth-Butterfield and Welbourne (2002) is that in peripheral processing, the "rule of thumb" is that more is better. In other words, if the judge in a debate round is not going to process your arguments centrally they will instead base their judgment on a heuristic, and that heuristic may likely be based on the number of arguments put forth by a particular advocate. Evidently debaters and debate coaches alike have instinctively recognized this and thus try to shoehorn into a speech as many arguments as absolutely possible. Thus, adding to the frustrating dilemma, almost all debate associations seem to battle against the excessive rate at which debaters speak. This higher speaking rate allows for the inclusion of more arguments in the round and therefore a favorable decision, particularly, it turns out, if the judge in the round is processing the message peripherally.

NARRATIVE THEORY

Walter Fisher shook up the communication field with his notions that we are just as much valuing beings as reasoning beings. He challenged the dominance of the rational model of human reasoning as developed from the time of Plato and Aristotle where individuals are persuaded and make decisions based on the quality of arguments and evidence. Rather, he suggests we better understand behavior through storytelling and narrative. He thus proposes we use the narrative as an analytical device and casts persuasion in narrative terms. All forms of communication fit the narrative paradigm. Stories may take the form of what we commonly understand them to be, such as poems, plays, movies, and the like, but they may also take the form of speeches and everyday conversation. He felt all of these narrative forms appeal to our reason. Therefore, Fisher's (1984) *narrative paradigm* is a synthesis of argument and artistic themes that challenge the notion that persuasive communication must be rational in structure and evaluated by the standard of formal logic alone. Fisher's theory fits the IPDA philosophy that stresses communication over strict reasoning. A key to

46 • *IPDA Textbook*

success in IPDA debate should be the debater's communicative ability. A good persuasive communicator, according to Fisher, is the one that is also a good storyteller.

But the narrative paradigm includes, rather than denies, the rational paradigm. Fisher simply felt the study of persuasion had inappropriately shifted to technical argument and formal logic and thereby excluded most people. In his view, it had become elitist and he wanted to return it to the rationality of everyday argumentation where consideration is given to all members of the community rather than just to the specialized few. In many ways this is a claim that can be made about much of the academic debate community from which IPDA is an offshoot. Debate association after debate association has battled the tendency to move from an all-encompassing rhetorical style, which values the narrative style, to the narrowly defined rapid fire strictly argumentative logic that can only adequately be evaluated and judged by the professionally educated judge (i.e., the expert debate coach).

Fisher wanted to return rhetoric (the study and use of persuasion) to the roots of human experience. According to Larson (2007), Fisher was frustrated with the focus of traditional approaches to communication. It had lost the conviction of the human experience by emphasis on the dissection of text (as well as speech) with systems of formal logic and argument. Larson put it this way, "The difference is like that between studying the human body in anatomy class by dissecting cadavers and studying it by examining living people—both approaches have value, but one misses the lived experience" (61). Fisher gives five assumptions associated with the prevailing rational paradigm: a) people are rational, b) people make decisions based on good arguments, c) the speaking situation determines the nature of our argument, d) rationality is based on knowledge and argumentative skill, and e) good rational analysis can solve the logical puzzles of the world. For Fisher this is too limiting. Rather, he proposes, for his narrative paradigm, five parallel assumptions to those of the rational paradigm. First, rather than rational he proposes people are essentially storytellers. Second, we make decisions based on good stories rather than just good arguments. Third, our history, culture, character, and other such variables determine what we consider to be good reasons rather than just the structure of formal logic. Fourth, narrative *fidelity* and *coherence* determine rationality. Finally, the world is a set of stories from which we choose rather than a set of logical puzzles we need to solve through rational analysis. So how is the narrative adjudged to be a success or a failure? For this, Fisher proposed we judge the narrative on the basis of its *fidelity* and *coherence*.

Fidelity, the first horn of Fisher's horns of rationality, focuses on how closely the story matches our sensibilities as to what is realistic and whether it is the type of thing that would really happen. Fidelity for Fisher (1987) is his *logic of good reasons*. In his text *Human Communication as Narrative*, Fisher's (1987) logic of good reasons focuses on five value issues. He says we are interested in the values embedded in the speech, how relevant those values are to the decision being made, the consequences of sticking to those values, the overlap of the narrative's values with our worldview, and finally, conformity with the audience member's concept of what is the appropriate basis for conduct. Em Griffin (2003) points out that ". . . when we judge a story to have fidelity, we are not merely affirming shared values. We are ultimately opening ourselves to the real possibility that those values will influence our beliefs and actions" (330). Debaters seeking to heed Fisher's admonition should structure the case so it overlaps the worldview of the judge. Since judges are unique, the advocate needs to focus on highlighting universally-held values and pointing to the consequences of such holding to those values. Fisher suggests the possibility of a permanent public or a universal audience that exists over time and possesses enduring values.

> It appears that there is a permanent public, an actual community existing over time, that believes in the values of truth, the good, beauty, health, wisdom, courage, temperance, justice, harmony, order, communion, friendship, and oneness with the Cosmos—as variously as those values may be defined or practiced in "real" life (Fisher 1987, 187–188).

Coherence, the second horn of Fisher's two horns of narrative rationality, relies on the degree to which a story is consistent within itself. Stories are coherent when we feel important details of the narrative have not been overlooked or omitted, and we feel the storyteller has not "doctored" the facts. Secondly, the characters in consistent stories have good reasons for their actions and the resultant impact of the setting also makes sense. Finally, it means the story is logically organized in that it has a beginning, middle, and an end.

To the debater, Fisher's concept of coherence, suggests we cannot discount logic all together. Logic provides the internal consistency a story needs to be persuasive. The advocate must wed this reasoning with plausible interpretation. It must be remembered, the judges in the round will not only compare our story against the opponent's but also the judge may have heard our story elsewhere on the same theme.

Fisher articulates a view of persuasion that better captures the common human experience than the more technical elitist approach that has dominated the debate community in the past. Stories are among the most powerful persuasive tactics available and a story aptly told counters many facts. Quentin Schultz (2006) suggests that every good speech has at least two good stories at its heart. Never underestimate the good story.

PRACTICAL CONSIDERATIONS

In conclusion I would like to suggest some practical advice to debaters based on these three modern theories of persuasion. From the dual processing theories, ELM and HSM, the following suggestions seem pertinent: First, consider whether the judge is likely to process information centrally or peripherally. This consideration needs to be made as you are eliminating the potential resolutions for the upcoming debate round, as well as considering whether or not you are in the preliminary rounds or the out-rounds. Since preliminary round judges are often "volunteers," they may lack the motivation necessary to centrally process your arguments. Of course this depends equally on the nature of the topic that remains after the elimination process. If a highly popular topic, which has been recently discussed in the news or on campus is selected, they may well have the motivation and ability to process the arguments centrally. At times, the nature of the resolutions themselves tend to encourage a certain processing route. Often abstract resolutions result in peripheral processing whereas the more concrete resolutions of fact and policy tend to encourage central processing. Knowing this can guide your case preparation after the resolution has been selected.

Second, when constructing the case, if you can develop a few strong arguments and you feel the judge is capable and can be motivated to process them centrally, then stick with those arguments. On the other hand, if the judge is likely to process them peripherally, or you do not have strong arguments then strive to make as many arguments as possible.

Third, when constructing the case don't only consider how to persuade through logic, and therefore the central route, but also consider how to cue into the peripheral route by the use of stylistic language devices. Likeability and dynamism have long been recognized as powerful persuasive tools. These characteristics can be brought forward by using powerful language that demonstrate, with clarity, not only your position on the resolution but also how you believe the judge should feel about your position or the opponents position. Richard Weaver categorized this type of language as "ultimate terms." He further divided them into god terms and devil terms. Words such as family, civil rights, progress, and security are god terms because they carry a positive connotation in American society. Words such as socialist, communist, reactionary are devil terms since they carry strong negative connotations. Nowhere in the attempt at appealing to our tendency to process peripherally, can the use of such "ultimate terms" be seen better than with the issue of abortion. Each side wants us to see their position as positive so they select positive terms to define themselves—pro-life and pro-choice. Likewise, they seek to define the other side negatively by their use of devil terms to describe the opposition.

Also, consider the use of euphemistic language and avoid powerless language to create the desired attitude towards your ideas. Using a term such as "downsizing" instead of "layoffs" can create a more congenial attitude towards an argument in support of making an organizational department more cost-effective and thereby contributing to the economic health of the overall company. Powerless language comes in the forms of vocal segregates, redundancies, excessive qualifiers, and personal apologies. Vocal segregates, such as "uhs, uhms, and you knows," will negatively impact the judge. Redundant repetition of words or phrases such as "judge" or "ladies and gentlemen" throughout the speech becomes annoying to the persons listening to the speech. Excessive qualifiers and personal apologies put doubts in the mind of the judge in the round as to the strengths of your case and your competence as a speaker.

Finally, while in the round, pay attention to the judge and his or her reactions. Are the judges taking notes and otherwise paying close attention to your arguments? If so, they are, at least attempting, to process your arguments centrally. On the other hand, if the little distractions in the room pull them from what you are saying, they are most likely going to render their decision on heuristics and are processing arguments peripherally. In this case you will need to adjust your presentation to appeal to these tendencies.

From narrative theory the following suggestions can be suggested. First, include at least one, if not two, pertinent stories; if you are able to make an extended analogy of a story to meet the thesis of the resolution, so much the better. Remember Fisher suggests the story itself has persuasive impact. It is noteworthy that much of the Bible utilizes the story to impart its persuasive message rather than just a series of arguments.

Secondly, structure the case in such a manner that it resembles a story that has a beginning, middle, and end. When making your arguments do your best to link them to culture, history, and human character; appealing to cultural premises serves to make the case more like a story and at the same time appeals to our peripheral processing tendencies. Ask yourself, "Does my case match what the average person would consider to be realistic and is it consistent within itself?"

Thirdly, as much as possible, utilize the stylistic devices of simile, metaphor, and rhythmical language. Such language makes the story of your case memorable. Along with these devices make use of common sayings that tend to be uncritically accepted by audiences.

Phrases such as "a bird in the hand is worth two birds in the bush" are effective methods of keeping the judge focused on your ideas.

In summary, remember judges process persuasive information along a continuum of high effort (central processing) to low effort (peripheral processing). Judges will often fluctuate between these methods when making decisions about your arguments; therefore, it is wise to consider how you can engage them no matter which mode he or she may use. Lastly, the story is a strong persuasive tool, so the closer you can bring the characteristics of effective stories, fidelity and cohesion, into the construction of your case and arguments the better.

REFERENCES

Booth-Butterfield, S., and J. Welbourn. 2002. "The elaboration likelihood model: Its impact on persuasion theory and research," in *The persuasion handbook*. James Dillard and Michael Pfau (eds.), Sage Publications, Thousand Oaks, CA, pp. 155–173.

Cacioppo, J. et al. 1996. "Dispositional differences in cognitive motivation: The life and times of individuals varying in need for cognition." *Psychological Bulletin,* 119: 197–253.

Chaiken, S., Giner-Sorolla, R., and S. Chen. 1996. "Beyond accuracy: Defense and impression motives in heuristic and systematic information processing." In P. M. Gollwitzer and J. A. Bargh (Eds.), *The psychology of action: Linking cognitions and motivation to behavior* (pp. 553–578). New York: Guilford Press.

Fisher, W. 1984. "Narration as a human communication paradigm: The case of public moral argument." *Communication Monographs,* 51: 1–22.

Fisher, W. 1987. *Human communication as narrative: Toward a philosophy of reason, value, and action.* University of South Carolina, Columbia.

Griffin, E. 2003. *A first look at communication theory.* Boston: McGraw Hill.

Larson, C. 2007. *Persuasion: Reception and responsibility.* (11th ed.), Belmont, CA: Thompson Wadsworth Publishing.

Penner, L., and B. Fritzsche. 1993. "Magic Johnson and reactions to people with AIDS: A natural experiment." *Journal of Social Psychology,* 23: 1035–1050.

Petty, R., and J. Cacioppo. 1981. *Attitudes and persuasion: Classic and contemporary approaches.* Wm. C. Brown, Dubuque, IA.

Petty, R., and J. Cacioppo. 1986. *Communication and persuasion: Central and peripheral routes to attitude change.* New York: Springer-Verlag.

Petty, R., and J. Cacioppo. 1986b. "The elaboration likelihood model of persuasion." In L. Berkowitz (Ed.), *Advances in experimental social psychology* (Vol. 19, pp. 123–205). San Diego: Academic Press.

Petty, R., and D. Wegener. 1999. "The elaboration likelihood model: Current status and controversies," in *Dual process theories and social psychology.* Shelley Chaiken and Yaacov Trope (eds.), Guilford Press, New York, pp. 44–48.

Schultz, Q. 2006. *An essential guide to public speaking: Serving your audience with faith, skill and virtue.* Grand Rapids, MI: Baker Academic.

Chapter 4 Sidebar

Modern Persuasion Sidebar

Shane Puckett

Louisiana Tech University

In addition to models of persuasion theory and the foundation of compliance gaining acceptance within individual audience member, you must also understand what the audience will accept as information and argument. Beyond understanding how an individual chooses to accept one argument over another, the arguer must first assess what parameters exist within the audience for acceptance of information. There are two postmodern philosophical argumentation theories that best exemplify Stephen Toulmin's concept of argument "fields" and Michel Foucault's concept of "knowledge." Once we understand the concepts and parameters of what the audience will accept as information or knowledge, we can then understand which arguments will best yield compliance.

Most know Stephen Toulmin's work by his "Toulmin Model," the argumentation model comprised of six interrelated components. However, in the construction of these components, Toulmin's philosophy of arguments' fields underpins what should be selected within the model for an audience. His model of practical arguments justifies claims rather than inferring claims from evidence (Toulmin 1958). Justification is a retrospective activity, while inference is a prospective one. Justification is concerned with how people share their ideas and thoughts in a situation that raise the question of whether or not those ideas are worth sharing (Janik, Rieke and Toulmin 1979). The idea that argument involves justification leads Toulmin to discuss the standards by which arguments succeed or fail to justify claims. An argument is deemed as justified, only if it is able to survive the criticism offered by those who participate in the rational enterprises of various fields (Toulmin 1972). Toulmin's use of the word "field" is his way of explaining that different situations and contexts will require different criteria and standards. While other perspectives assume that arguments are the same regardless of the field, Toulmin argues that some elements of argument differ from one field to another. Toulmin notes that fields can be described as disciplines that you subscribe to (i.e., training, education, or profession), or fields can be seen as the relationship when sociological entities come to share a constellation of practices (Willard 1982).

Understanding the fields that are associated with your judges within each debate round will help you access the information that they view as logical or right. In addition to the information that the judges will accept as most relevant to their fields, you can also assemble your argument in a logical arrangement which the judges will deem as "probable," "possible," or "necessary." Understanding what information the judges will accept and how to logically arrange it for them to perceive the information as "true" or "plausible" is the key to accessing the ballot and winning a debate round. Most common fields that are seen

50   Contributed by Shane Puckett. Copyright © Kendall Hunt Publishing Company

in a debate round can be the profession of the judge (i.e. professor, student, etc.) or group affiliations (religious organizations, political affiliations, marital status). These relationships give insight to which justification arguments are most likely to be preserved as valid by each judge.

Beyond the ideas and the arguments that judges affirm as true because they fit within the fields that the judges ascribe to, judges' opinions are also shaped by what society governs as knowledge. In order for a debater to access what can be seen as logical knowledge, a debater must understand what the judge sees as knowledge. Foucault explores why we allow certain concepts in the marketplace and why others are not allowed. In addition to understanding how information is deemed knowledge, Foucault also tries to determine why certain groups give alternate weight to the same marketplace concepts at different times. Thus, Foucault wants to know why certain ideas were important in the past, but are not given much weight in today's society.

Foucault first examines knowledge by trying to understand and define "discourse." He believes that discourse plays a central role in the creation of knowledge. Everything that can be spoken about in a particular discourse community is considered as knowledge (Lotringer 1989). This process occurs through "discursive formation," which is defined by the total set of relations that unite, at a given period, the discursive practices that give rise to epistemological figures, sciences, and possibly formalized systems (Foucault 1970). It is the grid or network that allows thought to be organized. In other words, discursive formation is a cultural code that is a characteristic system, structure, network, ground of thought, or style of organization that governs the language, perception, values, and practices of a system, a community or a historical period. Only one discursive formation can dominate at any one time because the structure governing the discursive formation is so fundamental that, in the age of one discursive formation, to think by means of another is extremely difficult.

Foucault explains that the nature of a discursive formation can be known through the discovery and articulation of the rules that characterize it (Foucault 1972). Knowledge can only exist if it follows certain rules. These rules, which are typically unconscious, and as a result often cannot be clearly and easily articulated, determine that one statement rather than another comes to be uttered in a particular discursive formation. They determine the possibilities for the content and form of discourse. While there are many of these rules for different contents and contexts, they usually are found in three categories.

The first of these categories for the rules that govern knowledge deals with the control over what is being talked about as/in a discursive formation. It governs both the discourse and appearance of the object. For example, rules in this category include prohibitions against talking about certain things—namely rules that silence certain dimensions of experience simply by not recognizing them as objects of discourse (Foucault 1972). For instance, in the Victorian Age, children's sexuality simply was not an object of discourse, therefore children's sexuality was not discussed, and that aspect of children's experience was repressed. Within intercollegiate debate, we see these governing rules in discursive formation when it is known that the judge will not listen to procedural arguments like topicality, or when we know that judges do not favor the idea of kritiks in debate. In order to access arguments and gain the "win" in a debate round, we must understand the governing rules of the people adjudicating. The more a debater understands what the judge considers "knowledge," the more probability the debater has at accessing the round with their arguments.

The second category of governing rules does not concern itself with what is being said, but who is saying it. These rules dictate that people listen to the discourses of certain individuals and reject the discourses of others. The discourses of those who are not heard are considered "null and void, without truth or significance, worthless as evidence, inadmissible in the authentication of acts or contracts" (Foucault 1972). Culture and society will only listen to the discourse of certain people and reject the rhetoric of others. Lawyers, for example, must pass the bar examination in order to practice law. Individuals listen to medical doctors speak about issues involving health because discursive rules attribute competence to medical doctors in this area, while the discourse of practitioners of alternative medicine is generally not heard because the practitioners have not fulfilled the conditions for competence established for speakers of medical discourse. We see this governing rule in intercollegiate competitive debate when debaters get into citation wars. Citation wars happen when debaters compare authors of their evidence in the round. Instead of the argument being the focus of debate, the debate shifts to which competitor has the best author. We see this also when adjudicators give the "win" to competitors with the justification "they had citations" or "they cited sources." This example explains how the argument was not the focus of the debate round, but rather the focus was on the authorship of the arguments.

The last of these governing rule categories concerns the form that the concepts and theories must assume to be accepted as knowledge. Some of these rules govern the arrangement of statements required for a discourse to be seen as knowledge, while others dictate the style and form of that discourse (Foucault 1972). When professors publish in academia, for example, they have to write in a way that adheres to the rules of the journal's style (i.e. APA, MLA, Chicago, etc.). If the article does not adhere to the proper form, style or arrangement, the information will be rejected as knowledge. The ideas of delivery, courtesy, and organization are all examples of how adjudicators examine form in intercollegiate competitive debate. When judges examine arguments about the resolution as they pertain to the trichotomy of propositions, they are assessing whether or not the information came to them in the appropriate form to be perceived as knowledge or truth. Many times, if a debate violates these forms, the judge will reject the competitor's access to the resolution.

While understanding the treatment of the persuasion process through a model helps us shape our rhetoric, we must also understand the information that will be accepted as knowledge by the listeners. As Toulmin explains, understanding the context and perspectives of the adjudicators and the "field" or lens that they view the world through will assist you in meeting the needs of the adjudicators' reality to persuade them. In a slightly different way, Foucault agrees with this idea. He examines what information to use due to governing rules that determines what is or is not knowledge. Beyond seeing persuasion as an object to be obtained, rather one can see persuasion as fluid, meeting the needs of realities for compliance-gaining.

WORKS CITED

Janik, A., Rieke, R., and S. Toulmin. 1979. *An Introduction to Reasoning.* New York, NY: Macmillan.

Fisher, Walter R. (1984). "Narration as Human Communication Paradigm: The Case of Public Moral Argument." in Communication Monographs 51. pp. 1–22.

Foucault, M. 1970. *The Order of Things: An Archaeology of Human Science.* New York, NY: Pantheon.

Foucault, M. 1972. *The Archaeology of Knowledge and Discourse on Language.* (A.M. Sheridan Smith, Trans.). New York, NY: Pantheon.

Foucault, M. 1972. "History, Discourse, and Discontinuity." *Salmagundi.* (A. M. Nazzaro, Trans.), 20, 225–248.

Lotringer, S. (Ed.). 1989. *Foucault Live (Interviews, 1961–1984).* (L. Hochroth and J. Johnson, Trans). New York, NY: Semiotext(e).

Petty, R. E., & Cacioppo, J. T. (1996). Addressing disturbing and disturbed consumer behavior: Is it necessary to change the way we conduct behavioral science? Journal of Marketing Research, 33, 1–8.

Toulmin, S. 1958. *The Uses of Argument.* Cambridge, UK: Cambridge University Press.

Toulmin, S. 1972. *Human Understanding, Vol I: The collective Use and Evolution of Concepts.* Princeton, NJ: Princeton University Press.

Willard, C. A. 1982. *Argument Fields: Advances in Argumentation Theory and Research.* Carbondale, IL: Southern Illinois University Press.

Chapter 5

Ethos: The Strongest Proof of All

Cole Franklin
East Texas Baptist State University

Aristotle defined rhetoric as "the power to observe the persuasiveness of which any particular matter admits" Aristotle (1991). He went on to identify three proofs available to the speaker in rhetoric: character or "ethos," disposition or "pathos," and the speech itself or" logos". While pathos and logos are discussed elsewhere in this text, this chapter focuses specifically on ethos. Aristotle believed that if a speaker was worthy of credence, that credence could be used as proof by the speaker. In fact, Aristotle said "character contains almost the strongest proof of all" Aristotle (1991). This chapter will address the elements of persuasion that are based upon ethos, some rules for ethical speaking, three dimensions of ethos and some practical strategies to improve speaker credibility.

ETHOS-BASED ELEMENTS OF PERSUASION

In order to understand ethos more fully, one must have a grasp of what elements are entailed in ethos. In his discussion of ethos, Aristotle identified three elements of this form of proof. In order for a speaker to truly have a high level of ethos, he or she must possess and demonstrate the characteristics detailed below.

First, speakers with ethos must demonstrate a sense of competence. They must show that they have knowledge of and experience with the subject at hand. Without a demonstration of competence, an audience is unlikely to believe what a speaker has to say.

Second, a speaker must demonstrate high moral character. The speaker must be honest and trustworthy in his or her presentation. Speakers must appear to hold to high ethical standards in their presentation. In order to do this, speakers should adhere to four standards for ethical speaking. According to O'Hair, Stewart, and Rubenstein (2010), there are four ground rules for ethical speaking: trustworthiness, respect, responsibility, and fairness. Trustworthiness "is a combination of honesty and dependability" (O'Hair, Stewart, and

Contributed by Cole Franklin. Copyright © Kendall Hunt Publishing Company

55

Rubenstein 2010, 71). Trustworthiness includes giving full disclosure and information to an audience. Respect means treating people in the right and proper way. Debaters must also have respect for both their judge and their opponent. Debaters should refrain from engaging in personal attacks and treat competitors in a respectful manner. Responsibility requires that speakers understand the power they have to influence others and use that power for the good of others even if a debater must support a resolution he or she does not personally support. Fairness involves being open-minded and seeing both sides of an issue. While it is important for a debater to see both sides of an issue, obviously, the affirmative or negative will present evidence that supports his or her respective side of the resolution. Being open-minded does not negate the necessity to present information supportive of your position on the resolution.

The third element of persuasion based on ethos is that of goodwill toward the audience. A speaker must demonstrate concern for the audience. While many times the only audience member in a debate round may be the judge, debaters should show an active interest in the judge and appeal to him or her. As Cirlin (2006) stated, "one of the most important intellectual skills IPDA can teach is how to anticipate the needs and desires of different audiences and adjust to them" (41). He went on to state that "the speaker with superior audience analysis will be much more likely to persuade the judge" (42). In order to understand the judge, a debater must be concerned for the goodwill of the judge and seek to tailor the message to the individuality of that particular judge.

DIMENSIONS OF ETHOS

McCroskey (2001) identified three dimensions of ethos that a speaker should be aware of, as these elements can be a significant factor in a judge's or audience's decision. The three dimensions are initial, derived, and terminal ethos.

Initial ethos is that which a speaker has before he or she begins speaking. According to McCroskey, one's "background, personal characteristics, and appearance all contribute to a source's initial ethos" (90). Cirlin (2006) makes some specific suggestions to assist the IPDA debater in enhancing his or her initial ethos: "Find out what you can and start doing some initial thinking about what this critic's biases are likely to be. Are we talking male or female? Old or young? Formal or informal? Student or teacher" (46)? Finding out what one can about the judge can enable to debater to make adjustments to enhance his or her initial ethos before speaking in the round even begins.

Derived ethos is that which a speaker creates by making modifications during a speaking encounter in an effort to raise his or her ethos in the mind of the audience, or judge, in the case of a debate round. McCroskey suggests that the use of effective supporting material or evidence, effective delivery, speaker sincerity, and message organization can all impact derived ethos. Speakers who utilize good evidence will have higher ethos than speakers who do not have good supporting materials. Good delivery is also necessary to higher ethos. This can be evidenced by the fact that in a debate round, competitors with higher speaker points generally will win the round.

Terminal ethos "is the product of the interaction between initial ethos and derived ethos" (McCroskey 2001, 95). It is the ethos a speaker or debater has at the conclusion of a speaking encounter or debate round. One's terminal ethos will influence one's initial ethos at

Chapter 5: Ethos: The Strongest Proof of All • **57**

the beginning of the next encounter. Or in the case of debate, a competitor's ethos follow-ing a round will influence the initial ethos of that competitor the next time the debater is judged by the same adjudicator.

IMPROVING ETHOS

Gass and Seiter (2003) offer some specific techniques that one can utilize to enhance cred-ibility. Some are offered below with particular tips for IPDA debaters.

1. Be prepared: The old adage says practice makes perfect. While that may not be entirely true, good preparation does lead to better performance, no matter what the activity or venue. IPDA debate provides competitors with 30 minutes of preparation time. Use it wisely. Even if you feel knowledgeable and comfortable with the resolution and your position, use your preparation time to outline your case, look for new research, ask others for any additional insight they might have into the topic. Going into a round ill-prepared will be evident to a judge and the lack of preparation will be a glaring shortcoming in a round. Learn as much as you can about your resolution and design a case that you feel comfortable presenting. This confidence will be evident to a judge and will lead to better results.

2. Cite evidence and supporting materials: While IPDA debate does not emphasize evi-dence as some other formats of debate do, evidence is still essential. Competitors who enter a round with little or no evidence to support their contentions will be quickly admonished by the opponent and the judge's comments on the ballot. Good evidence is always useful in a debate round and competitors should look for high quality, recent research that will form credible sources to enhance a case. Credible research will lend credibility to the speaker and raise the speaker's ethos.

3. Demonstrate honesty and sincerity: While it is difficult to gauge how honest or trustworthy one is in a 30-minute debate round, speakers who demonstrate good moral character can raise their ethos in the mind of a judge. Additionally, if the judge is familiar with a competitor, the terminal ethos established in prior interactions can have positive or negative carry-over into the current debate round.

4. Display goodwill toward your audience: Competitors should demonstrate a true interest in the judge during a round. As one former debate coach stated, "The only thing that happens in a debate round is what the judge hears." Additionally, if the judge feels that the competitors are truly interested in him or her, the judge will feel more of a connec-tion to the competitors and their ethos will rise in the mind of the judge.

5. Adapt language to the listener: Speakers should always strive to tailor their speaking style to the listener. The suggestion for debaters is the same. This includes avoiding slang and jargon (unless you know your judge well and believe that he or she is inter-ested in hearing jargon) and eliminating vocal interruptions such as "uhms" and "ahs", pauses and gaps. Additionally, speakers should pay attention to their rate of speech as some judges are opposed to fast speaking or "spreading."

6. Avoid powerless speech: Competitors should attempt to use powerful assertive language instead of powerless and weak language. Avoid the use of tag questions ("The admin-istration should lower taxes, shouldn't they?"), hesitations ("uhm," "uh"), and hedges

("kind of," "sort of," "maybe"). Speakers who use powerless language often seem weak to a judge. This weakness can greatly reduce a speaker's ethos or credibility.

7. <u>Try to increase listener involvement</u>: Speakers who can effectively demonstrate to a judge why this issue at hand is important are more likely to be successful in their persuasive attempts. Competitors should be able to explain to the judge exactly why the issue is relevant to him or her. This will lead to the judge becoming more involved in the subject and feeling more confident in the speaker and his or her perspective on this relevant issue.

While pathos, logos, and ethos are all useful to a speaker and debater, ethos often is the factor that sways a judge in a round. This influence could be due to the fact that speakers with high ethos generally incorporate logos and pathos in their presentations. As noted, if a speaker uses high quality evidence (logos) in a round, his or her ethos will rise. Likewise, speakers who demonstrate empathy and concern for their audience (pathos) also generally have higher ethos. IPDA debaters should never overlook the importance and influence of ethos in their rounds.

REFERENCES

Aristotle. 1991. *The Art of Rhetoric* (H.C. Lawson Tancred, Trans.). New York: Penguin Books.

Cirlin, A. 2006. *Audience Analysis*. In S. Jeffcoat and K. Peterson (Eds.), *Public Debate: A Guidebook to IPDA* (pp. 41–48). Thomson.

Gass, R. H., and J. S. Seiter. 2003. *Persuasion, Social Influence and Compliance Gaining*. Boston: Allyn and Bacon.

McCroskey, J. C. 2001. *An Introduction to Rhetorical Communication*. Boston: Allyn and Bacon.

O'Hair, D., Stewart, R., and H. Rubenstein. 2010. *A Speaker's Guidebook: Text and Reference*. Boston: Bedford/St. Martin's.

Chapter 6

Pathos: Emotional Appeals in IPDA Debate

Michael Ingram
Whitworth University

The classic television show and film series *Star Trek* featured two characters who argued from different points of view. Mr. Spock was the science officer who argued from logic. His claims were based on evidence and logical inferences and were detached from emotional considerations. He believed the only way to discover truth was to strip away all emotions and focus solely on logic. Dr. McCoy was the chief medical officer who argued from emotions and his heart. When both presented advice to Captain Kirk, McCoy consistently made emotional appeals, and considered how decisions would affect others emotionally. Perhaps some of Kirk's best decisions were made by listening to both logical and emotional appeals, and seeing where they could work together.

A survey of textbooks on argumentation and debate will reveal considerable coverage of logic, how to build intellectual appeals, and how to substantiate claims with external proof. Certainly there is a need for clear and ordered thinking in public discourse and in intercollegiate debate rounds. Yet there is also a need to recognize the prevalence of emotional appeals in common argumentation outside of debate rounds, and the proper role of such appeals inside the round. This chapter will provide guidance on how to use emotional appeals inside and outside of a tournament.

DEFINITIONS

The term **pathos** comes from Aristotle. It is one of his three artistic proofs, along with logos and ethos. Garver (1994) quotes Aristotle "The emotions are those things through which, by undergoing change, people come **to differ in their judgments** and which are accompanied by pain and pleasure." Golden et al. (2011) quote Aristotle "the hearers themselves become the **instruments of proof when emotion is stirred in them** by the speech; for we give our judgment in different ways under the influence of pain and joy, of liking and

Contributed by Michael Ingram. Copyright © Kendall Hunt Publishing Company

60 • IPDA Textbook

of hatred." An audience that feels anger, or may be inclined to feel anger, is likely to hear an argument differently than an audience that is not angry nor inclined toward it. Audiences will react differently to arguments depending on their emotions, and speakers can address those emotions to try and move the audience in a particular direction.

Aristotle believed speakers should know the emotional state of their audience and could use that to their advantage in making an argument. He described several emotions including anger, fear, shame, and pity. Debaters should know who their audiences are and what they are likely to believe. Direct appeals to these likely emotions of the audience can be persuasive.

Speakers use intentional appeals to emotion to stimulate an emotional response in the audience. Crowley and Hawhee argue "emotional appeals are based on the assumption that human beings share similar kinds of emotional response to events. . .(1999, 148)." An appeal to the pain resulting from the death of a child, or an appeal to the anger of injustice is likely to find similar reactions from diverse audience members. Thus emotional appeals are attempts to build a stronger connection between speakers and their audiences, as well as influencing audiences to believe the claims of speakers.

There are many occasions where speakers count **on audience emotions to help further their point**. Commencement speeches at graduation are full of emotional appeals, discussing themes like gratitude and using descriptive language to evoke memories of students' first days on campus and comparing them to the feelings of completing their degree. Ceremonial speeches of remembrance, like those at 9/11 commemorative events, evoke common feelings of loss, grief, and hope. Pastors and priests preach sermons calling on the faithful to believe and act with their whole heart.

Debaters may also use emotions to help judges and audiences better understand a point. They may refer to particular **emotional examples** to bolster a claim. They may describe iconic images, like flooding scenes from New Orleans after Hurricane Katrina, to help audiences see and feel the results of particular issues. Not all emotional appeals are fallacies of argument, and some appeals can be quite helpful.

While emotion has a place in argumentation, it should not be substituted for logic altogether. Speakers using emotional appeals alone are likely to craft arguments based on fallacies, and offer weaker claims. A stronger combination is to construct arguments of sound logic and evidence, and combine them with considerations of the audience's emotions.

FIRST APPLICATION: HUMANIZE THE CLAIMS IN A DEBATE ROUND

There are at least four ways debaters can use emotional appeals appropriately and effectively in rounds. <u>One way of using pathos appropriately is to tell a story that illustrates an argument.</u> On January 28, 2014, President Barack Obama delivered his annual State of the Union address to Congress, and to the American people via television and radio. Obama used an emotional story, which he hoped people could relate to, and thus connect more with his arguments.

I'm also convinced we can help Americans return to the workforce faster by reforming unemployment insurance so that it's more effective in today's economy. But first,

Chapter 6: Pathos: Emotional Appeals in IPDA Debate • **61**

this Congress needs to restore the unemployment insurance you just let expire for 1.6 million people.

Let me tell you why. Misty DeMars is a mother of two young boys. She'd been steadily employed since she was a teenager. She put herself through college. She'd never collected unemployment benefits. In May, she and her husband used their life savings to buy their first home. A week later, budget cuts claimed the job she loved. Last month, when their unemployment insurance was cut off, she sat down and wrote me a letter—the kind I get every day. "We are the face of the unemployment crisis," she wrote. "I am not dependent on the government. . .Our country depends on people like us who build careers, contribute to society. . .care about our neighbors. . .I am confident that in time I will find a job. . .I will pay my taxes, and we will raise our children in their own home in the community we love. Please give us this chance."

Congress, give these hardworking, responsible Americans that chance. They need our help, but more important, this country needs them in the game.

Obama hopes Congress will make a specific reform. He uses a story that stirs emotions, and builds a connection between his example and the likely emotions of the audience to persuade hearers to embrace his reform.

In many State of the Union addresses, the president will recognize someone present in the chambers who has accomplished something remarkable and is labeled as a hero. Often this leads to a standing ovation for the guest while sitting in the "hero's gallery." President Ronald Reagan began this rhetorical practice on January 26, 1982, by inviting Lenny Skutnik to the speech. Skutnik jumped into the freezing Potomac River to rescue a woman after an Air Florida jet had crashed in the water earlier that month.

We don't have to turn to our history books for heroes. They're all around us. One who sits among you here tonight epitomized that heroism at the end of the longest imprisonment ever inflicted on men of our Armed Forces. Who will ever forget that night when we waited for television to bring us the scene of that first plane landing at Clark Field in the Philippines, bringing our POW's home? The plane door opened and Jeremiah Denton came slowly down the ramp. He caught sight of our flag, saluted it, said, "God bless America," and then thanked us for bringing him home.

Just two weeks ago, in the midst of a terrible tragedy on the Potomac, we saw again the spirit of American heroism at its finest—the heroism of dedicated rescue workers saving crash victims from icy waters. And we saw the heroism of one of our young government employees, Lenny Skutnik, who, when he saw a woman lose her grip on the helicopter line, dived into the water and dragged her to safety.

And then there are countless, quiet, everyday heroes of American life—parents who sacrifice long and hard so their children will know a better life than they've known; church and civic volunteers who help to feed, clothe, nurse, and teach the needy; millions who've made our nation and our nation's destiny so very special—unsung heroes who may not have realized their own dreams themselves but then who reinvest those dreams in their children. Don't let anyone tell you that America's best days are behind her, that the American spirit has been vanquished. We've seen it triumph too often in our lives to stop believing in it now.

In each case, the president uses the hero as an emotional appeal to get the audience to both like the guest and to like his own message. Reagan uses the presence of a hero to bolster the power of his own claim.

Stories also stand out in **memory**. It is easier for most people to remember an emotional story or parable than it is to remember a logical proof or series of syllogisms that establish a claim. The emotion embedded in a story can help elongate the effects of the speaker on the audience.

Such stories can also convey the likely implications of an argument. Rather than describing the effects of a policy plan only in terms of numerical data, some integration of emotion in a specific context can provide a fuller picture. When the Social Security Administration raised the age of "full retirement" from 65 to 67 in 1983, there were logical reasons for the change such as saving money in the system and acknowledging the fact that the average American life span is longer than it was in the past. In 2015, two presidential candidates called for the full retirement age to be raised again, also in the name of saving money and preserving social security.

Opponents of such an increase might use emotional appeals to ask advocates of another increase to imagine telling this news to their own parents or grandparents. Such an appeal allows for a fuller consideration of the effects of a policy. It calls listeners to hear not only the facts but also the implications in a particular way. The claim "it is necessary for the federal government to raise the retirement age for social security full benefits" can be substantiated with various financial data. But to also put the counterclaim in the context of "imagine your elderly parents having to work three more years" or "your grandparents have worked for 43 years, and now the federal government wants them to work even more for benefits they already deserve" works to get listeners' attention. It requires audiences to think about the full implementation of a course of action.

Crowley and Hawhee note the power of stories. "Rhetors who can imagine the emotions evoked by a scene may stimulate similar emotions in their audiences by developing the power of **enargeia**, a figure in which rhetors picture events so vividly that they seem actually to be taking place before the audience (1999, 155)." A clear and powerful description of the actions of heroes, or effects of the raised retirement age, can be quite influential on audiences.

A second way of using pathos appropriately is connecting the claim to how the audience should feel. Consider debate over the Affordable Care Act (ACA). Speakers can overtly direct audiences to what they should feel about a claim, or they can indirectly lead audiences toward a certain emotional response. Debaters can tell the audience they should feel outrage or sympathy or pity.

In 2015, the Catholic charity "Little Sisters of the Poor" lost their suit in federal court. The ACA requires organizations to provide a type of health care for their employees that included contraceptives, which are contrary to traditional Catholic moral teachings. The federal government had exempted churches and some religious organizations, while offering religious universities and others religious organizations an exemption by using a third party who would provide the contraceptives to employees. The Little Sisters rejected this third party approach, believing it still forced them to act against their religious views.

Chapter 6: Pathos: Emotional Appeals in IPDA Debate • **63**

Speakers who favor the Little Sisters and their arguments might direct audiences to overtly feel sad at the loss of First Amendment religious freedoms for the Little Sisters. They might direct audiences to feel anger over the ruling, and toward the government agencies that did not uphold religious liberty. Speakers favoring the ACA third party exemption option might tell audiences to rejoice at the First Amendment not requiring everyone to hold a particular religious view at their job and to celebrate this verdict with joy. Debaters can tell audiences not only what to believe, but what to feel as well. Channeling the emotions of the audience may also shape future actions that debaters want the audiences to take.

Debaters can select from a wide range of emotions in telling audiences to feel joy, happiness, sadness, anger, or a myriad of others. In many IPDA debates about actions of the United States, or the United States Federal Government, common emotional appeals can include anger at a government action, sympathy for those suffering from discrimination and harm, or hope from a newly proposed law or policy. Not all audience members will follow the speaker's direction to feel a certain way while listening to a speech, but it is likely some audience members will.

A third way of using pathos appropriately is to consider the language in which you place arguments. Using a descriptive name can convey emotional meaning, whether in a positive way or negative way. In 2014, many Republican politicians called the ACA by a shorter and more evocative name of "Obamacare." When they campaigned against this legislation back home, they were able to invoke passions of their partisan audiences who were not supporters of President Obama. Attaching the name of a political adversary to a program can help persuade the audience to support their member of Congress simply on the basis of a common dislike of that person.

This can function as a **rhetorical shortcut** for arguments against a previously established position, and avoid simply being an ad hominiem attack. If Republican Congresswoman Cathy McMorris Rogers has already made a variety of arguments against Obama's policies, then the act of attaching his name to a potentially unfavorable policy, simply reinforces previously established arguments in the minds of her supporters in the audience.

Crowley and Hawhee note the power of **honorific** language, which treats people and things respectfully, and **pejorative** language, which disparages and downplays them (1999, 156). Debaters can use language of praise to elevate people and positions they advocate, such as "agreeing with the wise course of action proposed by the experienced and influential Senator X." Debaters could use pejorative language to disagree with "the mistaken views of the oft-confused Senator Z."

Using **descriptive language** can convey powerful emotional meaning. In 1963 Dr. Martin Luther King, Jr. spoke at the Mall in Washington, D.C. delivering his "I have a dream" speech. The speech contains emotional language that positions King's claims into ordinary situations where audience could connect with him.

But one hundred years later, the Negro still is not free. One hundred years later, the life of the Negro is still sadly crippled by the manacles of segregation and the chains of discrimination. One hundred years later, the Negro lives on a lonely island of poverty in the midst of a vast ocean of material prosperity. One hundred years later, the Negro is still languished in the corners of American society and finds himself an exile in his own land. And so we've come here today to dramatize a shameful condition.

64 • IPDA Textbook

The descriptive language and King's powerful delivery combine to make the case against racial discrimination more persuasive. He used another metaphor and description to further his claims.

> In a sense we've come to our nation's capital to cash a check. When the architects of our republic wrote the magnificent words of the Constitution and the Declaration of Independence, they were signing a promissory note to which every American was to fall heir. This note was a promise that all men, yes, black men as well as white men, would be guaranteed the "unalienable Rights" of "Life, Liberty and the pursuit of Happiness." It is obvious today that America has defaulted on this promissory note, insofar as her citizens of color are concerned. Instead of honoring this sacred obligation, America has given the Negro people a bad check, a check which has come back marked "insufficient funds."

> But we refuse to believe that the bank of justice is bankrupt. We refuse to believe that there are insufficient funds in the great vaults of opportunity of this nation. And so, we've come to cash this check, a check that will give us upon demand the riches of freedom and the security of justice.

Reprinted by arrangement with The Heirs to the Estate of Martin Luther King Jr., c/o Writers House as agent for the proprietor New York, NY.

Language can be used to direct the thinking of the audience. The Sapir-Whorf hypothesis suggests that language shapes a human's sense of reality. Human perceptions of the world rely on language. The descriptive words used by speakers are deliberate intentions to color a viewpoint. In recent years the "gambling" industry has recast itself as the "gaming" industry, hoping to change audience perceptions of their services. Gambling might sound risky and perhaps morally suspect, but gaming sounds like fun.

In 1987, the National Football League Players Association went on strike for three games. The NFL recruited new players, added them to rosters and played games for three weeks. The NFL referred to them as "replacement players" who were legitimate, new, and temporary employees of the league. The union referred to them as "scabs" who were there to take away the jobs of other men. In describing this situation and making an argument about management-union relationships, the very word choice reveals both the speakers' attitudes toward the topic, and how they want the audience to feel.

Consider the political position of those, like the National Abortion Rights Action League (NARAL) who believe that women ought to be allowed to make their own decisions over whether to have an abortion. They tend to be labeled "pro-choice" while for years the opposing side, including groups like the National Right to Life Committee (NRTC), were labeled "pro-life."

However, some NARAL sympathizers will use the expression "anti-choice" to describe the NRTC. The NARAL Pro-Choice America website tracks "anti-choice" legislators and legislation. Abortion is certainly a complex issue, and the powerful emotional language employed can shape viewpoints. Various groups who favor legal abortion use the language of "anti-choice" to convey an emotion that the other side does not subscribe to the freedom to choose, the current federal law or women's autonomy. Such groups might make an overt argument that the other side is "taking away freedom" and put that in emotional terms. And some NRTC sympathizers will use the expression "pro-death" to describe NARAL, and use descriptive language to describe the process of an abortion.

Debaters should be aware that emotional language can sometimes obfuscate the claim and hinder clear and effective communication. Emotional language can draw attention to itself and get in the way of the message. When opposing debaters resort to emotionally charged language in lieu of evidence and logic, or even with evidence and logic, the meaning can still be lost. Thus emotional language needs to be used carefully.

Finally, a fourth way of using pathos appropriately is to overtly address both the heart and mind. Speakers should let the audience know they are aware of both the intellectual and the emotional dimensions of an argument. Debaters should use both logos and pathos in arguing their case.

When some environmental groups like Greenpeace call for greater legislation to reduce or prevent pollution of the environment, they must demonstrate knowledge of the effects of chemicals in the air or water. They create logos-based arguments on the science of the chemicals, and use research-based proof to support their claims. Such speakers must combine this knowledge with an emotionally-based appeal to create a sense of urgency for audiences to believe and act. They must show reputable proof that environmental damage in the Arctic is caused by humans, and they may use stories of cute polar bears to help win a hearing and make their full case using emotions and logic.

One caution is that emotional appeals should not substitute substantial argumentation. It is easy to find a political debate where one politician simply repeats a slogan or an emotional statement, instead of providing a complete answer to a question, or a complete thought to a problem. It is also easy to find persuasive campaigns based on emotions alone. Resist letting the emotional appeal substitute careful and critical thinking.

SECOND APPLICATION: DELIVERY WITH EMOTION

First, emotion can be used in altering delivery patterns to convey **urgency** of a claim. Imagine the same arguments being delivered by two different speakers. The first speaker proceeds in a manner that is factual and clear, but uses little variance in vocal pitch, rate, or tone and has a monotone delivery. The second speaker presents the same argument but with some emotion in the voice. Passion and urgency are added to the presentation by using a wider range of vocal features. In many IPDA rounds, audiences are more likely to respond to debaters who have employed some emotion that demonstrates a commitment of the speaker to the argument, and establishes some urgency for the claims.

Good speakers use a full range of vocal patterns to make their case. Christian evangelist and speaker Beth Moore employs a wide range of volume, vocal pitch, and speed when speaking to audiences about the Christian faith. Making any sort of change to one's vocal cadence can help audiences realize that this section sounds different, and might be more important than the surrounding text. Speaking a bit faster or slower can grab the audience's attention. Raising or lowering the volume level, or making the vocal pitch higher or lower also gets the audience's attention. Such alteration signifies the particular importance of a passage, and can make the overall presentation sound more conversational.

Certainly there are settings where audiences are accustomed to hearing facts and arguments reported in an emotionless way, like physicians gathering medical clues on a complex patient case, or bankers evaluating reasons to purchase or not purchase a smaller bank. Yet when the time comes to make an argument and call for a course of action, speakers

66 • *IPDA Textbook*

who have a particular claim to offer will be better served by using emotions to convey the strength of their perspective.

Second, passionate delivery can help bolster ethos. Audiences want to see speakers who believe what they say. Speakers using passion or conviction in their voice are more likely to win a hearing. Integrating emotion conveys a life to the argument and works to increase the speaker's credibility. Again, this is not substituting emotion for the argument. It is calling on speakers to show some evidence of emotion in some parts of their presentation to demonstrate a commitment to the claims.

Speakers sharing a story from their own lives will often use emotions to emphasize the pains of particular trials they have faced. And they can use emotions to demonstrate joy and confidence when recounting how they overcame those trials.

In the final rebuttal speeches of IPDA debates, speakers can use passion to help their case. Debaters can blend confidence and power in their voice to strengthen the emotional force of their argument. In the dominant North American cultural context, debaters who look judges in the eye and speak slightly louder than normal and with urgency in their voice can foster emotional responses in the audience. Debaters who have been clear and organized, have used clear logic, and have presented good evidence will be even stronger by providing some emotion in their delivery to convince the audience of their viewpoint.

THIRD APPLICATION: AVOID LOGICAL FALLACIES

Debaters should be wary of emotional appeals that cloud judgment. Be careful not to stray into fallacies by using emotional appeals without logical proof. Speakers and debaters should avoid these types of emotional appeals.

First, avoid substituting emotional claims for authoritative proof. Using emotions alone for proof is insufficient. To argue "favorable emotions are associated with X; therefore, X is true" is to lack proof for the claim. Imagine a political candidate arguing, "We must make America great again—so vote for me and I will make America great!" There might be passion in the delivery and emotive words in the claim, but there is no presence of proof in this claim. A stronger claim would include evidence like "In my previous roles, I did X, Y, and Z which contributed to the increased greatness in my state."

Some advertisements use emotions without proof. Budweiser beer often uses television commercials featuring the Clydesdale horses and other winsome animals. These animals and images cannot offer proof as to why consumers should purchase Budweiser for its taste, value, or quality. While these commercials are often effective in getting people to remember their product, they do not offer evidence to support the claim. Such appeals are less successful during in-person debates than they are during Super Bowl advertisements.

Second, avoid ad hominem, where you attack the person and not the claim. If Person A argues X, and Person B attacks Person A and therefore claims X is false, the ad hominem fallacy is present. The person, or quality of the person making the argument does not prove that the argument is true or is false. Often ad hominem attacks use emotive language to describe someone in unflattering terms.

If the affirmative debater claims that "raising taxes will stimulate job creation," and the negative debater argues "you are from a small and academically-suspect state university so your judgment is suspect, and therefore we should not raise taxes" the fallacy has occurred.

If the affirmative debater argues "the United States should withdraw from NATO," and the negative debater argues "it is clear my opponent has a yellow streak of cowardice, so this conclusion must be set aside," the fallacy is present.

Using emotional appeals to attack the person (quite apart from legitimate concerns on credibility) is not helpful to the debate. Resist emotional attacks on other debaters and focus on addressing the claims, reasoning, and proof.

Third, avoid the appeal to popularity approach where something is purported to be true because "everyone" believes it. This is structured as "most people believe X (or have favorable emotions toward it) so X must be true." It is easy to clothe these appeals in emotional language. Debaters might hear "Proposition One has overwhelming support so it must be the right course of action" without any demonstrable proof of such support. Debaters might hear "Proposition One has overwhelming support from right thinking persons everywhere, so it is abundantly clear to intelligent people that it is certainly the right course of action." But the claim is not logically true and inserting emotional descriptors does not make it any more true.

This fallacy might also be seen where the popularity of a premise is also used as evidence for its truthfulness. The claim "everyone thinks the capital of Washington should be moved to Spokane, so it must be the right thing to do" does not include proof or reasoning why the move would be a good idea.

In times past, everyone believed the earth was flat and that the sun revolved around the earth. Both claims were upheld with fervent and emotional belief, and probably with emotional and evocative language. But simply having a majority of believers does not inherently mean the claim is true. Debaters should be quick to look for proof for a claim beyond the statement of emotions held by "everyone."

SUMMARY

This chapter has discussed emotional appeals inside and outside of a tournament. Remember:

- Pathos recognizes audiences differ in their judgments by the power of emotions, and audiences become instruments of proof in pathos-based appeals.
- There are many occasions where speakers and debaters will make overt appeals to emotions that fit the situation.
- Pathos can humanize claims by providing a story to illustrate an argument, by telling the audience how they should feel, by making intentional language choices to convey an argument, and to overtly address the heart and mind by using appeals to logos and pathos.
- Emotions can be used in delivery to convey the urgency of claims by varying all aspects of the delivery, and to help bolster ethos by communicating the commitment of the speaker to the claims.
- Avoid the fallacies of substituting emotional claims for authoritative proof, of attacking the person instead of the claims, and appealing to popularity. Emotional appeals can blend with each of these logical fallacies to create logically weak claims.

Just as *Star Trek* had the logic of Mr. Spock and the emotions of Dr. McCoy to advise Captain Kirk, effective IPDA debaters will use pathos along with logos to offer their best possible arguments in the round.

BIBLIOGRAPHY

Crowley, S., and Debra H. 1999. *Ancient Rhetorics for Contemporary Students*. 2nd ed. Needham Heights, MA; Allyn & Bacon.

Garver, E. 1994. *Aristotle's Rhetoric: An Art of Character*. Chicago, IL: University of Chicago Press.

Golden, J. L., Goodwin B., William C. and J. M. Sproule. 2011. *The Rhetoric of Western Thought*. 10th ed. Dubuque, IA; Kendall Hunt Publishing Company.

King, Jr., M. L. "I Have a Dream." Speech, Washington, D.C., August 28, 1963. http://www.americanrhetoric.com/speeches/mlkihaveadream.htm

Obama, B. "State of the Union." Speech, Washington, D.C., January 28, 2014. 2014 - Obama: https://www.whitehouse.gov/the-press-office/2014/01/28/president-barack-obamas-state-union-address

Reagan, R. "State of the Union." Speech, Washington, D.C., January 26, 1982. Reagan 1982: http://www.pbs.org/wgbh/americanexperience/features/primary-resources/reagan-union-1983/

Chapter 6 Sidebar

Pathos Sidebar

Lauren Raynor

University of Arkansas-Monticello

1. Emotions are a critical tool in persuading an audience. Emotions drive people to make the choices they do in everyday life. An effective speaker can convey any emotion to their audience.

2. Speakers use emotions in different ways. Some chose passion or anger to persuade the audience, while others use sympathy and empathy to persuade. Depending on the resolution of the debate round, a variety of emotions can be used to emphasize a point. For example, when speaking about clubbing baby seals a speaker would most likely use sympathy to persuade the audience. However, when speaking about the effects of global warming a speaker may use urgency and fear to persuade the audience.

3. A speaker must decide what emotions to use in each resolution. IPDA debate has a variety of topics within each round. Therefore, as mentioned in the above notation, each topic calls for different emotional deliverances.

4. Empathy is a powerful persuasive tool. When a speaker is able to make the audience "feel" the argument, the audience can relate to and understand what the speaker is advocating. When a person "feels" passionate about a topic, then that passion persuades them to act.

5. Always advocate with passion. A speaker is always more persuasive when passion and emotion is brought into the argument. The way a speaker presents the argument through vocal fluctuation and body language all conveys passion. Thus, when the audience reads the speaker's emotions, the audience will be persuaded by the speaker's passion for the argument.

Contributed by Lauren Raynor. Copyright © Kendall Hunt Publishing Company

Chapter 7

Logos in IPDA Debate

Keith Milstead
University of Arkansas-Monticello

Aristotle defines logos as the "power of proving a truth, or an apparent truth, by means of persuasive arguments" (Aristotle and Roberts 2011). The very simplicity by which this is stated may give one reason to believe that logic is easy to discuss. However, scholars have written volumes attempting to describe what is meant by logical argumentation. First, we must understand that logical text and logical argumentation is not the same thing. Scholars have insisted that logical text can use mathematical premises much in the way that we assign definitions to terms in a dictionary (Parker and Veatch 1959, 80–85). This is to mean that logic in its purest "written" form may need more structure and support than spoken argumentation in a debate round. The difference, of course, is a specific audience member: the judge. This chapter will discuss the necessity for, and manner and techniques by which logos may be used in IPDA in order for debaters to be seen as persuasive to a judge.

Debate in its purest sense is a game of chess between two competitors. If the affirmative can sense what the negative's case will be or vice versa and then prepare logical responses to their opponent's arguments, then they will have a better chance at convincing a judge of their position. This is not to mean that every argument can be preempted, just that seeing what your opponent will do or wants to do before they do it allows you to shape arguments in a manner that will be better defended and seem more logical in the mind of a judge. Look again at Aristotle's definition of logos. In IPDA debate, competitors rarely have the opportunity to "prove" their case to be true. If the affirmative or negative were able to prove their case to be complete truth, then there would be no reason to debate, nor by our own standards would there be "room to debate" and therefore would be deemed truistic in round. We should then aim for the other part of the definition. We should seek to persuade our audience with argumentation to expose an apparent truth.

EARLY CONTRIBUTIONS

Truth, at least absolute truth, in its very essence is an abstract term that scholars have deemed impossible to manifest. It is because of this, that we as debaters should make it

Contributed by Keith Milstead. Copyright © Kendall Hunt Publishing Company our sole goal to convince, or persuade, our judges that our analysis should be considered truth. It is for this reason that Aristotle coined the three divisions of rhetoric (ethos, pathos, and logos). Both Aristotle and Plato attempted to define and explain the purpose of rhetoric, especially as it relates to the ability to persuade and the importance of persuasion. A translation of Aristotle's *Rhetoric* shows that he defined it as "the faculty of observing in any given case the available means of persuasion" (Aristotle and Roberts 2011). Plato's definition, through translation, is slightly more insightful: "a universal art of winning the mind by arguments" (Jowett 1953). The importance of these terms and definitions allow us to better understand the role logos has in achieving them.

Freeley and Steinberg (2009) summarized Aristotle's four functions of rhetoric. Here, they conclude, "Aristotle pointed out that in some situations scientific arguments are useless; a speaker has to 'educate' the audience by framing arguments with the help of common knowledge and commonly accepted opinions" (Freeley and Steinberg 2009). This is perhaps why Aristotle suggested that logos was the superior form of appeal and that arguments should be judged on reasoning alone (Aristotle and Lawson-Tancred 1992). This gives us insight into the role that logos plays in IPDA debate. While we may use some facts, statistics, and expert opinions at times to strengthen our arguments and appeals, it is often our ability to logically induce that carries the most weight in the minds of judges. We will examine this further later in the chapter.

Terrell (1967) summarizes another early attempt to find truth through logic. The early philosopher, Zeno, attempted to prove that motion was an illusion with logic alone. Though he was unsuccessful in this experiment, two main conclusions can be drawn. First, everyone has the ability to judge the correctness or incorrectness of reasoning. Second, through sheer logic alone, the correctness and incorrectness of arguments can be determined (Terrell 1967). What we can conclude then is that through logic, every debate round should be conducted and officiated. With our ability to think critically, reason, conclude, and deduce, any debater should win an argument or round with sound logic.

INDUCTION AND DEDUCTION

One of the ways that debaters use logic in reasoning is by their abilities of induction and deduction. First, let us define each. Induction is "the form of reasoning in which we come to a conclusion about the whole on the basis of observations of particular instances," while deduction is "reasoning by which we establish that a conclusion must be true because the statements on which it is based are true" (Rottenberg and Winchell 2009). Both of these tools are essential to our abilities to use logic in debate.

Induction can be a very powerful form of reasoning for the IPDA debater in several ways. First, we can determine how terms might be defined, what types of weighing mechanisms might be used, or how a judge might respond to a particular argument all based on previous experiences with programs and competitors. Because IPDA uses a variety of topics at every tournament, it is very likely that one will see the same type of resolution more than once during the course of the season. Therefore, knowing how a topic was researched, how their opponent responded to certain ideas, or even what particular argument won or lost the previous round can provide valuable experience to the debate. This, on a large scale is inductive reasoning. By observing and/or participating in a large number of rounds, one gains useful insight and can therefore conclude certain facts about a topic area or opponent.

Chapter 7: Logos in IPDA Debate • **73**

On a smaller scale, debaters can certainly use inductive reasoning within their own argumentation. It is through the very nature of inductive reasoning that researchers provide probability or certainty figures to summarized observations. The scientific method tells us that the only way to know with 100 percent accuracy if something is true or exists is to observe all of the artifacts in question. For example, if you talk to 50 college athletes on your campus, and if most or all of them tell you that the most difficult part of being a college athlete is the workouts or training they must do, then you might conclude that for college athletes, this is the most difficult thing to deal with. However, unless you talked to all college athletes on your campus and each told you the exact same thing, you could not properly conclude this to be true on your campus, let alone on every college campus. It is this understanding that allows us to use logic in order to arrive at a level of probability through inductive reasoning.

It is inductive reasoning that allows us to make generalizations and conclusions based on what we believe to be true around us. The better sociological understanding that one might have allows them to persuade a judge through logic that something in their reasoning is true. For example, say that you are in a debate round and the affirmative has suggested that raising tuition costs would be a good thing in order to improve the level of technology in schools, and therefore increase the education of the students involved. On the surface, this seems to be a very good idea, given the possibility of increased education and learning for the students. The negative, however, could argue that, based on their knowledge of fellow college students and firsthand experiences, students can't afford an increase in tuition at this time. This argument becomes even more persuasive if the judge is also currently a student and the negative can therefore conclude that the judge wouldn't want to pay more for tuition and should not vote for the affirmative based on that fact.

One final thought on inductive reasoning is that through this type of argumentation, hasty generalizations and logical leaps can occur. We as debaters need to be aware of using too small a sample size within our conclusions, and asking a judge to believe something based solely on our experiences should be avoided. Flawed logic occurs most often through inductive reasoning and can therefore sometimes be defeated in argumentation based on that premise. In other words, if you feel your opponent has used inductive reasoning in their argumentation, be sure to point out if they have made assumptions too large to be acceptable or if their examples used too few observations to be true on a larger scale.

ANALOGICAL ARGUMENTATION

Sometimes, debaters use analogies to help others understand concepts better. Technically speaking, analogies can use deductive or inductive logic, but it is almost always inductive reasoning. Analogies help us illustrate concepts rhetorically in order to better understand ideals and sometimes even physical objects. Perella (1987) uses the example of using the human body to show the relationship between the three branches of government (298). Because it can be difficult to comprehend the symbiotic relationship that the legislative and judicial branches have, one could suggest that the legislative could be the brain while the judicial would be the heart, and so on. This type of logical strategy is very helpful for debaters to use in order to increase the understanding that a judge has. This can be especially helpful when speaking of theoretical premises and/or questions of value. When debating, for example, whether education is more important than experience, one can induce that without having changed a tire, simply reading about how to do it could be useless. This gives a judge a frame of reference in a real-world sense that can allow for better appreciation of additional arguments on the matter.

It is important to note that by their very nature, most analogies can be considered hasty generalizations (see the section on logical fallacies for explanation). That is to mean that when we attempt to make an analogy, we are often using a very small example or sample in order to maximize the effect of a much larger issue in question. It is for this reason that many deem analogies to be non-argumentative. For an analogy to be entered as an argument and not merely an illustration, it must meet certain criteria. First, it must meet some level of probability. This means it would need an adequate sample size in order to be applied to a larger population. Second, it must have common characteristics. This often means an apples-to-apples approach. When debaters argue that one is comparing apples to oranges, this means that the two ideals in question do not share enough common characteristics to merit the analogy. The branch of government/human body example would fail this criterion. Finally, the analogy must accept exceptions to the rule. This is to mean that no analogy can be all-inclusive and account for all individuals. There will be deviance within human nature that would choose contrary to popular thought.

SYLLOGISMS

It is through deductive reasoning that we get one of the best tools of logic for a debater, the syllogism. Freeley and Steinberg (2009) define a syllogism as "a systematic arrangement of arguments consisting of a major premise, a minor premise, and a conclusion." It is essentially an if-then statement that allows us to reach a conclusion based on the understanding of certain qualifiers. Full chapters can be written on syllogisms alone, so we will view an abbreviated discussion here. Often, syllogisms can be used to construct entire cases or contentions. It is important to realize that even the best syllogisms are not without fault. It is the ability to convince a judge with sound reasoning, or logic, which makes the syllogism an effective tool. Below are some basic examples of syllogisms.

Major premise: All US Presidents must be at least 25 years of age.
Minor premise: Barack Obama is a US President.
Conclusion: Therefore, Barack Obama is at least 25 years of age.

Major premise: All human beings are mortal.
Minor premise: Jason is a human being.
Conclusion: Jason is mortal.

The first element of the syllogism is the major premise. Major premises can be understood or fact-based with supporting evidence. In some instances, it is necessary to research evidentiary sources in order to fulfill the major premise. For example, let's say you want to have a major premise that "All states have had their education funding cut in the last year." This statement is likely not known or understood by all and therefore, a US government document that suggests this premise to be true may need to be cited as evidence to support the claim. From there, we might be able to suggest that a specific state needs an increase in education funding from additional warrants. On the other hand, many major premises can be cited as general knowledge. For example, "All US states have laws regulating drinking

Chapter 7: Logos in IPDA Debate • **75**

and driving" is a statement that can be made with confidence without the need for evidence because it is assumed knowledge that debaters and judges alike should be familiar with. From there, we can then propose additional regulation based on the knowledge that certain states have varying laws.

Just like the major premises, minor premises may be understood or fact- and evidence-based. For example, let's say you had a major premise of "Crime rates increase when the economy weakens" with a minor premise of "The economy weakened last year." From there, one would be able to suggest that the crime rate increased last year as a conclusion. You would likely need a source that supported the decrease in the economy last year for some judges and competitors though. From there, just as a side note, your opponent could still argue the premise even with evidence to support because there are so many factors that make up an economy and one or two factors may not indicate the entirety of the situation. As such, different experts may give different answers to that particular question. In some instances, however, evidence is not needed to support a minor premise and can be agreed by all given common knowledge. The example above uses the minor premise that Barack Obama is a US President. This statement should be assumed as factual by all parties.

Based on the acceptance of the major and minor premises, one can then state with certainty a conclusion. As mentioned previously, syllogisms can still be argued or questioned. Most importantly, one should note that a conclusion is predicated on the premises being correct. If one can show the fault of one or both of the premises, then the conclusion cannot be attributed as such. Often, a good debater is able to use cross-examination in order to provide support for their syllogisms. Premises can be disguised as individual questions within cross-examination whereas the conclusion can then be saved for contention during one's speech. For example, if a competitor can get their opponent to agree that their advocacy would lead to an increase in federal spending in order to fund a new program and then get them to agree that new program spending is bad in general, they could then argue in their speech that their opponent agreed that their own advocacy is a bad idea because new program spending is bad and they admitted they are asking for new program spending. This is an obvious example, but the more logical your approach in the round, and the more creative you can be with the phrasing of questions, the more successful you can be in supporting your syllogisms. It should be noted that many scholars have suggested that Aristotle's syllogism model implies absolutism. That is to mean that, technically speaking, probabilities cannot exist within them (Perella 1987).

ENTHYMEMES

Perhaps more useful to IPDA debate is another form of deductive reasoning: the enthymeme. An enthymeme has been defined as, "a syllogism based on probabilities, signs, and examples, whose function is rhetorical persuasion. Its successful construction is accomplished through the joint efforts of speaker and audience, and this is its essential character" (Bitzer 1959). Another description calls it a truncated syllogism whereby one of the premises or even the conclusion is not stated and merely understood or insinuated. For example, say an affirmative is arguing for wireless wiretaps to be used to stop suspected terrorists. One could expect their audience or judge to know that by its very nature, this would be a violation of our right to privacy, and therefore should be rejected based on the unconstitutionality of the argument. In this instance, the negative could argue that the minor premise is that wiretapping could be a violation and the conclusion would be that it should not be supported based on that alone. No major premise is necessary if you can assume that the judge knows or would agree that any violation of rights is bad. Note specifically that the enthymeme is based on probabilities, signs, and examples. One might suggest then that pure deductive reasoning, and logic in a greater sense, can be achieved without evidentiary support. This is primarily noted because it should be understood that good debaters can and should be able to win arguments without evidence.

The very essence of the enthymeme is the ability to understand and argue that premises are assumed and therefore need no additional explanation. This means that debaters can use examples without the necessity of fully developing arguments. To say that the economy has been in a depression would not need additional reasoning or support and therefore can be assumed in argumentation about a proposed advocacy to help the economy. This is a great tool for debaters in IPDA given the amount of time that each speaker has. Often, debaters will cite their abilities to assume knowledge as a tool that allows them to maximize their time management in a round. In short, the difference between the enthymeme and the syllogism is that it allows persuaders to base an argument on presumed knowledge or speak in terms of probabilities. When we say that people should go to school to learn, it is an enthymeme and based solely in logic and experience.

THE TOULMIN MODEL

A discussion of deductive logic would not be complete without some time devoted to a first cousin of the syllogism. This is called the Toulmin model. Philosopher Stephen Toulmin introduced a structure of elements that should be found in sound, explicit arguments. The ones that are most important are claims, data or support, and warrants (Toulmin, Rieke and Janik 1979). The three of these together can provide solid, logical reasoning by which persuasion is very likely to occur. In this model, the support or data are similar to the minor premise previously discussed while the warrant would be the major premise and the claim the conclusion. We will begin the discussion of the three main parts before looking at an example.

You may have noticed in the above description that the Toulmin model seems slightly backwards. This is because debaters often start with the claim. The claim is, as defined by Toulmin, what you are trying to prove, i.e., the conclusion. The ultimate claim in any debate round is the resolution itself. Ultimately, the resolution should serve as the claim for the affirmative, while the negative attempts to disprove it. Some affirmatives will use the Toulmin model within each main point or contention, whereas the main tagline is the claim. Claims should be found throughout the debate round by both sides for it is through claims that true debate occurs. Advanced debaters will sum up their claims at the end of their last speech to give judges an idea of what the round has been reduced to. It is here that great use of logic occurs because this is where, logically speaking, one can summarize the main arguments necessary to prove or disprove the resolution.

Data or support is the second element of the Toulmin model. It is sometimes referred to as grounds. Support, as defined by Toulmin, is the evidence and reasoning necessary to reach the claim. This is what we have to base our argument on. Where some debaters might want statistical data or evidentiary support, reasoning and logic play a large role here as well. Earlier, we discussed that sometimes arguments can be assumed as general knowledge without the necessity of evidence. Either way, it is logic that allows us to determine which support or data is necessary in order to prove our claim to be true. This is why some debaters will use their contentions, or main points as individual supports that can all independently prove the resolution true or false. Within these points, advanced debaters will use different examples that suggest a larger picture, or the resolution, to be right or wrong. Let us use the following example to illustrate:

Resolution: US democracy would be better with a viable third party.

Affirmative Contention 1: Third parties increase political activism.
Affirmative Contention 2: Third parties allow more voices to be heard.
Affirmative Contention 3: Third parties supply checks and balances to Republicans and Democrats.

All of these contentions would suggest that US democracy would be better or stronger with a more viable third party. At times, debaters will vary this "formula" for case construction based on the need for stronger support or warrants. In some cases, the affirmative might be able to imply that these three contentions prove the resolution true within an introduction or summary after presenting the main points of the case. Note also, that even in this example, each of the three "support" points could and should be considered three claims as well. In other words, in some instances, in order for support to be considered within the model, one might need to treat them as claims, where reasoning and additional explanation may be necessary.

In other cases, though, the affirmative might need to give warrants to "bridge the gap" between the support(s) and the claim(s). Toulmin described the warrant as the evidence and/or reasoning that is necessary to move from the support to the claim. In the previous example, the warrants might be summarized in the resolution analysis, introduction, or even in a summary at the end of the speech. In other words, one could logically suggest that political activism, having more voices heard, and providing checks and balances make US democracy better. However, in some instances, one might need to give support that suggests that political activism, hearing more voices, and supplying checks and balances does, in fact, improve democracy. It is perhaps here where the negative has the best opportunity to present their own case to disprove the affirmative's position. This means that if the negative can suggest that political activism has been known to hurt US democracy and so on, then they can effectively and logically disprove the very premises put forth by the affirmative.

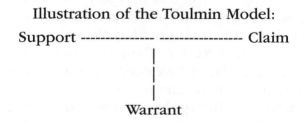

Illustration of the Toulmin Model:

Support ---------------- ---------------- Claim
                              |
                              |
                              |
                         Warrant

In some cases, additional steps or pieces to the puzzle may be necessary. It is for this reason that Toulmin described three additional elements that may be used in this model. First, there is backing, which is additional support that is needed for the warrant to be true. This is similar to the example given earlier about needing to supply additional information in order to prove that political activism does, in fact, strengthen democracy. Another element that was mentioned by Toulmin was modal qualification. Toulmin said that this was the degree of cogency by which our warrants can be ascribed. In other words, this means to what degree of certainty we have about the warrant we have argued. If one can say with complete certainty that the warrant is factual, then they have high cogency. The modal qualification can range from certainty to possibility. The final Toulmin element is simply the rebuttal or reservation. Debaters should be aware that rebuttal is a term that means "to show weakness in or contradiction to an argument with reasoning of the opposite."

Now that the Toulmin model and the syllogism have been discussed, a short description of the differences between the two is warranted. Rottenberg and Winchell (2009) give three differences between the two models. They suggest the first difference to be in the language that is used; specifically, that the word premise in the syllogism model implies that the fact is assumed true, whereas in the Toulmin model, the claim is assumed false without proper analysis of the support and the warrant. Secondly, they suggest that within the syllogism, the three parts are "locked into place" (337) and that in the Toulmin model, arguments move or progress from the support to the claim by way of the warrant. Finally, they suggest that the additional elements provided by Toulmin allow for a flexibility lacked by the basic syllogism. What this really means is that the Toulmin model is an updated, more useful tool for use in the debate world. Both, however, employ logic as a means to persuade, in that they allow us as debaters to arrive at a conclusion in an easily comprehendible manner in an if/then mode of thought.

A note of caution is required here with regards to the syllogism and Toulmin model. It is here where some debate formats have used these tools to make and presumably "prove" abstractions. This means that using these models without the assistance of logic can often lead to outlandish statements. For example, here is a Toulmin-shaped argument used in some formats of collegiate debate:

Support: US-Chinese Relationships are strenuous now.
Warrant: US support of (X) would fracture these relations because China does not support it.
Claim: This would cause backlash by the Chinese government and lead to war.

This example shows where almost anything can show a fracture in relations between the United States and China because the ideological systems are so different. It is through logic that one should suggest that any one action would not lead to war between the two countries, as decisions are made all of the time contrary to support by both governments. This is not to mean that these arguments are not worthy nor that other debate formats are incorrect in their structures, just that logic can be lacking within some argumentation. The IPDA constitution exclusively suggests that IPDA debate should mimic a real-world discussion with lay judges. The inclusivity of lay judges suggests that logic be a primary driving force behind our arguments especially when using these very helpful formulas of argumentation. Public debate, by nature, is intended to have a differing structure whereby propositions and arguments should "stimulate audience interest" and be judged by those with little experience in political matters (Lee and Lee 1989).

LOGICAL FALLACIES

No discussion on logos would be complete without some devotion to logical fallacies. There can be literally hundreds of classified logical fallacies and full books can be written describing them. For the purposes of this chapter, the most common and strategically argued will be included. A logical fallacy occurs when improper reasoning is used to reach a conclusion incorrectly. We as debaters are likely guilty of faulty logic within every debate round. This is not to mean that we are illogical per se, just that there are plenty of traps that exist when logic is used. The better understanding we have of these potential traps, the better we can avoid them. Additionally, knowing these can also allow us to draw attention when our opponents use them, thus suggesting that we are more logical to a judge.

Hasty Generalization: Perhaps the most common fallacy and easiest to decipher is the hasty generalization. Already referenced earlier in the chapter, the hasty generalization occurs most often when we reach a conclusion without enough evidence to support our claim. When we make assumptions about a group or activity based on our limited observation of them, we are committing a hasty generalization. It is for this reason that superstitions exist. Once we have a desirable or undesirable outcome, we look to explain it based on the circumstances that existed at the time. We must be sure that we can draw a particular conclusion based on sufficient evidence. This comes back to the scientific method of probability. If we argue that something can be considered truth within a certain level of probability, then we can often avoid the hasty generalization. When looking at studies or polls, one should be aware of the sample size in order and be sure that they include the margin of error as well. Another application of this principle is called a "leap in logic." This refers to when an argument goes from A to D while skipping over B and C. At times, debaters like to assume certain things can and will occur without explanation or at least some reference. An example of this might include when one argues that the passage of a bill will lead directly to specific results. The mere passage of a bill does not ensure the implementation of the legislature or the successful performance of an agent of action.

Appeal to Authority. The appeal to authority can occur for several different reasons and can therefore mean different things. First, it might mean that we have improperly cited a source that is not well-versed or educated in the context of their opinion. In other words, just because someone might be an expert in one thing, they are not then an expert in all things. Even though celebrities are used to sell products, they should not be considered experts on the products that they advertise. The second, and perhaps more alarming fallacy on authority appeal, occurs when a document or authority is cited in an effort to end discussion on the matter. In other words, because John Doe says this is correct, it must be and there is no arguing the fact. This happens in IPDA in two ways. If something is deemed unconstitutional or unlawful, it is often claimed that the action in question should not be pursued based on that fact alone. Remember, slavery was considered lawful at one point. Additionally, debaters will sometimes argue that because they have a source and their opponent does not, they are right about the subject matter. If Warren Buffett said it is justified to not pay taxes, would you assume he was correct just because of his expertise in money? Therefore, just because an expert believes something to be true, it is not automatically deemed so and when debaters claim that they have a source and their opponent does not, this is merely a logical fallacy and is nonresponsive.

Post Hoc: Post hoc comes from the Latin phrase *post hoc ergo propter hoc,* meaning "after the fact, therefore because of the fact." Sometimes this can be explained when we attempt to say something has a causal relationship when it is merely a correlation. To say that the sun rose at 6:30 this morning does not mean that the sun rose because it was 6:30 a.m. It some cases, it may suffice to say that events occur coincidentally. Here too, the analysis of superstitions earlier can help understand this fallacy. Debaters should be especially careful when claiming matters of social existence have causal relationships. This means that what is true of one segment of society may not be true of another. It is for this reason, again, that debaters should refer to levels of probability and not causal or absolute facts.

Slippery Slope: The slippery slope is one of the most common and regularly used fallacies in debate. This occurs when we argue that taking a first step inevitably leads to another and another, etc. It is found in some cases as a last resort in negative argumentation because we can attempt to theorize what might happen if a particular action is undertaken. We have seen slippery slope arguments even in the mainstream. Opponents of gun legislation have argued through the years that any regulation of gun ownership would lead to complete banning of guns. Even now, opponents of socialized health care have argued that it would lead to enormous governmental control over other sectors. Theoretically, any slippery slope argument could be deemed correct after years or decades, but inaction due to the possibility of negative ramifications would mean nothing was ever improved or created due to potential harms. Most importantly, slippery slope fallacies seem to ignore the various other factors that can affect the outcome of any particular action.

False Dilemma: The false dilemma fallacy occurs when we narrow a decision down to only two alternatives. There are any number of examples that can illustrate this fallacy, but often the affirmative will fall into the trap of arguing for their position and against the status quo. This line of analysis excludes any additional courses of action. Just as fallible, the negative will often exclude discussing any additional ideals as well, allowing the affirmative complete control of the discussion in the round. This does not mean that the negative should be free to argue additional advocacies (counter plans), just that often they are trapped into not allowing for a discussion about other status quo conditions that could be causing a problem. Say for example that the affirmative argues that repeal to "No Child Left Behind" is warranted given the current state of the education system. Within the affirmative case there can be an assumption that it is standardized testing that has led to the downfall of our education. The negative could argue that it is lack of teacher certification that has led to the demise in education and therefore repealing the NCLB would not fix the problem. Instead, the affirmative is successful in arguing against NCLB and the negative is obliged to argue for it, which results in a false dilemma.

Ad Hominem: The term *ad hominem* means "against the man." It is found in debate rounds typically in one of two forms. Either a debater may question their opponent's ability to speak with authority on a matter instead of addressing their arguments or they may question the source of evidence instead of the evidence itself. This does not mean that either of these challenges is without validity. However, simply arguing against the author or speaker should not dismiss the argument in theory. A question of someone's authority can be just as valid as the argument they make. If Charles Manson told you that murder was wrong, would you dismiss the notion based on his history of doing the opposite? Again, even though one may be improperly qualified to make a valid point, a qualified individual may make an invalid one. It is through logic that we should judge the statements made.

Bandwagon: Also known as the popular appeal fallacy, the bandwagon is simply arguing in support of an action because everyone else is doing it or arguing against an action because everyone else is against it. This is an easy trap to fall into because we can sometimes find overwhelming evidence in support of an action given the experiences of some segments of population or even whole populations. For example, during the debates about universal health care in recent years, proponents often cited the success that various countries had in implementation of a form of it. At times, debaters would find themselves arguing that because others had been successful with the system, we should also use it. The argument was fallible because it failed to acknowledge why it was working elsewhere and only that it was.

False Analogy: The false analogy fallacy, also referred to as the weak analogy, occurs when the comparison of two subjects in an analogy are improperly contrasted. This is very similar to the apples to oranges analysis that was discussed earlier. Often, advanced debaters will exaggerate the effects of an action within an analogy to make it seem much worse than it is. For example, in a debate about alternative forms of energy, an argument was made that nuclear energy should not be used because of the dangers that it possesses. The opponent then gave the analogy that, by that example, cars should be banned because they pose a danger. This analogy was fallible because it suggested that cars could be equated to an energy source and that the number of alternative energy sources was comparable to the modes of individual travel. To say that nuclear energy is dangerous is arguable and the risk should be weighed against the potential rewards. If cars were banned, it would have a colossal affect whereas if nuclear energy was deemed too dangerous, other energy sources existed. The very premise of the false analogy assumes that because two things share a characteristic, they must include far more similarities.

There are many more logical fallacies that debaters should be encouraged to learn about. Debaters should consult texts and other sources to become more familiar with these fallacies and how they can negatively affect one's ability to persuade with logic. When you can bring attention to an opponent's faulty logic, you can boost the credibility of your own, thereby making your arguments more believable.

CONCLUSION

In summary, logic can be the deciding factor of a debate round in a number of ways. From Aristotle's view on logos and reasoning to Toulmin's model of deductive logic, we can understand to some degree how logic and reasoning advance argumentation and allow us to settle disagreements. Remember that Aristotle said that through sheer logic, the correctness or lack thereof in argumentation can be determined. We as IPDA debaters should strive to allow logic to play a large role in determining the outcome of debate rounds. Too often, we can "refer to evidence and sources to determine arguments, and while they can certainly help, we should ask ourselves the validity of the entire lineage of the argument" (Rybacki and Rybacki 1996). This means that we should not allow the number of sources brought up in round to be a deciding factor in it. Logic, in practice, is a means of persuasion whereby we can connect with other people. When we connect with others, we can advance ideals and concepts much further to truly impact the world around us instead of just enumerating wins and losses or sources. There is definitely room for evidence in a debate round, but we should be deciding the issues based on the logical advancement of ideas. IPDA debate has pledged to teach real-world methods of discussion. There are few real-world discussions that fail to use syllogisms, analogies, or other tools of logic. As such, we all should be sure to champion logos as an integral part of our activity.

REFERENCES

Aristotle, and Roberts, W. R. (2011, September 27). *Aristotle's Rhetoric.* Retrieved April 10, 2012, from rhetoric.org: http://rhetoric.eserver.org/aristotle/index.html

Aristotle, and Lawson-Tancred, H. 1992. *The Art of Rhetoric.* London: Penguin.

Bitzer, L. F. 1959. "Aristotle's Enthymeme Revisited." *Quarterly Journal of Speech,* 45 (4): 408.

Freeley, A. J. and D. L. Steinberg. 2009. *Argumentation and Debate: Critical Thinking for Reasoned Decision Making* (12th ed.). Boston: Wadsworth Cengage Learning.

Jowett, B. 1953. "The Dialogues of Plato." In *The Dialogues of Plato: Translated and edited by Benjamin Jowett,* 261. Oxford: Oxford University Press.

Lee, R. E., and K. K. Lee. 1989. *Arguing Persuasively.* New York: Longman.

Parker, F. H., and H. B. Veatch. 1959. *Logic as a Human Instrument.* New York: Harper & Row.

Perella, J. 1987. *The Debate Method of Critical Thinking: an Introduction to Argumentation.* Dubuque, IA: Kendall/Hunt Publishing Co.

Rottenberg, A. T., and D. H. Winchell. 2009. *Elements of Argument* (9th ed.). Boston: Bedford/ St. Martin's.

Rybacki, K. C., and D. J. Rybacki. 1996. *Advocacy and Opposition* (3rd ed.). Boston: Allyn and Bacon.

Terrell, D. B. 1967. *Logic: A Modern Introduction to Deductive Reasoning.* New York: Holt, Rinehart and Winston.

Toulmin, S., R. Rieke, and A. Janik. 1979. *An Introduction to Reasoning.* New York: Macmillan.

PART 3
Public Debate

Chapter 8	Striking in IPDA Debate - Dale Sikkema & Patrick G. Richey	85
Chapter 9	Evidence in IPDA Debate - Jeffrey Dale Hobbs, Jodee Hobbs & Piengpen Na Pattalung	93
Chapter 10	Audience Analysis - Adam Key	103
Chapter 11	The Affirmative Case - Robert Alexander	121
Chapter 12	The Negative Case - Christopher M. Duerringer	141
	Preparing for Battle: Negative Sidebar - Anthony McMullen	148
Chapter 13	Cross-Examination - Robert Alexander	151
	Whose Cross-Examination Is This Anyway? - Anthony McMullen	164

Chapter 8

Striking in IPDA Debate

Dale Sikkema
Middle Tennessee State University
Patrick G. Richey, PhD
Middle Tennessee State University

While public debate is similar in many regards to other formats of debate, it is unique in its approach to topics of discourse. Lincoln-Douglass, public forum, and policy debate have a single long-term topic that debaters research well in advance. Public debate, like parliamentary debate, introduces new topics each round. In parliamentary debate a single topic is announced and the participants prepare a case fifteen minutes before the round begins. Public debate differentiates itself further by using a **strike sheet** with five potential topics per round that the debaters select from. The debaters have 30 minutes of preparation time to construct arguments.

At first, the five topic strike sheet approach may seem daunting. However, it gives the debaters much more flexibility to maneuver with topics rather than being stuck with an arbitrary topic. This chapter will focus on the topic selection. It will first examine the procedure of **striking** a topic from the strike sheet. Then this chapter will discuss methods of strategic topic selection. Finally, the chapter will conclude with some tips for ethical striking.

STRIKING PROCEDURES

The procedure of **striking** or removing a topic from the strike list is fairly simple. Each competitor must know in advance whether she or he is the affirmative or negative. This can be determined by checking the **posting sheet** (a document that has all the competitor pairings for a round). The tournament director will announce draw and the competitors will pair up. The director will hand the pair of competitors a strike sheet with five topics (see Figure 1) and time will begin for the round. It is important to remember that time begins when topics are handed out and that competitors need to use haste when selecting topics.

Contributed by Dale Sikkema and Patrick Gerhardt Richey. Copyright © Kendall Hunt Publishing Company   **85**

86 • *IPDA Textbook*

```
1. Superman is better than Batman.
2. We should lift the embargo against Iran.
3. Baseball players are paid too much.
4. It is better to be feared than loved.
5. The Electoral College should be abolished.
```
Fig. 1

The negative gets to strike the first topic (see Figure 2).

```
1. Superman is better than Batman.
2. We should lift the embargo against Iran.
3. Baseball players are paid too much.
4. It is better to be feared than loved.
5. The Electoral College should be abolished.
```
Fig. 2

The affirmative now gets to strike a topic (see Figure 3).

```
1. Superman is better than Batman.
2. We should lift the embargo against Iran.
3. Baseball players are paid too much.
4. It is better to be feared than loved.
5. The Electoral College should be abolished.
```
Fig. 3

The negative gets his or her final strike (see Figure 4).

```
1. Superman is better than Batman.
2. We should lift the embargo against Iran.
3. Baseball players are paid too much.
4. It is better to be feared than loved.
5. The Electoral College should be abolished.
```
Fig. 4

The affirmative now has two topics left to choose from. The affirmative will strike one topic and the topic left will be debated in the round. In the case of the example (see Figure 5) the topic of debate will be "Superman is better than Batman."

```
1. Superman is better than Batman.
2. We should lift the embargo against Iran.
3. Baseball players are paid too much.
4. It is better to be feared than loved.
5. The Electoral College should be abolished.
```
Fig. 5

TOPIC ANALYSIS

Debate rounds do not start in the room when the affirmative begins speaking. Rounds start when the negative makes the first strike. There is as much strategy in good striking to obtain a preferable topic as there often is in a round. A poorly chosen topic can end the round before a debater even walks into the room. The next section will provide pointers on how to approach topic selection and wise striking. The section will be divided into affirmative striking tips and negative striking tips.

Strike as Affirmative:

Strike all absolutes—Words such as <u>all</u>, <u>every</u>, <u>always</u>, <u>never</u>, and <u>absolute</u> are examples of absolute terms that the affirmative should avoid. The affirmative never wants to choose a topic in which he or she must defend an absolute position such as, "Love <u>never</u> fails." The "never" is the absolute word in the resolution; and the negative only has to show one instance where love could fail in order to win the round.

Strike poorly worded topics—Most tournament hosts will proofread the topic and make corrections to improper grammar and poorly worded topics. However, some errors may still appear on the strike sheet. These topics should be avoided because they can cause confusion or muddle rounds. Moreover, many judges prefer not to listen to long-winded topicality arguments about whether the author's intent was "fly" as in to board an airplane or "fly" as in to flap wings until flight is achieved.

Confusing—The affirmative should avoid confusing topics such as the aforementioned examples containing ambiguous language. Also avoid topics which lack subject-verb agreement in number or tense. Finally, avoid lengthy or wordy topics because each word adds to the ground the affirmative must define and defend. For example, with the resolution "Candidate A is better than candidate B because of his stance on immigration reform," the affirmative must define and defend the candidate A's immigration stance as well as candidate A as a whole. In effect, the affirmative may have to debate two topics at once.

Status quo or solved—The affirmative should avoid topics that have already been solved or are present in the status quo. **Status quo** means that something is currently happening. An example could be if the resolution stated, "We should invade Iraq." The opposition could argue that this is status quo since American troops are already in Iraq. By doing so the affirmative does not meet its obligation as the advocate of change (further defined later in this book). It is also abusive for the affirmative to take a stance on something already accomplished since this switches the burdens and takes away the negative's defense and wastes the negative's preparation time.

Negatives—The affirmative should avoid topics that have a negative or double negative in them. In addition to having the burden of proof (further defined later in this book), the affirmative is also the advocate of change. The affirmative creates and moves forward from the status quo (see above). A negative in a resolution often contradicts or negates change and is fundamentally flawed in debate. An example of such a topic could be, "We will <u>not</u> sanction North Korea." Since it is implied that "we" are currently sanctioning North Korea, the topic is already flawed as a status quo topic. It further muddles the round because the affirmative has to advocate a non-action, which is contradictory to the affirmative's burden as advocate of change. The poor topic also makes the burden of proof difficult since argumentation lies in void rather action. Even if there is ground for the affirmative to debate, negative resolutions create confusing, often frustrating, debates.

Non-directional or multi-directional—The affirmative should avoid topics that may be neutral/non-directional, or topics that call for multiple directions. Specifically, avoid topics that call for two kinds of action. The affirmative does not want to advocate for multiple positions at once, nor do they want to spend the entire round trying to convince the judge that there is any advocacy (direction) at all in the round. An example would be a topic such as, "The sky is blue." This resolution of fact gives the affirmative too much ground to try to define out and leaves the door open for the negative to make abuse arguments since the negative does not know which way the affirmative will go with the topic. A good debate round has a central core theme that the affirmative advocates throughout the round and the theme is obvious to the judge and negative.

Strike morally biased topics—Remember the affirmative has the burden of proof. It is not wise to choose a topic that forces the debater to advocate a position that most would find morally reprehensible. An example could be striking a topic such as, "Black History Month should be abolished" at a historically black college (HBC). While there may be grounds to construct an affirmative case, the affirmative should think about the prospect of having a lay judge and having to advocate a topic that could be construed as racist. This gives the negative a large advantage from the start.

Try to strike unfamiliar topics—Avoiding unfamiliar topics is a basic approach to any topic selection. Remember that the affirmative only has 30 minutes to research and craft an affirmative case or plan. The affirmative does not want to waste this small amount of time trying to research an unknown topic. It is best to try to strike unfamiliar topics and hope to get a familiar topic so that the affirmative can quickly start case construction. Debate is an event governed by the clock. The affirmative must work the clock to her or his advantage.

Strike topics that you may know your opponent or opponent's team is extremely knowledgeable about—Finally, the affirmative should try to avoid topics that the negative or the negative's team obviously has knowledge about. As an example, it could be known that the coach for Team X is a huge NFL football fan. Try to immediately strike football-related topics since the affirmative already knows the negative has a strong research advantage. This is one reason why it never hurts to make friends and get to know other debaters and their teams. Remember, the negative also tries to strategically strike topics that the affirmative may have extensive knowledge about.

This section discussed a few tips to approaching topics as the affirmative. The chapter now will examine some tips if the debater is on the negative.

Strike as Negative:

Aim for absolutes—This is really just the reverse of the affirmative's "avoid absolutes" strategy. The affirmative has a very heavy burden when arguing an absolute. The negative can provide counter-examples that logically refute the statement or simply show that the affirmative's limited examples are not broad enough to prove a universal rule. As negative, draw on the theme that "the world is not black and white," and that there are exceptions to every rule.

Poorly worded topics—These are not just bad for the affirmative. A poorly worded topic (as described earlier, one that is not a declarative sentence or suffers grammatical errors) leads to poor preparation on both sides, confusion during the round, little meaningful clash, and a frustrated judge. Unless a firm agreement is reached to interpret a typo or grammatical ambiguity one way or another, one team should strike those topics. Because topics phrased as negatives (i.e., "TH believes gun control would not work") upturn the roles of affirmative and negative, they can be included in this category.

Aim for status quo—As described earlier, a resolution may affirm the status quo if it offers an idea or practice that is already in place. The negative can argue that because the affirmative is not doing or changing anything, there is no real substance to debate at all. Another strategy that the affirmative might use is to interpret the resolution in a way that is slightly or incrementally different from the status quo. In this case, the negative may point to the mild and insignificant nature of these changes. For instance, suppose the resolution states "China should adopt capitalism," while China has already implemented many capitalistic policies, the affirmative might propose additional and incremental market reforms, but the negative can attack the significance of those reforms. There is no point in debating a plan that barely modifies the status quo. Finally, if the affirmative brings up harms in the status quo that must be solved, the negative can point out that the status quo still has not solved those harms. Continuing the previous example, negative may state, "If prior market reforms still cause the harms in question, further market reforms will not help."

Emotionally loaded—Pay attention to the moral sympathies and emotional biases you may face from your judges and audience. Whether to strike charged social or political topics may depend on the region or religious affiliation of the host school. Also pay attention to recent news; if a recent factory shutdown, caused by union disputes, recently led hundreds to lose their jobs, that may lend the affirmative an advantage on a topic like "TH believes unions kill jobs."

Familiarity—There are three questions to ask about topic familiarity. First, is the affirmative or the affirmative's debate team knowledgeable about the topic? That could be dangerous. Second, are you or your team knowledgeable about it? Finally, if you are knowledgeable, can you apply that knowledge in a readily understandable way, without jargon and technical details? For example, the topic may be that "TH would replace the income tax with a national sales tax." Many economics majors would jump on this. However, many judges will remain unmoved by sophisticated comments about *marginal propensity to consume* or other highly field-specific language.

ETHIC OF STRIKING

Striking is not ethically void. Since striking well is critical to winning a debate, the temptation may arise to unfairly strike or abuse an opponent. This section of the chapter will review some tips to help insure ethical striking.

Courtesy—The ethics of striking are grounded in principles found in the IPDA constitution (2013). Be *polite*. Be *civil*. Be *professional*. Debate is a community, and one's conduct while striking either builds up or tears down the ethos of the individual and his or her team. Take a moment to offer a simple, but courteous introduction when you meet your opponent. Basic interpersonal comfort can lead to a more fruitful and honest clash, even in an adversarial setting. It is also customary and courteous to allow the affirmative to keep the strike sheet. Since the affirmative must define the terms, it is fair to allow them to keep the strike sheet in case they need to refer to it for exact wording.

Disclosure—The affirmative discloses by revealing to the negative, prior to the round, information about how the topic will be interpreted. This information can range from definitions of specific terms to a summary of the plan that will be proposed. There is never any formal obligation to disclose; however, there are many situations in which, for both practical and ethical reasons, one *ought* to disclose. A metaphorical topic could be so

90 • IPDA Textbook

open-ended that the negative receives no opportunity to prepare any arguments (i.e., "TH should take the road less traveled."). If the affirmative's interpretation left the negative no room to prepare arguments for the debate, the negative may be justified in calling it abusive (that is, so unfair that it merits voting for the negative). Disclosing the interpretation, on the other hand, preempts that complaint.

Moreover, a debate round consisting mostly of **meta-debate**, debating about debating, contains very little clash. Instead of arguing about the road less traveled, the round disintegrates into a messy dispute over fairness and disclosure. This applies to any open-ended topic. Occasionally, the policy goal mentioned in the topic could be expressed in a variety of radically different ways (i.e., "TH would close the gender gap.") Alternatively, the definition of "this house" may refer to a number of groups or institutions. In all of these cases, disclosure leads to a fairer round with more fruitful clash and less meta-debate.

It is also important to remember the receiving side of disclosure. Remember, it is not a rule to disclose, but a courtesy. Abusing disclosure will ensure that no one will disclose in the future. The negative should refrain from using an "apriori disclosure critique" on anyone who does not disclose. This is no different from debaters automatically running topicality in parliamentary or policy debate rounds and usually leads to a muddled and uncivil debate.

The negative should also refrain from arguing with the affirmative if the affirmative is kind enough to disclose. At a recent Pi Kappa Delta (PKD) National Tournament a negative debater argued with the affirmative debater for 15 minutes during the strike period after she disclosed. The affirmative's preparation time was severely limited and the public display reflected poorly on the negative debater and his team. Such issues should be resolved cordially in the debate round. It is as unprofessional for a debater to argue with their opponent before the round as it is to argue after the round.

Time—Be on time for the draw. The IPDA constitution (2013) specifies that tournament directors have discretion over how to handle debaters who show up late to draw. Often, after a few minutes, the team that is present will choose the topic and go off to prepare, and the missing team will have to go to extra lengths to even discover the topic. When striking begins, do not spend an unreasonable amount of time examining the sheet. Feel free to take a strategic moment to consider them, but be able to make each separate strike in less than half a minute.

This chapter has examined how to strike, striking tips, and ethical striking. With the information gained, it is hoped that debate rounds start smoother with a better understanding of the round before it begins.

Terms:
Disclosure
Posting sheet
Meta-debate
Status quo
Strike sheet
Striking

Exercise

Create four to five topic strike sheets with evenly balanced topics. Have a person strike as the affirmative and one strike as the negative. While each person strikes, have them write down why the person chose to strike a certain topic. When the strikes are complete, have an open discussion as to why certain topics were chosen and others struck. Class participation is a must for this activity.

REFERENCES

IPDA Constitution. 2013. *International Public Debate Association constitution.* Retrieved from: http://www.ipdadebate.info

Chapter 9

Evidence in IPDA Debate

Jeffrey Dale Hobbs, PhD
Phuket Rajabhat University
Jodee Hobbs, MA
Andover Central High School
Piengpen Na Pattalung, PhD
Phuket Rajabhat University

The purpose of this chapter is to provide individuals involved in debate with practical suggestions concerning how to gather and use evidence. This chapter will provide information on the importance of using evidence, the characteristics of good evidence, types of evidence one can use, finding evidence, and using evidence in the debate round.

THE IMPORTANCE OF USING EVIDENCE

Putting it succinctly, evidence is required to create an effective argument. Debates are contests involving the creative use of arguments. Argumentation involves the application of reasoning to evidence for the purpose of making a claim (Freeley and Steinberg 2005). This definition is well-supported and exemplified by Toulmin's (1980) seminal model of argument. Toulmin posits that the minimum components required for a complete argument are data, warrant, and claim. Data are the evidence or grounds for the claim. The claim is the conclusion argued. And, the warrant is the permission given by the audience that allows the claim to be established by the evidence provided. For example, John will die (claim) because John is a person (data) and we know that all people die (warrant). Or, I will go to college (claim) because statistics show that college graduates tend to earn more than high school graduates (data) and I want to earn a lot of money (warrant).

Toulmin's model of argument is acknowledged as a judicial or audience-based model of argument, and it is designed to be practical in nature as it attempts to explain how people actually argue in daily life. A jury trial provides an excellent illustration of the model's usefulness because, for all practical purposes, the defendant is guilty only when the jury (audience) says the defendant is guilty. If the jury says "guilty," the defendant goes to

Contributed by Jeffrey Dale Hobbs, Jodee Hobbs and Piengpen Na Pattalung. Copyright © Kendall Hunt Publishing Company

jail—whether or not he or she actually committed the crime. The jury members must agree that, according to their understanding of the law as presented in the trial (the warrants), the evidence presented in the trial means the defendant is guilty. Similarly, in a debate, the judge must agree that the evidence and reasoning you present means that the claims you make are true. If the judge doesn't agree, you will not win the debate no matter how "true" your arguments are.

It serves no useful purpose for the lawyer to say that the jury members were wrong because they failed to vote for the "truth" contained in the lawyer's evidence—the lawyer's client is still going to jail. The key is for the lawyer to give evidence and warrants which will convince the jury. Likewise, it does no practical good for a debater to complain that the "stupid judges" made the "wrong decision" because the judges failed to recognize the "truth" contained in the debater's arguments. The key is to provide evidence and warrants that those judging agree prove the points in contention.

THE CHARACTERISTICS OF GOOD EVIDENCE

The Toulmin model specifies that evidence must be presented in order to have a complete argument. Without evidence, all a debater has is an unsupported assertion. So, what are the characteristics of good evidence? While there are many characteristics that could be discussed (see Freely and Steinberg 2005), this chapter discusses a few of the most crucial ones. Good evidence is acceptable to the audience, follows the rules of the argumentative situation, tells a consistent story, is verifiable, is recent, and is worthy of belief.

Good evidence is acceptable to the audience. This is one of the main implications of the Toulmin model of argument. It makes common sense to use evidence that your audience will agree to. Can you reasonably expect a Bible verse to convince an atheist or a quote from a liberal Democrat to convince a staunch Republican?

Good evidence follows the rules of the argumentative situation. Just as there are rules that govern what type of evidence can be presented in a trial (for example, evidence gained in an illegal search cannot be used in a trial), there are rules for evidence use in IPDA debate. According to the preamble of the IPDA constitution, "The use of evidence cards and/or verbatim written materials is prohibited. Such materials may be studied, memorized, and/or paraphrased, but they may not be physically present in the round. The 'reading' of such materials should be highly penalized." These rules are further clarified in the bylaws:

Contestants may not bring written reference materials into the round with them. No 'reading' of evidence will be permitted. They may only bring and reference case outlines and limited notes which they may have worked up during the preparation period before their round. Evidence must be memorized or paraphrased for use during debates. This is another case where judges should be made aware of this rule and instructed to count off for abuses. Serious violations of this rule should cause the judge to automatically award the decision to the opponent.

Good evidence tells a consistent story. Walter Fisher (1987) argues that humans are storytellers who base beliefs, values, and actions on the stories they accept as true. For instance, people who accept the story of creation often believe, value, and act differently than people who accept the story of evolution. According to Fisher, people test or judge the quality of stories on the bases of narrative probability and narrative fidelity. A narrative that has probability is internally consistent—it does not contradict itself. A narrative that has fidelity is externally consistent—it is consistent with the stories already accepted as true; that is, it is true to one's life experiences. Fisher's narrative theory provides additional support to the idea that evidence must be acceptable to the audience and the theory helps to clarify what makes evidence acceptable—it is internally and externally consistent. A debater should not present evidence that contradicts itself. In a debate witnessed by one of the authors of this chapter, a debater presented testimony from two experts concerning why the death penalty should be abolished. One expert was cited as saying the death penalty was cruel and unusual punishment. The other expert was quoted as saying that the death penalty was too easy on criminals—not cruel enough. This expert argued that criminals would face harsher punishment with a life sentence where they had to sit and think about what they had done for a lifetime. Do you see the contradiction? Is the debater's story about abolishing the death penalty to be believed?

Good evidence is verifiable. People should be able to check for themselves if something is true or not. If a debater cites a fact, he or she should be able to give the source of that fact. The requirement for verifiable evidence is common in many areas of human activity. One example of this is the requirement that scientific researchers provide a detailed account of their research methodology when they report their data. This allows for the experiment to be replicated and the results verified if anyone should question the results. Also, hearsay evidence is generally not allowed in trials as it is not verifiable. NDT and CEDA debaters are required to give citations for all of the evidence they read in a round.

Good evidence is recent. Recent is a relative term. The evidence you use should be up-to-date, and nothing should have occurred that invalidates the truth or relevance of the evidence between the time the evidence was produced and when it is used. Some things change slowly and some things change very quickly. Statistics regarding the health of the United States' economy can be outdated by happenings on Wall Street in a matter of minutes. Some philosophical questions remain timeless—allowing for the quoting of even the most ancient of philosophers.

Good evidence is worthy of belief. As an IPDA debater, you should make the personal decision to use evidence worthy of belief Aristotle, (1984). In other words, you should decide to be honest and ethical in your attempts to secure the ballot. Be fair and honest in presenting evidence. If you are not sure about a fact, don't use it. Never lie or make up evidence. To paraphrase the golden rule, present the kind of evidence you want others to present to you when you are faced with an important decision. If you were buying a car, would you want the salesperson to make up "facts" about the car's safety, reliability, and gas mileage?

TYPES OF EVIDENCE

Evidence can be classified in a variety of different ways. The classification system we have chosen for this chapter is common knowledge, examples, statistics, and testimony (Campbell and Huxman 2003). All four of these types of evidence can be used in IPDA sponsored debates.

Common knowledge is sometimes known as shared premises. It is knowledge or beliefs shared by the speaker and the audience. For example, we all know, or share the premise, that the world is round. However, common knowledge is a weak form of evidence in a debate. All it takes to invalidate common knowledge is for the evidence to be questioned or challenged. By definition, the evidence is no longer a shared premise as soon as someone says that he or she disagrees. By its very nature, debate calls for this type of disagreement, even playing devil's advocate for the sake of the debate. Relying on shared premises does not always guarantee the results you are looking for because people often hold contradictory premises. One example of a person holding contradictory premises is a person who believes both that "opposites attract" and "birds of a feather flock together." Thus, you should only rely on a shared premise when you are certain everyone in the debate will agree with the premise and when no contradictory premises are likely to be held by the judge.

Examples are specific instances that illustrate the point in question. You might think of them as a "statistic" of one. They can vary in degree of detail and they provide more psychological than logical proof (Campbell and Huxman 2003). In choosing examples as evidence, a debater should choose real examples over hypothetical ones and should make sure that the example is a typical instance of what is being illustrated. Real examples provide more proof than hypothetical ones because real examples demonstrate that something actually happened; hypothetical examples only raise the possibility of an event. Due to the degree of difference in proof, a debater should identify hypothetical examples as being hypothetical—it is the ethical thing to do. Also, make sure the examples you use are typical instances. We are all familiar with the diet advertisements on television that end with the phrase "results not typical."

Statistics are numbers. Think of them as a large collection of "examples." Statistics tend to provide more logical proof than psychological proof (Campbell and Huxman 2003). Numbers, for the most part, lack the ability to involve our emotions. When was the last time you had a really good "cry" over a probability value of <.05? Thus, a good rhetorical strategy involves combining statistics and examples together. The example provides the psychological or emotional proof and the statistic provides the logical proof—the likelihood or frequency of the event illustrated in the example. There are many questions that one should ask when choosing statistics to use as evidence. We will discuss two of these questions. First, one should ask how the population was sampled to develop the statistic. In other words, is the sample unbiased and representative of the population in question? A statistic is only as good as the sample involved. A statistic cannot tell you what is true about the population unless it represents the population in question in a fair and unbiased manner. Phone-in survey questions during the local news are viewed as invalid because they involve a biased, self-selected sample—only those who are extremely interested in the subject of the poll will take the time to make the call. Second, one should ask how the variable reported in the statistic was defined. Some statistical variables are fairly tangible and straightforward—inches, pounds, degrees, etc. But, many statistical variables in the social sciences are not so well defined and researchers do not agree on how these variables should be measured. For instance, how do you measure love, religious commitment, or critical thinking? Sometimes statistics disagree with each other because the variable in question has been defined differently by the researchers who gathered the statistics. Hypothetically, if one researcher defined marital love as how many times a person says "I love you" to his or her spouse and another researcher defined marital love as the number of times one did something nice for his or her spouse, the person who did many nice things for his spouse but didn't say "I love you" would be counted as loving his or her spouse in one study but not the other. Since the above two tests of statistics are so important, you should only use statistics as evidence when you can explain how the population was sampled and how the variables were defined.

Testimony involves the quoting of another person's words. Testimony involves the sharing of another person's experience, expertise, and opinions. It is important that debaters rely on the testimony of experts when using testimony as evidence—quote people who are qualified to render opinions on the subjects in question. Internet sources must be carefully vetted—anyone, expert or lay, unbiased or biased, with a computer can be "published" on the internet. In contrast, for instance, information published in academic journals has been tested by the process of peer review. Also, the use of testimony requires that a debater pick sources to quote that are viewed as credible by his or her judge. The use of testimony involves the use of an authoritative warrant (Brockriede and Ehninger 1960). If the source of the testimony (data) is not viewed as having ethos, the judge will not give the warrant, or permission, needed for the data to prove the claim. Advertisements use authoritative warrants in commercials involving celebrity endorsements. For example, I am going to wear Hanes (claim) because Michael Jordan said I should (data/testimony) and I want to be like Mike (warrant). The advertisement only works with people who like Mike—those who view him as a credible or authoritative source. Finally, when using testimony, be sure to avoid the use of conclusionary evidence—evidence that cites only the author's conclusions without giving the reasons for these conclusions. Conclusionary evidence leaves the question of "why" unanswered. By citing reasons along with conclusions, you can often add motivational and substantive warrants to the authoritative warrant gained by quoting a particular source.

FINDING EVIDENCE

This section will briefly discuss the topic of research. Many different general research strategies exist and you can find an excellent discussion of such strategies in Booth, Colomb, and Williams (2008). We will not repeat those strategies here—instead, we will focus on advice we believe is particularly relevant to the practice of IPDA debate. Also, we don't feel the need to explain how to use the computer to do research on the internet to a generation raised on computers. The organizational scheme for this section is to take a look at the best way to spend research time before, during, and after the tournament.

How should the debater spend research time before the tournament? Debaters are frequently associated with the talent of being able to think fast on their feet. This is only partially true. Yes, good debaters are smart. But, excellent debaters are smart and prepared. It is through thorough preparation and research that a debater looks quick on his or her feet. To prepare to debate at an IPDA tournament, you should research rhetorical theory, debate theory, current events, and philosophical systems.

First, to be prepared to debate, one must research rhetorical theory. Public debate is designed to be an activity that gives individuals a chance to both learn and practice better ways of communicating with others. Theory informs practice. For example, researching Aristotle (1984) provides information on "... the faculty of observing in any given case the available means of persuasion" (24). According to Aristotle, the means of persuasion are ethos (speaker credibility), pathos (emotional appeals), and logos (logic). Researching

Perelman and Olbrechts-Tyteca (1969) exposes you to one of the best essays written on how to debate about values. They write: "When a speaker wants to establish values or hierarchies or to intensify the adherence they gain, he [sic] may consolidate them by connecting them with other values or hierarchies, but he [sic] may also resort to premises of a very general nature which we shall term loci" (83). These loci, or lines of argument, include quantity, quality, order, the existing, essence, and the person. Researching Fisher (1987) provides insight into argument as a story which any audience can judge according to narrative probability (internal consistency) and narrative fidelity (external consistency). Researching Foss' and Griffin's (1995) essay on invitational rhetoric provides you with an alternative rhetorical paradigm based in the feminist values of equality, immanent value, and self-determination. Yes, the goal of debating can be something other than winning. It can be about sharing perspectives and developing relationships.

Second, to be prepared to debate, one must research debate theory. Debate, as a subset of rhetoric, has developed some specialized theories of its own. For example, the requirements we place on counterplans are unique to the debate world. In the work world, you do not reject a colleague's suggestion because it is topical or because it is not net beneficial to the idea you suggested. Excellent debaters will become experts in debate theory. Additionally, as practitioners of debate, you have the opportunity to be involved in the creation of debate theory. This is especially true in an organization as young as the International Public Debate Association. This time, practice informs theory.

Third, to be prepared to debate on the negative, one must research current events. IPDA topics are frequently about current events—both foreign and domestic. For example, the resolution might state: "The United States should cut federal income taxes." As a public debater, you need to know about current trends in economics, education, government, and technology. If you do not know about a topic, you cannot enter into an intelligent debate about the subject. Without specific facts, it is impossible to accurately weigh costs and benefits in a policy round. Watch and read the news daily.

Fourth, to be prepared to debate on the negative, one must research different philosophical systems. IPDA topics are often broad philosophical topics. The resolution might state: "Postmodernism is a dangerous philosophy." Additionally, philosophical systems can be used as critiques of the affirmative's position, such as a feminist critique, and as ways to argue for alternative criteria, such as arguing the debate should be decided on the philosophy of utilitarianism.

When researching rhetorical theory, argumentation theory, current events, and philosophical systems, it is wise to find a way to keep track of what you have learned and organize it in a way that is easy to find and use at the debate tournament—preparation time at a tournament is precious and it passes quickly. In essence, you need to develop a reliable filing system for your evidence. While keeping and carrying hard copies of debate evidence briefs and important articles is possible, it is probably advisable to develop an electronic storage system. Some teams develop a personal website that keeps their teams' research briefs on file for easy access at tournaments.

How should the debater spend research time during the tournament? Ideally, you should be able to spend preparation time selecting the specific evidence (gained from research before the tournament) that best fits the needs of your scheduled debate. In other words, you have done your research before the tournament so that you can spend preparation time selecting and organizing your best arguments with the help of your coach and colleagues.

Chapter 9: Evidence in IPDA Debate • **99**

However, this is not always possible. No matter how good you are at predicting the future, sooner or later you will end up with a topic you had not thought of before the tournament. Thus, the next best thing is to spend time researching "links" between the current topic and the arguments you have prepared to debate. If you know a lot about economics and the topic is education, what are the links, or relationships, between education and the economy? With the right evidence, you can turn an education debate into a debate on economics—the subject you are better prepared to debate because you researched it before the tournament. With this goal in mind, you should consider researching several generic topics that can be linked to a variety of subjects. The key to success is preparation—it is impossible to become an expert on a completely new topic during 30 minutes of preparation time.

How should the debater spend research time after the tournament? A debater's research is never done. Evidence is the grounds for arguments. New evidence is needed for new and creative arguments. If you stop researching, your arguments will become stale, predictable, and ineffective. Thus, keep researching the topics already mentioned: rhetorical theory, debate theory, current events, and philosophical systems. However, after each tournament, the debate topics faced at that tournament can help shape the direction that research should take for the next set of tournaments. Ask yourself what topics were the subjects of debates at the tournament. You are likely to see the same topics or, at least, similar topics again. Prepare for these topics by doing specific research on the subjects involved—especially those you have not researched before. Prepare an evidence brief addressing the issues of each topic. A debate team will find it helpful to make weekly research assignments to help share the research burden that such preparation demands. Another productive use of research time after a tournament is to spend time verifying the evidence used by your opponents—especially the evidence that did not sound quite right to you. Researching the evidence your opponents used will help you to be prepared to answer their arguments in future rounds.

USING EVIDENCE IN THE DEBATE ROUND

Much of what has been written in this chapter already addresses the topic of how to use evidence during the debate round. However, there are a few more bits of advice that we would like to share regarding the use of evidence.

First, make sure that you have evidence for each argument that you want to advance in the debate. According to Toulmin, without data, there is no argument. In fact, it is preferable to present a variety of data for each argument you offer in the debate. Our advice is that you go for depth rather than breadth of arguments. Debate a few things well rather than many things poorly.

Second, give a way to weigh, or choose between, competing evidence in the debate. Your evidence says one thing and your opponent's evidence says another thing. So, which is the better evidence? What criteria should the judge use to weigh evidence? Using the ideas presented in this chapter, you might be able to demonstrate that your evidence is the better evidence because it is more consistent, more recent, or more verifiable than your opponent's evidence. As a word of caution, preponderance of evidence is a poor criterion to use in debates because it begs the question. Criteria need to help the judge make a decision regarding what really counts as evidence toward proving or disproving the resolution. The simple existence of evidence does not demonstrate that it is acceptable evidence for determining the truth of the proposition. For example, dogs bark. Let us say that I present this fact as evidence in the debate round for the resolution: "A dog is a good pet." My opponent does not disagree. So, by preponderance of evidence, I have won that point. But what have I proven with regards to the resolution? I haven't proven anything. Real criteria have to be presented. Whether or not the fact that dogs bark makes them a good pet depends on how you define good—not from the sure fact of having presented more evidence than the other side. The evidence must be interpreted by criteria that actually define "good." If the criterion used was "protection," then barking would mean that a dog is a good pet. If the criterion used was "does not disturb neighbors," then barking would mean that a dog is not a good pet.

Finally, we want to remind you to use evidence ethically—to make your arguments worthy of belief. This is a personal decision that a debater has to make on his or her own. IPDA debate encourages ethical argumentation, but enforcement is left up to the individual debater. If you act ethically, you can be proud of your success in the activity. What is considered to be unethical uses of evidence? Obviously, falsifying evidence is unethical—avoid the temptation to invent tailor-made evidence for your case. It is also unethical to tell half-truths by taking evidence out of context or by leaving out relevant details. The arguer denies the judge an authentic choice because the judge's decision is based on false or misleading information. The judge is tricked into accepting a position (Brockriede 1972). Additionally, it is unethical to use evidence without citing the source of that evidence—it is called plagiarism.

CONCLUSION

The difference between an unsupported assertion and an argument is evidence. A debater should ask the following questions when selecting evidence for use in an IPDA debate round:

1. Is the evidence acceptable to the judge?
2. Is the evidence consistent with the rules expressed in the IPDA constitution?
3. Does the evidence tell a consistent story?
4. Is the evidence verifiable?
5. Is the evidence recent?
6. Is the evidence worthy of belief?
7. If using a shared premise, does everyone agree with the premise and are no contradictory premises held?
8. If using an example, is the example a real and typical instance of the subject being illustrated?
9. If using a statistic, does the statistic come from a source that used representative and unbiased sampling and clearly defined variables?
10. If using testimony, does the testimony come from an expert who is viewed as credible by the judge?
11. If using testimony, does my evidence cite the author's reasons along with the author's conclusions?

12. Have I thoroughly researched the evidence I want to use—do I know what I am talking about?
13. Do I have sufficient evidence for each argument that I want to make?
14. Do I have a way of demonstrating that my evidence is superior to the evidence of my opponent?
15. Is my use of evidence ethical?

REFERENCES

Aristotle. 1984. *The Rhetoric and the Poetics of Aristotle.* Trans. W. R. Roberts. New York: McGraw-Hill, Inc.,

Booth, W. C., Colomb G. G., and J. M. Williams. 2008. *The Craft of Research,* 3rd ed., Chicago: The University of Chicago Press.

Brockriede, W. 1972. "Arguers as Lovers." *Philosophy & Rhetoric,* 5(1): 1–11.

Brockriede, W., and D. Ehninger. 1960. "Toulmin on Argument: An Interpretation and Application." *Quarterly Journal of Speech,* 46(1): 44–53.

Campbell, K. K., and S. S. Huxman. 2003. *The Rhetorical Act,* 3rd ed. Belmont: Wadsworth/Thomson Learning.

Fisher, W. R. 1987. *Human Communication as Narration: Toward a Philosophy of Reason, Value, and Action.* Columbia: University of South Carolina Press.

Foss, S. K., and C. L. Griffin. 1995. "Beyond Persuasion: A Proposal for an Invitational Rhetoric." *Communication Monographs,* 62(1): 2–18.

Freeley, A. J., and D. L. Steinberg. 2005. *Argumentation and Debate,* 11th ed. Belmont: Wadsworth Publishing Company.

International Public Debate Association. "The Constitution of the International Public Debate Association." http://www.ipdadebate.org/const.html. Accessed 27 April, 2009.

Perelman, C., and L. Olbrechts-Tyteca. 1969. *The New Rhetoric: A Treatise on Argument.* Trans. John Wilkinson and Purcell Weaver. Notre Dame: University of Notre Dame Press.

Toulmin, S. 1958. *The Uses of Argument.* Cambridge University Press.

Chapter 10

Audience Analysis

Adam Key
Texas A & M

In his penultimate work on persuasion, *The Art of Rhetoric*, Aristotle stated, "Speeches have more effect through their style than through their intellectual content." While Aristotle firmly believed, as many do now, that having better argumentation than your opponent should ideally be the deciding factor in persuasion, he recognized the inherent importance of one's delivery to the process of attitude change. Indeed, he acknowledged that the emotional impact of a speaker is just as important, if not more so, as the intellectual accuracy of his or her argumentation.

While the importance of emotion has been recognized since the times of the ancient Greek orators, very little empirical research has been conducted relating the recognition of emotional expression in an audience to persuasion. And while there has been extensive research into adapting a speech towards an audience, the scholarship in this area almost exclusively concerns reaching out to larger audiences as opposed to individuals (Morgan 2003). The one exception to this is the relatively young research field of personal selling. To date, an exhaustive search of available literature has yielded a single study empirically relating the ability to adapt to an audience's emotional expression to the persuasion of individuals (Byron, Terranova, and Nowicki 2007).

Beyond personal selling, one area that would benefit from such research is intercollegiate debate. A verbal competition in which two sides vie to persuade a single judge to support their position, debate is a laboratory for the use of persuasive tools. While the overwhelming majority of research into debate stems from the field of rhetoric, the field of interpersonal communication's research into understanding emotion and adaptability could uniquely inform debate scholarship.

There currently exist four chief intercollegiate debate associations within the United States: the National Debate Tournament (NDT), the Cross-Examination Debate Association (CEDA), the National Parliamentary Debate Association (NPDA), and the International Public Debate Association. Each organization is the central organization for a particular style of debate. CEDA, for instance, focuses on policy debate which requires heavy amounts of research and preparation of detailed governmental plans. In contrast, NPDA focuses on adaptability within a limited framework, all the while following British parliamentary procedure.

Contributed by Adam Key. Copyright © Kendall Hunt Publishing Company

Of the four, only IPDA focuses on specifically on "real-world application" (International Public Debate Association 2009, para. 1). Public debate is primarily focused on delivery style, audience adaptability, and speaker credibility. For this reason, judges at IPDA tournaments are primarily lay people from the surrounding community. Rather than both speakers and judges conforming to preexisting schema for evaluating argumentation, debaters are instead required to adapt their communication style to the lay judge. These particular aspects make IPDA the ideal organization in which to examine the effect of emotional adaptability to an individual person on the ability to change that person's attitude.

The purpose of this study is to examine the relationship of the ability to recognize emotional micro-expressions, to persuasion, in regular season tournaments of the International Public Debate Association. This study specifically examines the relationship of the aforementioned factor to differences in both win/loss and speaker point allocation within preliminary debate rounds.

LITERATURE REVIEW

Public Debate Format

While not exclusively an intercollegiate organization, IPDA is the most recent addition to an ongoing series of competitive intercollegiate forensic organizations within the United States (Cirlin 2007). Beginning with NDT, each organization would begin with an emphasis on communication skills, but over time would devolve into rapid-fire delivery, and technical jargon replaced rhetoric and audience analysis (Freeley and Steinberg 2005). As this transformation reached a zenith, frustrated coaches and debaters would begin a new organization (Eldridge 2008).

The Novice division is open to any interested competitor who has participated in less than eight competitive debate tournaments since entering high school and who has not earned a four-year baccalaureate degree. The Varsity division is open to any interested competitor who has not earned a four-year baccalaureate degree. The Professional division is open to any interested competitor, including those who possess degrees, and has no entry restrictions (International Public Debate Association 2009).

A traditional IPDA tournament includes either six or eight rounds. For each round, individual competitors are matched against a competitor from a different program or university and preassigned the position of the Affirmative or the Negative. The Affirmative must advocate in favor of the resolution, while the Negative's duty is to argue against it. Thirty minutes before the round begins, each pair of competitors is given a list of five resolutions. Beginning with the Negative, each takes turns striking two resolutions, leaving the final resolution to be debated during the round. Following that, competitors spend the remainder of the 30 minutes using the internet, their teammates, and coaches to prepare arguments (Richey 2007).

Each preliminary round consists of two competitors being adjudicated by a single judge. The order of speeches is as follows: 5-minute Affirmative constructive, 2-minute cross-examination by the Negative, 6-minute Negative constructive, 2-minute cross-examination by the Affirmative, 3-minute Affirmative rebuttal, 5-minute Negative rebuttal, 3-minute Affirmative rebuttal. Following the conclusion of the round, the judge chooses a winner and assigns both competitors a speaker point rating. Speaker points consist of rating from 1 = *Very*

Weak to 5 = Superior in eight areas for a range of 8 to 40 total points. The eight areas include delivery, courtesy, appropriate tone, organization, logic, support, cross-examination, and refutation (Alexander 2010).

A certain number of competitors, not exceeding more than half, will advance to elimination rounds. Advancement to rounds is determined by overall record, with ties in records broken based on the cumulative speaker point totals. For instance, if a division has 32 competitors, the 16 debaters with the best records will advance.

Under normal circumstances, each competitor will be assigned the Affirmative and Negative position an equal number of times. However, as competitors generally cannot compete in a preliminary round against the same competitor more than once at the same tournament, nor debate a member of his or her own program, the distribution of sides may not always be equal. Additionally, when an odd number of competitors is entered into a division at a particular tournament, one person per round receives an automatic win, called a 'bye,' thereby producing an uneven distribution of sides.

Emotional Expression

Competitive debate has existed in some form since the birth of democratic society in Greece. Even at its very beginnings, orators recognized the importance of nonverbal communication when debating (Golden, Berquist, and Coleman 1989). Pronuntiatio, delivery style, was one of the five pillars of speechmaking (Kennedy 1980). It was considered of equal value to the other pillars including inventio (information), disposito (dispositional organization), elocution (word selection) and memoria (memory) (Golden, Berquist, and Coleman 1989).

More recent research verifies the orators' beliefs. The use of emotional language has been empirically demonstrated to affect both understanding and appreciation of ideas (Marlin 2002). Cicero, widely considered one of the most preeminent Roman speakers, held emotion to be the most important part of any attempt to change minds (Haslings 1976). He correctly asserted that in order to effectively deliver persuasive messages, the study and understanding of facial expressions was necessary.

History and Universality

Paul Ekman (2001) theorizes that nonverbal cues about a person's behavior are resultant from emotional and cognitive sources. His field of research indicates that during periods of increased cognitive load (Vrij, Edward, and Bull 2001) or emotional experience (Ekman and Friesen 1974), individuals will readily and involuntarily display emotions nonverbally.

There is some degree of dispute over which nonverbal cues are the most reliable when attempting to detect emotions. Scherer (1986) claimed vocal cues, which are less controllable, were more accurate, while Ekman and Friesen (1969) originally held that the body itself was of equally reliable value. Further research has determined that both body and vocal cues are context and culture dependent. Facial expressions, however, have been shown to be reliable indicators (Ekman, Friesen, and O'Sullivan 1988).

Rather than context-dependent emblematic gestures which carry with them meanings that vary across culture, emotional facial expressions are both universal and objectively measurable (Ekman and Friesen 1975). When humans experience emotion, one of seven different emotional expressions is involuntarily triggered (Ekman, Levenson, and Friesen 1983). Sadness, for instance, involves the triangularis muscle which pulls the lip corners downward in conjunction with the medial frontalis muscle which raises the inner corners of the eyebrows (Ekman and Friesen 1975). Happiness is expressed through the Duchenne smile, named for the researcher who first empirically examined facial expressions through an examination of true and false smiles (Ekman, Friesen, and O'Sullivan 1988). The common belief is that a smile that merely employs the zygomatic major muscle to raise the corners of the mouth upward indicates happiness. Duchenne found that that muscular movement by itself could be easily duplicated, despite a lack of happy emotion. Instead, the activation of the orbicularis oculi, the muscle that causes crinkling around the eyes, must also activate to indicate a genuine smile (Duchenne 1862).

The seven universal expressions include happiness, sadness, disgust, fear, surprise, anger, and contempt (Ekman and Friesen 1969). Despite the fact that humans are trained from an early age to conceal emotion, these expressions inevitably occur (Ekman 2001).

Ekman's research traces its origin to the work of Duchenne and his contemporary, Charles Darwin (Ekman, Friesen, and O'Sullivan 1988). Darwin, following his many travels, noted that human emotions appeared to be innate (Darwin 1872). Visiting a large and diverse group of cultures, many of whom had very limited exposure to anyone outside their own social unit, Darwin noted that facial expressions remained the same. He was unable to understand the language they spoke, but was able to understand the emotions their faces expressed. Both emotions and the accompanying universal expressions, Darwin argued, were the product of human evolution.

According to Darwin, humans who could both experience and nonverbally communicate emotions were more likely to survive than those who could not. For instance, experiencing the emotion of fear helped individuals avoid dangerous situations. Likewise, the ability to nonverbally express fear of a dangerous situation allowed others, who viewed the emotional display, to also avoid impending danger.

Initial empirical tests, however, failed to confirm Darwin's assertions. Infants often displayed inconsistent and inappropriate facial expressions in response to emotional stimuli (Sherman 1927). Adults, too, displayed inappropriate expressions, most often smiling when subjected to surprise, embarrassment, or disgust (Landis 1924). By the mid-twentieth century, social scientists generally regarded facial expressions as the result of social learning, dependent on culture instead of biology (Bruner and Tagiuri 1954).

In the early 1960s, researchers began showing pictures of faces posed to express Woodworth's (1938) emotional clusters, finding an overarching agreement as to which expressions reflected particular emotions (Tomkins and McCarter 1964). Other researchers began replicating these experiments across various countries on four continents, finding near-identical results (e.g., Izard 1971). Responding to criticism from the academic community, Ekman and his colleagues conducted similar experiments with the Sadong tribe in Borneo and the Fore tribe in New Guinea (Ekman, Sorenson, and Friesen 1969). Both tribes were incredibly isolated and had almost no contact with Western culture, making it nearly impossible that they could have learned the expressions from Westerners or the media. As with the previous experiments, there was strong agreement as to which expressions represented each emotion. Additionally, congenitally blind children, who could not possibly have seen others making emotional expressions, have been shown to display the same expressions when experiencing spontaneous emotions (Eibl-Eibesfeldt 1973).

Micro-expressions

Ekman theorized that involuntary facial expressions exist in two separate varieties: subtle expressions and micro-expressions (Ekman and Friesen 1975). Subtle expressions, better termed as emotional leakage, occur when partial expressions appear momentarily only employing part of the face while the rest remains masked (Ekman and Friesen 1975). These are the most reliable when muscle groups that are difficult to control voluntarily, especially the forehead and brow, are part of the expression. It is improbable that these muscles could be activated during feigned emotion nor deactivated when emotions are masked. The measurement of subtle expressions does suffer from two flaws. First, not all facial expressions employ involuntary areas. Second, certain individuals are curiously able to control those particular muscles voluntarily (Ekman 2001). For these reasons, subtle expressions by themselves cannot be considered objectively reliable.

Micro-expressions are the more reliable of the two varieties (Ekman 2001). Unlike subtle expressions, micro-expressions occur across the entire face (Ekman and Friesen 1969). The length, however, is significantly shorter. When a micro-expression occurs, a person will display one of the seven universal emotional expressions across their entire face for a period of time between one-fifth and one twenty-fifth of a second (Frank and Ekman 1997). The majority of individuals are incapable of noticing micro-expressions without training (Ekman and O'Sullivan 1991). The single study currently available linking persuasive ability to emotion recognition deals exclusively with macro-expressions (Byron, Terranova, and Nowicki 2007). No available study examines the relationship between persuasion and the ability to recognize emotional momentary micro-expressions.

Benefits of Emotional Detection

The ability to accurately assess the emotional states of others is positively correlated with a host of benefits including better social adjustment (Carton, Kessler, and Pape 1999), improved mental health (Rosenthal, Hall, DiMatteo, Rogers, and Archer 1979), and increased workplace effectiveness (Halberstadt and Hall 1980). Additional positive correlations have been noted with gregariousness (Toner and Gates 1985), mental capability, social style, self-monitoring (Mufson and Nowicki 1991), and social desirability (Cunningham 1977). Further research reveals benefits for specific fields across a wide and diverse range including elementary school principals, therapists, human service workers, physicians, and business executives (Nowicki and Duke 1994). Indeed, the ability to recognize emotion is one of the central elements of both emotional intelligence (Matthews, Zeidner, and Roberts 2002) and affective social competence (Saarni 2001).

The ability to recognize emotion is crucial to adaptability within social situations (Halberstadt, Denham, and Dunsmore 2001). Adaptability, in turn, is of primary importance in the persuasion process (Gass and Seiter 2007). Awareness of the emotions of others produces messages responsive to the desires of your audience (Burleson 1989). During debater rounds, judges are required to remain silent and refrain from conversation with the competitors during the round (International Public Debate Association 2009). Thus, in order to adapt, competitors must be able to recognize emotions conveyed nonverbally by judges. When judges attempt to suppress emotional responses to what the competitors are saying, micro-expressions are likely to occur (Ekman and Friesen 1969). Debaters who are able to detect these expressions are likely better able to adapt their speaking, thus increasing the likelihood of persuasion.

In light of this information, the following hypothesis is offered.

H1: The ability to recognize micro-expressions will have a positive correlation with a win being awarded in a debate round.

While research suggests that the recognition of micro-expressions, in general, may contribute to persuasion, it is unknown which specific expressions may be valuable. Therefore, the following research questions are presented.

RQ1a: What effect, if any, does the ability to recognize the fear micro-expression have upon the result of a debate round?

RQ1b: What effect, if any, does the ability to recognize the surprise micro-expression have upon the result of a debate round?

RQ1c: What effect, if any, does the ability to recognize the happiness micro-expression have upon the result of a debate round?

RQ1d: What effect, if any, does the ability to recognize the sadness micro-expression have upon the result of a debate round?

RQ1e: What effect, if any, does the ability to recognize the anger micro-expression have upon the result of a debate round?

RQ1f: What effect, if any, does the ability to recognize the disgust micro-expression have upon the result of a debate round?

RQ1g: What effect, if any, does the ability to recognize the contempt micro-expression have upon the result of a debate round?

Audience Adaptability

Audience adaptability is effectively measured through the lens of person-centered communication (Applegate 1990). Person-centered communication schemas have been constructed to evaluate the adaptability of a speaker based upon audience feedback within various persuasive situations (Applegate 1982). Similarly, in public debate, each speaker is given a speaker point rating by the individual judge during each preliminary round. Scores range from one to five, five being the greatest, in the areas of delivery, courtesy, appropriate tone, organization, logic, support, cross-examination.

These schemas distinguish low levels of adaptation in which speakers do not meaningfully appreciate the perception of their audience to high levels where the speaker's entire argument molds to audience expectations (Delia, Kline, and Burleson 1979). The most notable factors identified within measures of person-centered communication are supporting the audience's positive identity and framing the message to coincide with the perceptions of the audience (Waldron and Applegate 1994). Nonverbal decoding ability has been previously correlated with person-centered communication (Woods 1996).

In light of this information, the following hypothesis is offered.

H2: The ability to recognize micro-expressions will have a positive correlation with the speaker point rating in a debate round.

While research suggests recognition of micro-expressions, in general, may contribute to speaker points, it is unknown which specific expressions may be valuable. Therefore, the following research questions are presented.

RQ2a: What effect, if any, does the ability to recognize the fear micro-expression have upon the speaker point rating in a debate round?

RQ2b: What effect, if any, does the ability to recognize the surprise micro-expression have upon the speaker point rating in a debate round?

RQ2c: What effect, if any, does the ability to recognize the happiness micro-expression have upon the speaker point rating in a debate round?

RQ2d: What effect, if any, does the ability to recognize the sadness micro-expression have upon the speaker point rating in a debate round?

RQ2e: What effect, if any, does the ability to recognize the anger micro-expression have upon the speaker point rating in a debate round?

RQ2f: What effect, if any, does the ability to recognize the disgust micro-expression have upon speaker point rating in a debate round?

RQ2g: What effect, if any, does the ability to recognize the contempt micro-expression have upon the speaker point rating in a debate round?

Adaptation in relation to persuasion has been studied extensively within the area of personal sales (Marone and Lunsford 2005). Personal selling is most often a dyadic communication event (Evans 1963) that occurs in a face-to-face setting (Soldow and Thomas 1984) whose success is dependent on the adaptability of the speaker (Fine 2007). The field is relatively young and has rarely been approached from a communication perspective (Williams and Spiro 1985). However, the similarity of circumstances to intercollegiate debate creates relevance within the findings of this field.

Weitz, Sujan, and Sujan (1986) define adaptive selling as the "altering of sales behaviors during a customer interaction based on perceived information about the nature of the selling situation" (175). This coincides directly with Gass and Seiter's notion of moving the message to the audience as part of successful audience adaptation (2007).

While the reviews concerning the relationship between adaptive selling measures and job-related performance measures have been varied (Park and Holloway 2004), this is likely due to the failure to use performance-based measures (Byron, Terranova, and Nowicki 2007). Instead, the majority of adaptive selling research relies on self-reports (Rozell, Pettijohn, and Parker 2004). The only study to examine the empirical link between accurate recognition of emotion and sales performance found a significant positive relationship (Byron, Terranova, and Nowicki 2007). In light of this information, the following research questions are offered.

RQ3a: The ability to adapt to customers will positively correlate with winning a debate round.

RQ3b: The ability to adapt to customers will positively correlate with the speaker point rating in a debate round.

METHOD

This study is designed to investigate differences in competitive equity based on the ability to recognize emotion and adapt to an audience during the Fall 2009 regular season tournaments of the International Public Debate Association. This investigation focuses on two primary areas. First, the study examines the win/loss allocation to individuals based on their ability to recognize micro-expressions, their ability to adapt, their sex, and their position of advocacy. Second, this study examines the relationship between speaker point evaluation and the aforementioned categories.

Participants

Participants were competitors participating in public debate at regular season tournaments sanctioned by the International Public Debate Association during the Fall 2009 semester, from August through December, within the states of Texas, Arkansas, Louisiana, Tennessee, and Mississippi. These states were selected because the majority of IPDA sanctioned tournaments occur in these states. Of the 16 regular season tournaments scheduled for the 2009–2010 season, only two were scheduled outside these states. During the Fall 2009 semester, only one tournament, in Idaho, was scheduled outside the selected states.

During the Spring semester, packets containing surveys and accompanying research materials were distributed to coaches of university-affiliated debate teams that had at least one student compete during the Fall semester. Coaches were requested to administer the surveys to the students who had competed during the Fall and return them to the author, either by mail or in person. Of the 181 surveys distributed, 36 were returned. The Sam Houston State University Institutional Review Board approved the contents and administration of the survey.

The sample ($N = 36$) consisted of 12 females and 24 males. Subjects were asked to provide their names in order to pair their results with their records from the Fall tournaments. Other than verifying that each subject was over the age of 18, no other personal information was collected.

Unlike other forms of research, when studying a competitive event like debate, the opponent must be taken into account in order to achieve valid results. If one were examining the effect of gender on the answers to a survey or the grade received on an assignment, it is assumed that their individual results are their own and independent of outside interference. In a debate round, however, the other competitor directly and purposively influences all results. There is only a single win to go around between the two competitors. Additionally, there is a distinct likelihood that the other debater additionally affects speaker points, if only by comparison.

The skill level of the other competitor, therefore, should be taken into account in order to provide accurate analysis. It is axiomatic that any individual will have a significantly more difficult time obtaining the win and high speaker points against a national champion than a novice. Without some method to account for the other competitor's effect, the results cannot be considered accurate.

Therefore, rather than competitors being examined individually, debate rounds were examined as a whole using dyadic analysis (Kenny, Kashy, and Cook 2006). Sex and position of advocacy were assessed through cumulative sheets encompassing 1,719 rounds, yielding 3,438 cases ($N = 3,438$). Of the available rounds, 635 contained at least one of the competitors who returned a survey, generating 693 cases for direct analysis of the effects of micro-expressions and audience adaptation. Finally, returned surveys included both competitors in 58 rounds, yielding 116 cases for comparative analysis.

Independent Variables

The independent variables employed in this study consisted of the ability to recognize micro-expressions, adaptability to judges, sex, and the position of advocacy.**Ability to Recognize Micro-expressions**

A modified version of the Japanese and Caucasian Brief Affect Recognition Test (JACBART) (Matsumoto et al. 2000) was employed. The measure consisted of 49 digital video clips that embed a.2 second exposure to an image displaying one of seven universal emotional expressions within a four-second clip of the same expresser's neutral face. This format eliminated after-images of the target expression (Matsumoto et al. 2000). This instrument differed from the original JACBART by extending the length of the neutral clip from a single second to four seconds to allow the subject more time to view the neutral expression in order to differentiate it from the emotional expression. JACBART has been shown to have good validity and reliability (Matsumoto et al. 2000).

Following the 49 clips of micro-expressions, the measure consisted of seven images displaying one of each universal emotional expression for 10 seconds each. This was performed to verify the subject's ability to identify emotional expressions in order to ensure validity of the micro-expression testing results.

The expressive images were obtained from Japanese and Caucasian Facial Expressions of Emotion (JACFEE), while the neutral images of the same expressers are from Japanese and Caucasian Neutral Faces (JACNeuf) (Matsumoto and Ekman 1988). All images were coded by the Facial Action Coding System to ensure validity in both the correct emotion and emotional intensity levels (Ekman and Friesen 1978).

Fifty-six individuals were depicted, each with a neutral face and one expressing an emotion. No individual was depicted more than once. Emotions were each depicted eight times, equally divided between males and females and between Japanese and Caucasian expressers. The order of all 56 images was randomly sorted and modified so that no emotion appeared twice in a row. No other criteria were used in sorting the images.

An orienting tone and a presentation number were displayed three seconds prior to the image being displayed. Participants were given an answer sheet that corresponds to the presentation numbers. For each image, participants were given a forced-choice option to answer Fear, Surprise, Happiness, Sadness, Disgust, Contempt, and Anger and "none of the above." Providing a "none of the above" option has been demonstrated to eliminate the tendency of individuals to choose an expression when they do not believe they observed one (Frank and Stennett 2001). Participants were told to mark the expression they believe they have observed, and to answer regardless of their degree of certainty. The video was paused after each image to allow time for answering.

Participants were instructed to watch the video in small groups. No discussion was permitted until the measure was completed.

Accuracy scores were calculated for each participant for the following categories: Micro-expressions, Fear, Surprise, Happiness, Sadness, Disgust, Contempt, and Anger.

Adaptability to Judges

The ability to adapt to judges was evaluated by employing modified versions of Spiro and Weitz's (1990) ADAPTS scale and the derivative ADAPTS-SV scale developed by Robinson, Marshall, Moncrief and Lassk (2002). The ADAPTS scale is a 16-item measure that "measures five facets of adaptive selling that include: a) recognition that different sales approaches are needed for different customers; b) confidence in the ability to use a variety of approaches; c) confidence in the ability to alter approach during interaction; d) collection of information to facilitate adoption; e) actual use of different approaches" (Meredith 2007). The ADAPTS-SV scale is modified version of the adapts, using a five-item scale that uses only five of the original ADAPTS items to examine behaviors and beliefs. The original facets of the ADAPTS scale are further refined by the ADAPTS-SV, making it the preferred measure for adaptive selling (Chakrabarty, Brown, Widing, and Taylor 2004). Sample items include

112 • IPDA Textbook

"When I feel my presentation style is not working, I can easily change to another style," "Basically I use the same approach with most judges," and "I try to understand how one judge differs from another."

The only modification made to both scales is the replacement of the term "customer" with "judge" and the phrase "sales" with "persuasion." Both scales were employed to increase reliability.

Dependent Variables

The dependent variables consist of the win/loss result and the speaker point rating given to each individual during a particular round. Both variables were determined based on tournament cumulative sheets made available by IPDA (Alexander 2010).

RESULTS

Data Analysis

Data entry was performed by employing Olsen and Kenny's (2006) pairwise double-entry method. Each competitor's scores during the round were treated as a separate set of scores, as each score was an independent observation by a judge in a particular round.

For the ADAPTS, ADAPTS-SV, and each micro-expression measured by the JACBART, each competitor scored between 0 and 7. Additionally, an overall micro-expression score was calculated by averaging the micro-expression scores.

To examine the effect of the difference in scores upon the dependent variables, the opponent's score was subtracted from the subject's score to yield a difference score. As SPSS is incapable of handling negative numbers, all scores were increased by 8. Therefore, for each round a competitor participated in, they possessed a difference score of 1 to 15 for the JACBART, ADAPTS, and ADAPTS-SV.

For dyads, if Competitor A and Competitor B participated in a debate round, the entry would consist of the following. On the first line, Competitor A would be the subject. His or her division (Novice, Varsity, or Professional), sex (Male or Female), position of advocacy (Affirmative or Negative), results (Win or Loss), speaker point rating (8–40), JACBART score as a whole and for each micro-expression, ADAPTS, and ADAPTS-SV score would be listed. Additionally, Competitor B's speaker point rating, JACBART score as a whole and for each micro-expression, ADAPTS, and ADAPTS-SV score would be listed. Finally, difference scores, subtracting Competitor B's score from Competitor A's and adding 8 to the final score, for the JACBART scores, ADAPTS, and ADAPTS-SV would complete the line. On the second line, the same data from the round would be listed, but using Competitor B for the subject instead of Competitor A.

Data was analyzed using SPSS, using logistical regression to conduct analysis of the win/loss allocation and linear regression using speaker point allocation.

H1

H1 predicted that a positive correlation existed between the ability to recognize micro-expressions and a win being awarded by a judge during a debate round. Results indicated a positive correlation between the ability to detect micro-expressions and the ability to obtain a win during a debate round, β =.36, p =.002. Difference scores between competitors indicating a positive relationship between having greater micro-expression recognition ability than your opponent approached but did not achieve significance, β =.39, p =.06. H1 was partially supported.

RQ1

RQ1 examined the effects of the ability to recognize individual micro-expressions upon the result of a debate round. Results indicated a positive correlation between the ability to recognize the contempt micro-expression and the ability to obtain a win during a debate round, β =.09, p =.02. Difference scores between competitors indicated significant effects between having greater ability to recognize the happiness (β =.93, p =.02) and anger (β =.29, p =.01) micro-expressions than your opponent. No other significant results were obtained.

H2

H2 predicted that a positive correlation existed between the ability to recognize micro-expressions and the speaker point rating by a judge during a debate round. Results indicated a positive correlation between the ability to recognize micro-expressions and speaker point rating during a debate round, β = 1.62, t = 5.85, p <.001, partial η^2 = 048. No significant results were obtained regarding difference scores. H2 was partially supported.

RQ2

RQ2 examined the effects of the ability to recognize individual micro-expressions upon the speaker point rating by a judge during a debate round. Results indicated a positive correlation between the ability to recognize the fear (β =.37, t = 2.23, p =.01, partial η^2 =.014), happiness (β = 1.05, t = 2.34, p =.02, partial η^2 =.01), sadness (β =.26, t = 2.44, p =.008, partial η^2 =.009), and contempt (β =.64, t = 6.72, p =.01, partial η^2 =.067) micro-expressions and speaker point ratings during a debate round. A negative correlation was observed regarding the ability to recognize the disgust micro-expression, β = -.31, t = -2.1, p =.04, partial η^2 =.007. No other significant results were obtained.

RQ3

RQ3 examined the effects of the ability to adapt to judges upon the result and speaker point rating awarded by a judge during a debate round. No significant results were obtained.

Discussion

Micro-expressions

In general, the ability to recognize micro-expressions, both generally and specifically, positively correlated with both the abilities to achieve a win and high speaker ratings in a debate round. Additionally, the ability to recognize specific micro-expressions more accurately than your opponent had a positive correlation with the ability to win a debate round. These findings are notable for a number of reasons.

The observed effects on the ability to recognize micro-expressions on the ability to win a debate round is important to research concerning persuasion and social influence. Rather

114 • IPDA Textbook

than attempting to adapt to the general idea of who an audience is, it is apparent that the ability to recognize and respond to the reactions of the audience during a presentation provides a speaker with a crucial persuasive tool.

While there were no significant effects found between either measure of audience adaptation and the result of the round, the lack of finding does not negate the likelihood that competitors who are able to recognize micro-expressions are using the observed responses to adapt to judges. In general, the adaptation levels of all subjects were very high ($M = 4.63$, $SD = 1.08$), indicating that adaptation is common to the surveyed public debaters.

This confirms and expands on Sayer's (1974) research concerning the ability of debaters to perceive nonverbal stimuli. As opposed to Sayer's method which asked speakers to generically observe a judge's nonverbal reaction and predict the result of the round, this study solidifies the finding by testing competitors' abilities to read the most reliable nonverbal indicators.

Concerning the ability to win, the ability to recognize the contempt micro-expression as well as superior abilities in recognizing the happiness and anger micro-expressions were observed. This likely indicates that successful competitors are able to recognize the judge's dislike, evidenced by contempt and anger, and appreciation, evidenced by happiness, of specific arguments.

Unlike competitors who are blind to these expressions, competitors are likely able to use these skills to shape their own arguments, emphasizing the points to which the judge responded with the happiness micro-expression and dropping or rewording points that receive contempt or anger micro-expressions. Competitors might also benefit by attacking the points of their opponent to which the judge responded with either angry or contemptuous responses.

With regard to the effect of micro-expression on speaker points, a positive correlation exists between the ability to recognize micro-expressions, both generally and specifically, with higher speaker point ratings. It is apparent that competitors who are rated highly in speaker points possess the ability to recognize a wide variety of micro-expressions including fear, happiness, sadness, and contempt. Intriguingly, a negative correlation was demonstrated between the ability to recognize the disgust micro-expression and speaker point ratings. While these findings are significant, it is unlikely that sadness and fear would appear on a judge's face during a debate round. Future research is needed to examine which expressions are likely to be made by debate judges during rounds. Finally, it should be noted that competitors in general, were better able to recognize micro-expressions than the general population. Facing similar tests, competitors, on average, were able to correctly identify 86 percent of micro-expressions, compared to 65 percent during the original JACBART study (Matsumoto et al. 2000).

CONCLUSION

In summation, several factors were demonstrated to affect the result and speaker point rating of debate rounds. Micro-expression recognition abilities (general, specific, and specific in comparison to the other competitor) were shown to affect the result of the round. Contempt, anger, and happiness were demonstrated to have specific relevance to the result. Speakers with the ability to recognize micro-expressions, both generally and specifically, were rated higher with regards to speaker points. A negative correlation was shown between speaker point ratings and the ability to recognize the disgust micro-expression.

Chapter 10: Audience Analysis • **115**

Overall, the findings suggest that the ability to recognize momentary micro-expressions can function as a powerful persuasive tool in the hands of a speaker.

Limitations

The results, however, are by no means conclusive. This study suffered from several limitations that have the possibility to bias the results. The amount of cases varies depending on the independent variable analyzed. A total of 1,719 rounds were coded in from the data on cumulative sheets, yielding a total of 3,438 total cases for analysis. Unfortunately, the only usable data from those sheets were competitor identifiers, sex, win/loss result, speaker point, and opponent identifier. Ideally, each of those cases would have been available for analysis. Unfortunately, the small fraction of surveys returned made that impossible. Only one university that regularly fielded more than 10 competitors sent in completed surveys. Additionally, of the universities that did respond, the sample suffered from subject mortality as individuals who had competed during the timeframe were unavailable due to graduation, lack of time, and lack of interest in continued membership on their respective teams. While the surveys returned generated a large number of rounds and cases, less than 10 percent of the rounds were against other individuals who responded to the survey. Therefore, sex and position of advocacy provided the most cases, followed by micro-expressions and audience adaptation, and finally difference scores. The difference in the number of cases may affect the validity of the results.

Secondly, there was no attempt to assess the judges themselves. While each case is a judge's observation of a particular individual in a particular round, the only available information on judges came from their ballots which were conglomerated into the cumulative sheets. No attempt was made to measure the frequency or type of micro-expressions made by a judge during a particular round. As micro-expressions are involuntary, it would be useless to survey judges to ask which expressions were made during a round. Additionally, it would be entirely unfeasible from a time and cost standpoint to videotape the judge during each of the 1,719 rounds, comprising almost 900 hours of video, and then have each micro-expression FACS coded.

While there is a definite correlation between the ability to recognize momentary micro-expressions and both winning debate rounds and achieving higher speaker points, there is a lack of evidence that the ability is the cause for the other. Competitors received no specific training in how to recognize micro-expressions or respond to them, nor were they surveyed as to whether or not they responded to emotional expressions during the round. Therefore, there is no assurance that competitors who are able to recognize micro-expressions were using them to achieve wins and higher speaker points. Finally, this study was conducted over a single semester. By limiting the selected tournaments to a timeframe of a few months, it is possible that an inaccurate picture of the effects of the various variables studied could have been generated.

Directions for Future Research

Future research should serve to both expand on this study and provide solutions for its limitations. As a correlation between micro-expressions and the results and speaker points in debate rounds has been established, future studies should examine the possibility of causation. For instance, two groups of competitors of roughly equal skill could be selected, teaching the experimental group to recognize and respond to micro-expressions while depriving the control group of this education. A longitudinal study would then examine the overall effect of micro-expression recognition on performance in debate rounds.

Additionally, the judges themselves should be examined. While it would likely remain time- and cost-prohibitive to videotape and code judges' reactions during all rounds, a pilot study examining several randomly selected rounds could illuminate which expressions are utilized by judges as well as frequencies of utilization. In doing so, research could be narrowed to training competitors to recognize and respond to expressions used most by judges.

REFERENCES

Alexander, B. 2010. *Tournament Results.* Retrieved from IPDA Debate Resource Page: http://sites.google.com/site/ipdadebate/Home/tournament-results

Alexander, B., Ganakos, J., and T. Gibson. 2009. "Participation and Success Rates for Women and Minorities in IPDA Debate." *Journal of the International Public Debate Association* 3 (1): 36–45.

Applegate, J. L. 1982. "The Impact of Construct System Development on Communication and Impression Formation in Persuasive Contexts." *Communication Monographs* 49: 277–299.

Applegate, J. L. 1990. "Constructs and Communication: A Pragmatic Integration." In G. Neimeyer and R. Neimeyer (Eds.), *Advances in Personal Construct Psychology* (Vol. 1, pp. 203–230). London, England: JAI Press.

Bond, C. F., and B. M. DePaulo. 2006. "Accuracy of Deception Judgements." *Personality and Social Psychology Review* 10: 214–234.

Burleson, B. R. 1989. "The Constructivist Approach to Person-Centered Communication: Analysis of a Research Exemplar." In B. Dervin, L. Grossberg, B. J. O'Keefe, and E. Wartella (Eds.), *Rethinking Communication Volume 2: Paradigm Exemplars* (pp. 29–46). Newbury Park, CA: Sage.

Bruner, J. S., and R. Tagiuri. 1954. "The Perception of People." In G. Lindzey (Ed.) *Handbook of Social Psychology* (Vol. 2, pp. 634–654). Reading, MA: Addison-Wesley.

Bruschke, J., and A. Johnson. 1994. "An Analysis of Differences in Success Rates of Male and Female Debaters." *Argumentation and Advocacy* 30: 162–174.

Byron, K., Terranova, S., and S. Nowicki. 2007. "Nonverbal Emotion Recognition and Salespersons: Linking Ability to Perceived and Actual Success." *Journal of Applied Social Psychology* 37: 2600–2619.

Carton, J. S., Kessler, E. A., and C. L. Pape. 1999. "Nonverbal Decoding Skills and Relationship Well-Being in Adults." *Journal of Nonverbal Behavior* 23: 91–100.

Chakrabarty, S., Brown, G., Widing II, R. E., and R. D. Taylor. 2004. "Analysis and Recommendations for the Alternative Measures of Adaptive Selling." *Journal of Personal Selling and Sales Management* 24: 125–133.

Cirlin, A. 2007. "Academic Debate v. Advocacy in the Real World: A Comparative Analysis." *Journal of the International Public Debate Association* 1 (1): 3–18.

Cunningham, M. R. 1977. "Personality and the Structure of the Nonverbal Communication of Emotion." *Journal of Personality,* 45: 564–584.

Darwin, C. 1872. *The Expression of Emotions in Man and Animals.* New York, NY: Philosophical Library.

Delia, J. G., Kline, S. L., and B. R. Burleson. 1979. "The Development of Persuasive Communication Strategies in Kindergartners through Twelfth-Graders." *Communication Monographs* 46: 241–256.

Duchenne, G. B. 1862. *The Mechanism of Human Facial Expression.* New York, NY: Cambridge University Press.

Dudash, E. 1998. "At the Speed of Sound: Rate of Delivery as a Dividing Factor in Debate." Paper presented at the Central States Communication Association: Chicago, IL.

Eibl-Eibesfeldt, I. 1973. "The Expressive Behavior of the Deaf-and-Blind Born." In M. von Cranach and I. Vine (Eds.) *Social communication and movement.* San Diego, CA: Academic Press, 163–194.

Eldridge, D. 2008. "IPDA: Academic Debate's Minority Group." *Journal of the International Public Debate Association,* 7–10.

Ekman, P. 2001. *Telling Lies: Clues to Deceit in the Marketplace, Politics, and Marriage.* New York, NY: W.W. Norton & Company, Inc.

Ekman, P., and W. V. Friesen. 1969. "Nonverbal Leakage and Clues to Deception." *Psychiatry* 32: 88–105.

Ekman, P., and W. V. Friesen. 1974. "Detecting Deception from the Body or Face." *Journal of Personality and Social Psychology* 29: 288–298.

Ekman, P., and W. V. Friesen. 1975. *Unmasking the Face.* Englewood Cliffs, NJ: Prentice-Hall, Inc.

Ekman, P., and W. V. Friesen. 1978. *Facial Action Coding System.* Palo Alto, CA: Consulting Psychologists Press.

Ekman, P., Friesen, W. V., and M. O'Sullivan. 1988. "Smiles when Lying." *Journal of Personality and Social Psychology* 54: 414–420.

Ekman, P., Levenson, R. W., and W. V. Friesen. 1983. "Autonomic Nervous System Activity Distinguishes among Emotions." *Science* 221: 1208–1210.

Ekman, P., and M. O'Sullivan. 1991. "Who Can Catch a Liar?" *American Psychologist* 46: 913–920.

Ekman, P., Sorenson, E. R., and W. V. Friesen. 1969. "Pan-Cultural Elements in Facial Displays of Emotions." *Science* 164: 86–88.

Evans, F. B. 1963. "Selling as a Dyadic Relationship—A New Approach." *The American Behavioral Scientist* 6: 76–79.

Fine, L. M. 2007. "Selling and Sales Management." *Business Horizons* 50: 185–191.

Frank, M. G., and P. Ekman. 1997. "The Ability to Detect Deceit Generalizes across Different Types of High-Stake Lies." *Journal of Personality and Social Psychology* 72: 1429–1439.

Frank, M. G. and J. Stennett. 2001. "The Forced Choice Paradigm and the Perception of Facial Expressions of Emotion." *Journal of Personality and Social Psychology* 80: 75–85.

Freeley, A. J., and D. L. Steinberg. 2005. *Argumentation and Debate: Critical Thinking for Reasoned Decision Making* (11th ed.). Belmont, CA: Thomson.

Gass, R. H., and J. S. Seiter. 2007. *Persuasion, Social Influence, and Compliance Gaining* (3rd ed.) Boston, MA: Allyn & Bacon.

Golden, J., Berquist, G., and W. Coleman. 1989. *The Rhetoric of Western Thought.* Dubuque, IL: Kendall-Hunt.

Horn, G. 1994. *Why Are Programs Leaving CEDA?* Paper presented at the meeting of the Speech Communication Association. New Orleans, LA.

Halberstadt, A. G., and J. A. Hall. 1980. "Who's Getting the Message? Children's Nonverbal Skill and their Evaluation by Teachers." *Developmental Psychology* 16: 564–573.

Halberstadt, A. G., Denham, S. A., and J. C. Dunsmore. 2001. "Affective Social Competence." *Social Development* 10: 79–119.

Haslings, J. 1976. *The Audience, the Message, the Speaker* (2nd ed.). New York, NY: McGraw-Hill.

Izard, C. E. 1971. *The Face of Emotion.* New York, NY: Appleton-Century Crofts.

International Public Debate Association. 2009. *IPDA Constitution.* Retrieved from International Public Debate Association Web site: http://uamont.edu/IPDA/const.html

Jarzabek, M. G. 1996. "The Double Standard in CEDA: A Feminist Perspective on Gender Stereotyping in Intercollegiate Debate." Presented at the Annual Meeting of the Southern States Communication Association. Memphis, Tennessee.

Kennedy, G. 1980. *Classical Rhetoric and its Christian and Secular Tradition from Ancient to Modern Times*. Durham, NC: University of North Carolina Press.

Kenny, D. A., Kashy, D. A., and W. L. Cook. (2006). *Dyadic Data Analysis*. New York: The Guilford Press.

Landis, C. 1924. "Studies of Emotional Reactions: II. General Behavior and Facial Expression." *Journal of Comparative Psychology* 4: 447–509.

Marlin, R. 2002. *Propaganda and the Ethics of Persuasion*. Peterborough, Canada: Broadview Press.

Marone, M., and S. Lunsford. 2005. *Strategies That Win Sales: Best Practices of the World's Leading Organizations*. Chicago, IL: Dearborn.

Matsumoto, D., and P. Ekman. 1988. *Japanese and Caucasian Facial Expressions of Emotion (JACFEE)* [Slides]. San Francisco, CA: Intercultural and Emotion Research Laboratory, Department of Psychology, San Francisco State University.

Matsumoto, D., LeRoux, J., Wilson-Cohn, C., Raroque, J., Kooken, K., Ekman, P., et al. 2000. "A New Test to Measure Emotion Recognition Ability: Matsumoto and Ekman's Japanese and Caucasian Brief Affect Recognition Test (JACBART)." *Journal of Nonverbal Behavior* 24: 179–209.

Matthews, G., Zeidner, M., and R. D. Roberts. 2002. *Emotional Intelligence: Science and Myth*. Cambridge, MA: MIT Press.

Mazure, M. A. 2001. "Women in Parliamentary Debate: An Examination of Women's Performance at the National Parliamentary Debate Association's National Tournament." *The Journal of the National Parliamentary Debate Association* 8: 31–36.

McClure, E. 2000. "A Meta-Analytic Review of Sex Differences in Facial Expression Processing and their Development in Infants, Children, and Adolescents." *Psychological Bulletin* 126: 424–453.

Morgan, N. 2003. *Working a Room: How to Move People to Action through Audience-Centered Speaking*. Boston, MA: Harvard Business School Press.

Meredith, M. J. (2007). Building and expanding the influence of business communication: Identifying gaps and seizing need opportunities for differentiation in the discipline. Paper presented at the annual conference of the Association for Business Communication, Washington, D.C.

Mufson, L., and S. Nowicki, Jr. 1991. "Factors Affecting the Accuracy of Facial Affect Recognition." *The Journal of Social Psychology* 131: 815–822.

Nowicki, S. Jr., and M. P. Duke. 1994. "Individual Differences in the Nonverbal Communication of Affect: The Diagnostic Analysis of Nonverbal Accuracy Scale." *Journal of Nonverbal Behavior* 18: 9–35.

Olsen, J.A., and D. A. Kenny. 2006. "Structural Equation Modeling with Interchangeable Dyads." *Psychological Methods* 11: 127–141.

Park, J., and B. Holloway. 2004. "Adaptive Selling Behavior Revisited: An Examination in Learning Orientation, Sales Performance, and Job Satisfaction." *Journal of Personal Selling and Sales Management* 23 (3): 237–249.

Richey, P. 2007. "IPDA Longevity: 10th Year Anniversary, an Analysis of Former Champions." *Journal of the International Public Debate Association* 1 (1): 26–35.

Robinson Jr., L., Marshall, G. W., Moncrief, W. C., and Lassk, F. 2002. "Toward a Shortened Measure of Adaptive Selling." *Journal of Personal Selling and Sales Management* 22: 111–119.

Rosenthal, R., Hall, J. A., DiMatteo, M. R., Rogers, P. L., and D. Archer. 1979. *Sensitivity to Nonverbal Cues: The PONS Test*. Baltimore, MD: Johns Hopkins University Press.

Rozell, E. J., Pettijohn, C. E., and R. S. Parker. 2004. "Customer-Oriented Selling: Exploring the Roles of Emotional Intelligence and Organizational Commitment." *Psychology and Marketing* 21: 405–424.

Saarni, C. 2001. "Cognition, Context, and Goals: Significant Components in Social-Emotional Effectiveness." *Social Development* 10: 125–129.

Sayer, J. 1974. "Debaters' Perception of Nonverbal Stimuli." *Western Speech* 38: 2–6.

Sherman, M. 1927. "The Differentiation of Emotional Responses in Infants. ii. the Ability of Observers to Judge the Emotional Characteristics of the Crying of Infants, and of the Voice of an Adult." *Journal of Comparative Psychology* 7: 335–351. doi: 10.1037/h0070458

Soldow, G. F., and G. P. Thomas. 1984. "Relational Communication: Form Versus Content in the sales Interaction. *Journal of Marketing* 48: 84–93.

Spiro, R. L., and B. A. Weitz 1990. "Adaptive Selling: Conceptualization, Measurement, and Nomological Validity." *Journal of Marketing Research* 27: 61–69.

Scherer, K. R. 1986. "Vocal Affect Expression: A Review and a Model for the Future." *Psychological Bulletin* 99: 143–165.

Tomkins, S., and R. McCarter. 1964. "What and Where are the Primary Effects? Some Evidence for a Theory." *Perceptual and Motor Skills* 18: 119–158.

Toner, H. L. and G. R. Gates. 1985. "Emotional Traits and Recognition of Facial Expression of Emotion." *Journal of Nonverbal Behavior* 9: 48–66.

Vogt, D. S., and C. R. Colvin, C. R. 2003. "Interpersonal Orientation and the Accuracy of Personality Judgements." *Journal of Personality* 71: 267–295.

Vrij, A., Edward, K., and R. Bull. 2001. "Stereotypical Verbal and Nonverbal Responses while Deceiving Others." *Personality and Social Psychology Bulletin* 27: 899–909.

Waldron, V. R., and J. L. Applegate. 1994. "Interpersonal Construct Differentiation and Conversational Planning." *Human Communication Research* 21: 3–-35.

Weitz, B. A., Sujan, H., and M. Sujan. 1986. "Knowledge, Motivation, and Adaptive Behavior: A Framework for Improving Selling Effectiveness." *Journal of Marketing* 50: 174–191.

Williams, K. C., and R. L. Spiro. 1985. "Communication Style in the Salesperson-Customer Dyad." *Journal of Marketing Research* 22: 434–-442.

Woods, E. 1996. "Associations of Nonverbal Decoding Ability with Indices of Person-Centered Communication Ability." *Communication Reports* 9: 12–22.

Woodworth, R. S. 1938. *Experimental Psychology*. New York, NY: Henry Holt.

Chapter 11

The Affirmative Case

Robert Alexander
Bossier Parish Community College

Academic debate has a language of its own. Though effort has been made to decrease the amount of jargon included in the following discussion, many "debate-world" terms (i.e., topicality, solvency, etc.) creep into the following pages on occasion. The purpose of including these terms is two-fold: to help the reader to learn the meanings of these terms as they relate to the affirmative case (in case you hear them referenced by others) and to assist in the reader's ability to cross-reference these concepts in other debate texts. If you are new to the world of debate and find these terms confusing, there is a key terms section at the end of this chapter to assist in your understanding. If you have experienced other formats of debate, try to use these contextual discussions to develop your methods of reference without using such terms. Regardless of your level of experience, one key communication concept should be taken to heart: words only have meaning as far as the listener grants them meaning. To that extent, since public debate is designed to be persuasive to the. . .well, public. . .jargon should be avoided as much as possible during all of your speeches (and explained when it is unavoidable). In determining what is "jargon," Justice Antonin Scalia and Bryan Garner explain "The key is to avoid words that would cause people to look at you funny if you used them at a party" (2008, 113).

Being "affirmative" simply means that the speaker has been designated to support the topic chosen for the round. During a typical debate tournament, you will be assigned the affirmative position for half of the debates you compete in (for example, if there are six rounds of debate competition, you will affirm a resolution three times and negate a resolution three times). As the affirmative you have a tremendous advantage: you get to set the tone and the primary focus of the debate. This is an opportunity that should not be squandered—use the information on the following pages to help you to become an effective advocate. The advocacy skills that you can refine through academic debate can be of use far beyond the context of competitive debates.

Contributed by Robert E. "Bob" Alexander. Copyright © Kendall Hunt Publishing Company

BURDENS OF PROOF

Initially, it is important to distinguish between a burden of proof and the burden of proof. For each claim advanced by either the affirmative or the negative during the course of the debate, the advocate is said to have a burden of proof to demonstrate that claim to be valid. However, when discussing the burden of proof, this uniquely applies to the affirmative. For this concept, debate essentially mirrors the criminal court system (where a defendant is said to be "innocent until proven guilty"), and the resolution is assumed to be false until proven true (a concept known as presumption; for example: in policy debates the status quo is "presumed" to be the best approach, unless a plan can be demonstrated to be more desirable). To use a baseball metaphor, the tie goes to the runner (or negative speaker).

When seeking to meet one's burdens, it is important to not overstate one's case. "Once you have worked long and hard on your case. . .you'll probably be utterly convinced that your side is right. That is as it should be. But the judges haven't worked on the case. . .and are likely to think it much more of a horse race than you do. . .You'll harm your credibility—you'll be written off as a blowhard—if you characterize the case as a lead-pipe cinch with nothing to be said for the other side. Even if you think that to be true, and even if you're right, keep it to yourself" (Scalia and Garner 2008, 13). Furthermore, the avoidance of overstatement is important in one's quest for accuracy when supporting their ideas. "Scrupulous accuracy consists not merely in never making a statement that you know to be incorrect (that is mere honesty), but also in never making a statement you are not *certain* is correct. So err, if you must, on the side of understatement, and flee hyperbole. Since absolute negatives are hard to prove, and hence hard to be sure of, you should rarely permit yourself an unqualified 'never.'. . .Inaccuracies can result either from deliberate misstatement or carelessness. Either way, the advocate suffers a grave loss of credibility from which it's difficult to recover" (Scalia and Garner 2008, 13–14).

Scalia and Garner begin their text on persuading judges within the court system by noting that "Judges can be persuaded only when three conditions are met: (1) They must have a clear idea of what you're asking the court to do. (2) They must be assured that it's within the court's power to do it. (3) After hearing the reasons for doing what you are asking, and the reasons for doing other things or doing nothing at all, they must conclude that what you're asking is best. . ." (xxi). This advice rings true as well for the burdens that an affirmative must also meet; the application of the first and third points to academic debate are clear, and point number two applies at the level of a jurisdictional analysis of topicality (we must demonstrate that our case falls within the scope of the resolution or it is not within the debate judge's authority to vote for us). Meeting these three conditions is the key to effective affirmative cases.

The author would argue that meeting the burden of proof extends beyond simply providing all of the information that can neatly fit into a checklist. In the opinion of the author, academic debates too often come down to fact versus fact, without an overall application of all elements of persuasion. In the lead editorial of the 2008 issue of the IPDA journal, Web Drake lamented a lack of rhetorical appeal that is present in most academic debates, and urged the IPDA community to integrate the principles of Aristotle—appealing not only to logic, but establishing credibility and emotional appeals as well. This lamentation is not new to the world of academic debate. Nearly a century ago, Freeburg voiced concern that "fifteen or twenty years ago debating contests between colleges were not calculated to enlist the admiration of the professor of Christian ethics" (1915, 578). Freeburg continued to voice an appeal similar to Drake's that debate contests should be seen as a means (focusing on developing the power of the rhetor) and not an end (focusing strictly on what it takes to win a ballot). To that extent, if we are truly to meet our "burdens" in round, we must hold ourselves higher than a standard of strictly presenting the facts—but ensuring that our sources are credible, our contentions are logical, and that we also appeal to appropriate levels of emotion. This concept has been heralded outside of academic debate—for example, in addressing courtroom strategy, McBaine chose to use the terms "Burden of Proof" and "Burden of Persuasion" interchangeably—and thus should be incorporated into our strategy if we are to truly develop as rhetors (1944).

CHOOSING A TOPIC

Great affirmative debaters know that winning affirmative cases begin before preparation time; in fact, they begin before the topic is chosen. In IPDA debate, you are given two topic strikes (or vetoes) which should be strategically employed. Many debaters want to immediately strike the topic that they may know little about or that concerns a subject they do not wish to debate; however, this is not the most strategic usage of your veto. The author's suggestion is that you should use your first strike for bias, and your second strike for these preference issues. After all, the negative may dislike the same subject matter as you—and if they choose to strike the topic you would have struck for "preference," then you have essentially earned yourself an additional strike. Even if the result is that with your final strike you are left with two subject areas that you may not be familiar with, it is far better to be debating a resolution that is not worded in a manner that is biased against your position, than it is to be debating a biased resolution about a topic that you may enjoy (note: a lack of "familiarity" here does not imply that you should choose a topic when you do not have any idea what it may be referencing to, as that topic may indeed be extremely biased, but your lack of understanding may result in an inability to spot that bias until you start researching it).

What is a "biased resolution?" Often the resolutional wording of value resolutions places the affirmative in a position where only 1 of 3 possible advocacies can result in an affirmative victory. For example, were we to debate the topic "Resolved: that sunny days are better than rainy days," the affirmative would win the round if the judge agreed that sunny days are better. However, the negative would win the round if s/he could convince the judge that a) rainy days are preferable, or b) neither is preferred, but there are desirable circumstances for each. Ultimately, any time a negative has a topic that has some derivative of "X is better than Y" wording, the negative has twice as many ways to win, and thereby the resolution is biased against the affirmative. Conversely, the more vague a topic is in its wording, the more that topic is said to be biased for the affirmative. Because of the affirmative's right to define, the more ambiguous wording a resolution has, the greater the opportunity the affirmative has to shape the topic. Furthermore, the affirmative has an advantage of using their entire preparation time focused on debating the issues they plan to introduce, whereas the negative must spend time attempting to anticipate what the affirmative will argue. Thereby, vague or metaphorical resolutions are said to be biased for the affirmative.

Additionally, debaters should consider bias based upon judge analysis. Though judges should ideally render a disinterested decision, in reality, personal views often shape the decision, or, at a minimum, serve as a lens for the way in which judges view information introduced in the round. Included within this judge analysis should be a consideration of your role in the debate. Scalia and Garner offer a list of objectives for oral argument before courts that also apply to academic debate. Among a speaker's burdens (in descending order of importance) are "to demonstrate. . .by the substance and manner of your presentation, that you are trustworthy, open and forthright; to demonstrate. . .by the substance and manner of your presentation, that you have thought long and hard about this case and are familiar with all its details; to demonstrate. . .mostly by the manner of your presentation, that you are likable and not mean-spirited" (141). Consider what topics will best allow for straightforward argumentation and honest dialogue on the subject, as these are keys to effective persuasion. The more creative you are with your interpretation, you may momentarily stump your opponent, but you will also generate a level of sympathy for your opponent with the judge. Consider the wording of the resolution, the burdens that you will have and how you will relate these to the judge as you determine which topic(s) will be least desirable for you to argue.

Which do I strike first? Potential for judge bias should serve as a layer of consideration for all topics. However, because the level of certainty of bias, strength of bias, and impact that the bias will have on the round all are variables that must be considered, the weight that you assign the potential bias will vary widely in the topic strike procedure. With all things equal from a judge analysis perspective of bias, if as the affirmative you are given a situation where there is but one of the "X is better than Y" style of resolutions available, for the aforementioned reasons, this should be the first topic struck. However, if you have two or more of these resolutions in your slate, you should strike the resolution with the most specific wording first (remember—the more vague the topic, the greater the opportunity you will have to shape the debate as the affirmative). Finally, if you have multiple "X is better than Y" style resolutions, and each have the same level of specificity, now subject matter comes into play. However, again you should be looking first for potential bias in subject matter, not for your preference of subject matter. For example, while we might be quite fond of jelly doughnuts, most of us could concur that with the topic "Resolved: that national security is more important than jelly doughnuts" the affirmative would have a much easier burden than with the topic "Resolved: that national security is more important than individual liberty." All things equal, if you have multiple "X is better than Y" resolutions, each of the same level of specificity, and there is no bias of subject matter, then preference comes into play on the first strike—simply strike the topic that you would least prefer to debate.

USAGE OF PREPARATION TIME

The limited preparation time of public debate helps to develop one's ability to think quickly, to process information efficiently, and to construct argument on the fly. To do this, a debater must make efficient use of their preparation time. Often inexperienced debaters find themselves spending too much time on a single element of the preparation and, within the zero-sum scenario of limited preparation, this time comes at the expense of the other elements of preparation. In discussing trial preparation, Scalia and Garner note that if the only deadline you set for yourself is the one externally provided, you will inevitably fail to devote enough time to one or more of the elements involved in the preparation process (2008, 66–67). To that extent, develop a rationing of time that works best for you during preparation with approximate windows of time for how long you will spend on researching, defining, thinking of cross-examination questions, pre-flowing the case, etc. An important element to include within this time structure is thinking through the case before you begin actually constructing it. Simply put, begin to develop your central idea and "think not just about your affirmative case but also about the case you can expect from your adversary and the responses you have available. Don't produce a first draft too soon. That tends to freeze the deliberative process, closing off alternative approaches that ought to have been explored. Jot down new ideas as they occur to you, but don't begin writing or even outlining. . .until you have fully exhausted the deliberative process" (Scalia and Garner 2008, 69–70).

Start preparing the First Affirmative by thinking of the last Affirmative Rebuttal. Strong affirmative advocacy considers not just "why" a proposition should be adopted, but also addresses "why not." Effectively answering potential negative arguments in the first speech is essential for five reasons: 1) if the judge thinks of these objections, it appears that you've overlooked obvious problems; 2) responding only after obvious counterarguments have been made makes you look reluctant to address the issues; 3) by going on the offensive you can put the negative debater into a defensive role; 4) you get the chance to frame the issues; and 5) your willingness to initiate discussion of potential weaknesses of your advocacy will enhance the perception of your trustworthiness (Scalia and Garner 2008, 16).

In most trial systems, the prosecution has the opportunity to speak both first and last, which "is consistent with the general theory that the party bearing the burden of proof is entitled to the last opportunity to talk to the jury and, thus, get a last chance to convince the panel" (Mitchell 2000). The time structure of IPDA debate follows this same format and, as a consequence, the affirmative has a couple of advantages that should be capitalized upon: the primacy effect and the recency effect. Generally speaking, there are two ways in which individuals judge information—either information is judged by forming a hypothesis based on what is first heard about an issue and then adjusting that hypothesis based on future data (the primacy effect), or complex information is judged by standards established by what is last heard on an issue (the recency effect) (Dennis and Ahn 2001; Lopez, Shanks, Almaraz and Fernandez 1998). Because of the speech structure in public debates, an effective affirmative speaker attempts to capitalize on both primacy and recency if he or she begins by thinking about their rebuttal speech (and offer the foundation in their first speech as well as driving the point home in their final rebuttal). However, in exchange for these benefits the negative gets longer speaking time during his or her two speeches. In timed competitive debates, many rounds are decided by effective time allocation. Because both the second and final affirmative speeches are shorter in duration than the negative speeches they follow, an effective affirmative must be able to efficiently address both the issues raised by the negative as well as the affirmative's central arguments. As a result, effective affirmatives must accomplish as much preemption (or anticipating negative arguments and answering those arguments before they are made) during their first constructive speech as possible, otherwise they may be placed into a situation where they are unable to argue both the negative's positions as well as their own in future speeches. "No general engages the enemy without a battle plan based in large part on what the enemy is expected to do. Your case must take into account the

126 • *IPDA Textbook*

points the other side is likely to make. You must have a clear notion of which ones can be swallowed (accepted but shown to be irrelevant) and which must be vigorously countered on the merits. . .you must decide which of your adversary's points are so significant that they must be addressed in your opening presentation and which ones can be left to your. . .rebuttal" (Scalia and Garner 2008, 10).

Effective preemption begins during the preparation time. An affirmative should consider not only the resolution, but the null-resolution as well (or what would essentially be the negative's burden). For example, if the resolution states "that the Securities and Exchange Commission should be scrapped," then the null-resolution would be "that the Securities and Exchange Commission should *not* be scrapped." Consider the opposing arguments and then find ways of preempting them during your first speech. This is a practice which is not limited to effectiveness for intercollegiate debate rounds, but serves as an effective tool for persuasion in general. As a public, we are subjected to preemption in persuasive messages all the time. For example, consider the typical advertisement for an automobile. One of the primary objections raised by consumers are variations of "this car is too expensive." However, the typical car automobile advertisement seeks to preempt this argument by directly addressing the issue of up-front expense (by offering "factory incentives," "special financing packages," "lease options," etc.) or by arguing that the vehicle's expense is justified as an investment (by explaining "fuel efficiency," "higher resale value," "increased safety," etc.). Generalizing the automobile advertisement example to intercollegiate debate, the affirmative has capitalized upon the primacy effect by getting their arguments articulated before the objection has been raised. Furthermore, this provides the affirmative with the option during future speeches of referring back to their arguments made during the first constructive speech (thereby saving the time it would take to initially develop the argument during latter speeches, and staying ahead in the time allocation warfare). Additionally, one must consider the sequencing of preemptive arguments during the affirmative constructive speech. Scalia and Garner suggest that effective preemption best occurs in the middle of your presentation, as opposed to at the beginning, which could create a perception of defensiveness at the outset, or at the end, which can leave the audience thinking about the counterarguments rather than your advocacy (15–16).

Furthermore, because there are not any breaks between speeches, the only available time that you will have to focus exclusively on your rebuttal speech will be during preparation time before the debate begins. Of course you will not always anticipate everything that will occur during a debate, but an effective affirmative begins by thinking of an "ideal circumstances rebuttal" and then adapts that rebuttal as the debate progresses. Ultimately, this gives you the opportunity to set up the arguments of your final speech during the earlier speeches, and will lead to much better speeches during the brief, but very crucial, final rebuttal.

I HAVE SO MUCH TO SAY

Before discussing the actual case structure for an affirmative, it is important to take another issue into consideration: rate of delivery. Students who have backgrounds in other formats of competitive debate may be conditioned to speak as quickly as possible and to include as much information as one can in their speeches. However, remember that the judges for public debates are typically "real world" members of the public—they come from all backgrounds and levels of experience. Therefore, this approach generally will not be effective in communicating your ideas to the judge. "Most people can process information only at a moderate rate. When ideas—even the best ideas—come tumbling forth too fast, they're apt to induce either headache or inattention" (Scalia and Garner 2008, 142). Public debaters should strive to speak comprehensibly, and to adapt their speaking style to the judge (for example, if the judge is not taking an exhaustive "flow" of the round, then memory devices such as restatement and analogies are of extreme importance—they cannot agree with you if they cannot understand you). Accordingly, effective affirmative speakers must craft their cases in a manner that allows them to sufficiently discuss their advocacy, but also to be able to adapt to the feedback they are receiving from their judge(s).

Included within this consideration is the quantity of main points that you use to support your case. Often we may be able to develop numerous reasons that our advocacy is supported, but including too many will ultimately harm your effectiveness. As McElhaney advises "your case is judged by its weakest points. Better to have two or three good ones than a bushel of mediocrity" (2008). Further, even if you perceive the quality of your arguments to be good, Scalia and Garner advise that "scattershot argument is ineffective. It gives the impression of weakness and desperation. . ." (2008, 22). Following McElhaney, Scalia and Garner's advice, use preparation time to limit your main points to those that are the strongest. Limiting the number of main points also assists in a secondary goal of time allocation. Simply put, if you have fewer main ideas in your first speech, you're able to discuss each of these in greater depth in the allotted time; and, furthermore, your burdens in subsequent speeches will include fewer points to defend as you are answering negative responses and "off-case" arguments. Additionally, consider the sequencing of your arguments and, when logic permits, place your strongest argument first (though sometimes logic necessitates the discussion of prerequisite points) so that you make an effective first impression (Scalia and Garner 2008, 14).

CASE INTRODUCTIONS

The introduction to the resolution is the affirmative's opportunity to set the tone for the round, to establish relevance of the topic and/or to establish meaning. Introductory statements should not be too drawn out (as to come at the expense of developing supports for the plan/case statement), but should effectively give the judge a reason to care about the debate that will soon develop. Consider the following example of the first 30 seconds of an affirmative constructive speech for the topic "Resolved: The Time is Now."

First, I would like to thank the judge for considering my advocacy during this round, my opponent who I am sure will be well-spoken, and the audience for choosing to observe this debate.

In today's modern geopolitical environment, contexts and variables change quickly, and one must adapt to those changes with an eye always fixed on what one can do in the present and the future implications of such action. That is why I stand firmly "Resolved: The Time is Now." Clearly, the indication of this topic is that while we must always be aware of our past (so as to avoid the cliché of "those not knowing history being doomed to repeat it"), we must keep a constant eye on the future.

To that extent, my advocacy will be embodied in one broad argument: that while the benefit of hindsight bias may make it easy to point out things that could have gone better with the conflict in Iraq, we must instead focus on the present if we are to progress.

Too often debaters move directly from "thank you's" to providing definitions that establish a bureaucratic feel to the speech. By contrast, inserting a case introduction before the definitions allows the debater to establish an issue's focused tone. In the above example, the second paragraph serves as an introduction to the round, setting a tone of focusing on the future, and the third paragraph provides a transition to the definitions that would follow in a typical affirmative case. As a side note, the norm of providing "thank you's" at the start and finish of the round can be an effective manner of expressing sincere appreciation, but these "thank you's" should be kept brief both to avoid a patronizing tone (Scalia and Garner 2008, 166, 174) as well as to preserve time for establishing your case. Furthermore, when providing these "thank you's," statements such as "there's probably other things you'd rather be doing," that occasionally are offered in attempt to connect to judges, should be eliminated as at best they serve to marginalize the importance of the event you have chosen to participate in and at their worst can alienate the judge (who may be there because they enjoy the event).

The case introduction is analogous to an opening statement in a courtroom setting (scaled appropriately to fit the compressed time requirements upon affirmative constructive speeches). In discussing the key to effective opening statements, McElhaney noted that "The job of the lawyer in the opening is not to tell the whole story. It's to set out a hook that will make the jury want to hear the details they'll use to fill in the blanks during the rest of the trial." Similarly, effective case introductions provide a thematic overview, but the supports for this theme lie within the body of the affirmative constructive.

When effectively crafted, the thematic overview can also serve to bolster your credibility and the emotional appeal of your case. Bell and Loftus noted that vividness (imagery-provoking language) positively correlates with audience perceptions of credibility of a speaker as well as the overall effectiveness of an appeal due to adding an emotional component (1975). To that extent, this is an excellent opportunity to begin the overall rhetorical message that was discussed in the concluding paragraph of the "burden of proof" segment of this chapter.

An additional consideration for the case introduction is the inclusion of the resolution. In the above example for "Resolved: The Time is Now," the resolution is included midway through the second paragraph. One may argue that since the topic is typically written on the board and/or on the judge's ballot, and the debaters involved also know the resolution, this is unnecessary. However, from a rhetorical sense, this establishes your primary advocacy for the round and is an important inclusion. In sum, "Debaters should consider three major principles when constructing the introduction for their affirmative case. First, the introduction should capture the attention of the judge. . .Second, the introduction should be concise. . .Third, the proposition should be stated accurately" (Hill and Leeman 1997, 230–231). Furthermore, the case introduction should be delivered from memory (as opposed to read from the flowsheet), both because this is an important time to connect with your judge(s) as well as to combat the natural levels of apprehension that can occur when beginning a presentation (Scalia and Garner 2008, 167).

THE RIGHT TO DEFINE

Among the limited rules for public debate is a statement that gives the affirmative the right to offer reasonable definitions for the round. These definitions are typically offered during the early segments of the first affirmative constructive speech, and they are extremely important for the round. Again though, it is important to remember the varied backgrounds of judges and thereby to offer truly "reasonable" interpretations. Ultimately what makes a definition effective is acceptance. As opposed to policy formats of debate where extreme creativity in interpretation may be rewarded, with general members of the public you are more likely to get nods of disapproval than accolades. In recent years there has been a trend toward disclosure (letting the negative know the affirmative interpretation during preparation time) that the author believes is a positive one because it typically results in greater clash of arguments. Choosing to disclose does not eliminate the advantage that an affirmative gets from an ambiguous resolution (because the affirmative maintains the ability to choose the specific focus, but they have simply alerted their opposition of that focus while the negative has time to prepare for it) nor does it free the affirmative from the responsibility to defend the resolution (a negative may choose to argue topicality if they feel that the case does not uphold the resolution).

In creating your interpretation, you obviously want to look for the examples that best support the resolution, but you must be careful that your definitions do not limit the debate so severely that there is no room for reasonable opposition. To that extent, affirmatives need to ensure that their interpretation is not a truism (when an idea is advanced that is accepted on face by a majority of people). For example, if an affirmative defending the resolution "Violence is never justified" chose to limit the resolution to "rape," the negative would be put into a position where their direct counter-advocacy would be to adopt the moral low-ground of defending rape—a position that a majority of people would definitively reject on face. To that extent, this interpretation could be said to be truistic and thus not allowing for sufficient debate. When defining, it is important to establish ground for argumentation (room for debate) on both sides of the issue (in order to ensure debatability).

Three reasons why definitions are important: 1) Foundation. When debaters rush to a discussion of merits without a clear definitional foundation, there is a tremendous potential for confusion. The result of this confusion is often that each debater may present his/her case, and the two cases do not directly relate to each other. For example, if the term "we" is not defined in the topic "Resolved: that we should do more to assist the poor," the affirmative may argue the need for more individual actions, while the negative may focus on the responsibilities of governments. Both may have valid points, but the points simply do not clash with each other. Furthermore, this resolution necessitates a definition of the ambiguous term "assist"—are we debating "financial assistance," "medical assistance," or some other derivative?

2) Lens. At other times, the definitions serve to establish the lens through which merit should be determined. For example, is golf a "sport" or a "game?" In debating the relational resolution of fact "Resolved: that golfing requires allot of energy," one may need to establish this lens as a prerequisite for relational claims. Consider the arguments that as a "sport," golf may require less physical energy than football, but as a "game," golf may require more physical energy than chess. Note also within this resolution the need to define the term "energy"—are we debating "physical energy," "mental energy," or some other derivative? Ultimately, the better job the affirmative constructive does of clarifying the debate via definitions, the better quality of debate that will result.

3) Forgone **opportunities become openings for the negative.** If the affirmative fails to capitalize on their opportunity to provide definitions within their first speech, then the door is opened for the negative to offer their own interpretation. This is problematic both from a time allocation standpoint and a primacy effect standpoint. From a time allocation standpoint, an affirmative placed into a scenario of debating negative interpretations of the resolution, as well as the negative positions and their own central arguments during their shorter speeches will have a difficult time effectively covering the issues in a manner persuasive to their judge. Furthermore, recalling the "primacy effect" discussed earlier, one can infer that the interpretation offered first may be the most prominent in the judge's mind and thereby the affirmative has ceded one of their chief advantages by allowing the negative to capitalize on this effect.

Connotative and Denotative Definitions. The denotative meaning of a word is the literal definition associated with the term (an objective definition), whereas the connotative meaning includes the emotional associations that one may have with such a term (a subjective interpretation). When choosing to narrow the scope of the resolution, one may look beyond the literal definition of terms (especially when considering metaphorical resolutions). For example, if given the topic "Resolved: that the rebel flag should be removed from our public institutions," one may denotatively define "rebel flag" as "the flag flown in battle representing the Confederate States of America." However, it is unlikely that the debate would focus on the literal merits of this "flag" but rather the symbolic nature of the controversy (i.e., is it a "reference to heritage" or a "symbol of hate?"). To that extent, this item is said to have a strong connotative meaning beyond just the literal definition. Along these lines, affirmatives should also consider the language choices they make when defining terms, and take into consideration the emotional connections that their judge may have with terms that are introduced during the debate.

Considering Grammatical Context. Many terms are inherently ambiguous, yet their meanings become clearer when evaluated within terms of their grammatical placement. For example, there is a huge difference between saying that "I am dead" versus "I am dead tired." To that extent, when developing definitions do not be satisfied just with defining the individual terms, but first take a look at the overall wording of the resolution to guide you to the proper meaning. Scalia and Garner offer the examples of the concepts of "Noscitur a sociis" and "Ejusdem generis" to illustrate these points. "Noscitur a sociis. 'A word is known by the words with which it is associated.' In the phrase 'staples, rivets, nails, pins, and stakes,' the word 'nails' obviously does not refer to fingernails. Ejusdem generis. 'Of the same kind.' A general residual category following a list of other items refers to items of the same sort. In the phrase 'staples, rivets, nails, pins, stakes, and other items,' the 'other items' don't include balloons, but only other types of fasteners" (45–46).

Criteria for Good Definitions. For virtually any term, a plethora of potential definitions and sources are available. Smith (1995) establishes multiple guidelines to consider when determining which definition(s) are best for your advocacy. The first rule is that definitions should not be too broad. For example, if you defined a circle as "a figure all of whose

Chapter 11: The Affirmative Case • **131**

points are equidistant from a given point" you encounter the problem that the definition "includes not only circles, but arcs and spheres as well" (6). When seeking limitations, you must be wary of the second guideline that definitions also should not be too narrow. For example, if one defined a "thief" as "a person who steals money," the definition would be too narrow because the limiter of the term "money" excludes other acts of thievery (6). Furthermore, some definitions can be both too broad and too narrow simultaneously. For example, if one defined a novel as "a prose narrative about people," the first half of this definition "a prose narrative" could potentially include things such as short stories (making it too broad) whereas the limiter of "about people" artificially eliminates the potential of other subjects (6). An additional guideline to test the effectiveness of definitions is to apply the "all and only" test (asking if the definition applies all possible circumstances and only to the term defined). For example, with the aforementioned circle definition, the statement is true of all circles, but is not limited only to circles; with the aforementioned definition of thief the statement is true only of thieves, but not true of all thieves; and finally, with the aforementioned definition of novel it is neither true of all novels nor is it true only of novels (6). Furthermore, definitions should state the essential characteristic of the term being defined; for example, if "person" was defined as "an animal that can (has the capacity to) build automobiles" one could say that this is true of all persons and only of persons, however this is not the essential defining characteristic of a person (6–7). Next, a definition should avoid circular reference by not using a term to define itself (e.g., "a line is a linear path") (7). Finally, definitions should avoid metaphorical and figurative language (e.g., "a camel is the ship of the desert" or "the lion is the king of the beasts") which can further obscure meaning (7).

CASE STATEMENTS AND PLANS

Typically, after the definitions have been established, the affirmative will state their advocacy for the round. In nonpolicy rounds, these take the form of a case statement. The case statement is essentially a thesis statement for the affirmative—the over-arching theme that they attempt to demonstrate en route to upholding the resolution. The case statement must advance an issue that is debatable. For example, if debating the topic "Resolved: that Americans need to fly the flag," a case statement such as "the American flag is intended to be attached to ropes and raised on a flag pole," may be rejected as being a truism. An effective case statement for the flag resolution may be "Our citizens need to rally behind our Commander-in-Chief during times of war." This statement offers a thesis that can be debated (during the 2004 elections, in the wake of the war in Iraq, many argued that it was their patriotic duty to oppose a leader who had taken what they believed to be an "unjust action"). In the example offered at the end of the case introductions segment, the third paragraph offers a case statement for the topic "Resolved: The Time is Now." This case statement narrows the focus to the conflict in Iraq and how the affirmative advocates viewing the issue. In a policy debate, the affirmative typically offers a plan of action in lieu of the case statement (though one may choose to offer a case statement in the introduction as well, in order to establish the value foundation that is used to justify the policy that unfolds later in the case) which is discussed more in the "policy resolutions" segment later in this chapter.

Arguing for Different Types of Resolutions

Fact Resolutions. Often, inexperienced debaters greet resolutions of fact as challenges for developing a plan of action to address an unstated need. However, one must realize that factual debates can themselves be stimulating and earth changing (quite literally). For example, it was once a "fact" that the world was flat, but thanks in part to effective advocacy, that "fact" has come to be disproven. This is similar to the burden of an affirmative during a fact resolution, where the affirmative will be challenged to defend the truth of a "fact," or the truth of a "relationship" (remember the relational fact resolution of "Golfing requires a lot of energy" previously discussed). Because a debate on a resolution of fact typically mirrors the standards of a civil trial (determining what the most likely "truth" is), the civil standard of "Balance of Probabilities" often provides the best criterion for determining the victor. "Balance of Probabilities" is used to make factual determination to a degree of probability—in other words, if we view truth on a scale of 0 being absolutely false and 1 being absolutely true, with the balance of probabilities standard, advocates would need to prove their case to be true at a level of.51, or more likely true (Redmayne 1999). In American civil courts, this standard is often referred to as "Preponderance of Evidence." However, because this term is often misconstrued in academic debate as referencing a standard based on quantity (eliminating an evaluative function of quality), the author has chosen to reference the "probabilities" standard here. Indeed, this misconception is not limited to academic debate, but has been improperly construed from the criterion in evaluation of legal standards as well, as Redmayne noted the "evidence" standard "...might be thought to imply that the plaintiff needs to produce more evidence than the defendant, but this interpretation does not appear to have any current support. Indeed, it would be odd if it did, because it would imply that there was some way of quantifying evidence, as opposed to the effect that evidence has on belief" (168).

For a factual resolution that only asserts a factual claim, the affirmative is simply tasked with providing descriptive arguments. For example, with the topic "Resolved: Elvis Presley died of a drug overdose," the affirmative could develop contentions such as: 1) Elvis had multiple drugs in his system at the time of death; 2) many of those drugs were reported to have independently surpassed lethal levels; 3) Except for the ingestion of these drugs, there is not a reason to believe he would have died at such a relatively young age.

For a factual resolution that asserts a relationship, the affirmative must provide both relational and descriptive arguments. For example, the topic "Resolved: that increased ice cream sales leads to more juvenile crime" indicates a causal relationship between the first variable (ice cream sales) and the second variable (juvenile crime rates). With this type of resolution, the affirmative could begin with a descriptive base (i.e., "ice cream contains sugar, which can trigger hyperactivity") and then seek to establish the relationship (i.e., "statistics show that whenever ice cream sales increase, juvenile crime rates increase as well"). One issue the affirmative must be aware of when constructing the relational case is that of a spurious relationship between the two variables (when two variables may change together, but there is not a causal relationship between the two). With the above example, the negative may argue that the relationship is spurious, that ice cream sales typically increase during the summer months, which is also the time that juveniles are not in the school system, and therefore the reason for the increased crime rates is opportunity, not ice cream. Therefore, an effective affirmative must attempt to anticipate when/how a negative may make claims of "spurious relationships" and seek to preempt those during their first constructive speech.

Value Resolutions. Value debates occur at a more complex level of argumentation. Indeed, the prerequisite "facts" are often pivotal to the claim, so effective advocacy for factual claims are necessary to effective argumentation on the resolution of value. The additional layer of advocacy in a value resolution includes a determination of qualities. "Reasoning about whether something is good or bad, better or worse, functional or dysfunctional, beautiful or repulsive—and all other such claims about the qualities of things—is reasoning about values" (Corbett and Eberly 2000, 95). With any type of value claim there is an inherent ambiguity (how does one determine "good" or "beautiful"), and, thus, the evaluative claim must be based upon a criterion. Criteria are perhaps best understood when illustrating the concept through a syllogism. For example, if we look at the syllogism: 1) the bank statement is easy to read, 2) things that are easy to read are good, therefore 3) the bank statement is good, "good" represents our evaluative term and the minor premise ("things that are easy to read are good") represents the criterion in the syllogism (Corbett and Eberly 2000, 98). Of course, one may look at this syllogism and choose to dispute the validity of the criterion (perhaps one could argue that "good" should be determined from an ecological perspective and, therefore, printed statements would not be "good"), so the advocate must not only provide the criterion, but must also be prepared to defend why it provides the ideal mechanism for determining the truth of the value claim. "As the ancient sophists first pointed out, the same wind can feel warm to some people and cool to others. That the same phenomenon is judged differently by different people, different communities, and different cultures should be no surprise. But when reasoners are called upon to make judgments, sometimes ranking or weighting the criteria for evaluation can help reasoning proceed" (Corbett and Eberly 2000, 107).

Value resolutions ask the affirmative to establish a hierarchy of merit, either explicitly or implicitly. At times the hierarchy is determined by the resolution. For example, with the topic "Resolved: that national security is more important than individual liberty," the affirmative would be tasked with proving why national security is of greater importance. At other times the hierarchy is more implicit. For example, with the topic "Resolved: that strengthening our national security would be desirable," the affirmative may again debate the security versus liberty implications, but may also be faced with alternate hierarchical claims such as security versus economic stability, as the issue of "desirability" typically implies a contrast of options.

Ultimately, the value resolution asks the affirmative to establish evaluative arguments in defense of the topic. For example, when debating the topic "Resolved: that reinstituting the draft would not be desirable," the affirmative may argue issues of individual choice, the effectiveness of a volunteer military, political support, etc. Independently one may agree that each of these points is worthy. Since these arguments do not explicitly establish a value hierarchy, the "at the expense of what" question can be established by the negative's argumentation. At that point, it becomes the duty of the affirmative to explain why the issues that s/he advocated are of greater importance than those advocated by the negative. An effective affirmative will seize on this opportunity to shape the debate by answering the obvious objections as a part of their first constructive speech (see previous discussion of preemption in the "usage of preparation time" segment).

In determining the value that one may choose to uphold, or the relationship between values (which are means and which are ends), one may consider the works that others have contributed to the literature. For example, Milton Rokeach developed a listing of instrumental values and terminal values that have been tracked with degrees of applicability to adult Americans through generations. Rokeach's list of "terminal values" provides a range of areas for value advocates to consider; the list includes: a comfortable life, an exciting life, a sense of accomplishment, a world at peace, a world of beauty, equality, family security, freedom, happiness, inner harmony, mature love, national security, pleasure, salvation, self-respect, social recognition, true friendship. and wisdom (Rokeach 1974, 226). Similarly, one may consider the work of Costanza et al. that built upon Maslow's hierarchy of needs to develop a system of measuring quality of life. Costanza et al. advocate that basic human needs include subsistence, reproduction, security, affection, understanding, participation, leisure, spirituality, creativity, identity, and freedom (Costanza et al. 2008). Furthermore, in considering criteria one may become familiar with traditional business evaluative mechanisms like "Cost Benefit Analysis" but may also choose more philosophical foundations such as those that seek universal rules (see Immanuel Kant's deontological perspective), the greatest good for the greatest number of people (see Jeremy Bentham and John Stuart Mill's discussions of utilitarianism) or the establishment of blind justice (see John Rawls' discussion of veil of ignorance). While there is no substitute for seeking an in-depth exploration of these concepts, one website that may be of assistance is "squashed philosophers" (located at http://www.btinternet.com/~glynhughes/squashed/), which provides annotated versions of the works of many philosophers.

Policy Resolutions. Policy resolutions can usually be spotted by their inclusion of agents, actions, and the term "should" within the wording of the resolution. For example, the topic "Resolved: that the United States Federal Government should substantially increase its border control efforts" includes an agent (the United States Federal Government) and an action (increase border control efforts). However, the resolution allows the affirmative the ability to choose her/his specific plan of action (what branch of the government, what efforts, etc.). The term "should" allows debaters to argue the merit of an action as opposed to the possibility of an action actually occurring under the current system. The term "fiat" is used to explain this process of assuming that a plan would be adopted in the manner that an affirmative proposes, so that the focus of the debate can instead be placed upon what *should* happen. Policy resolutions make the affirmative go a step further than value resolutions. While with the value resolution the affirmative ultimately is faced with proving desirability, in a policy resolution the affirmative must not only prove desirability, but must also successfully advocate a course of action.

With a policy resolution, the affirmative must specify a plan that they will advocate during the debate. The plan of action should consist of at least four elements: agent, mandates, enforcement, and funding. The agent is who will be taking the action (the Environmental Protection Agency, the American Red Cross, the United Nations, the Supreme Court, etc.). The mandates are the action that the affirmative is advocating (increasing enforcement of automobile emissions regulations, providing additional aid to hurricane victims, taking action based on the Universal Declaration of Human Rights, declaring the campaign finance reform legislation unconstitutional, etc.). In a majority of policy debate rounds, debaters claim that enforcement (who will enforce the plan and how the plan will be regulated) will be done through "normal means;" however, if the affirmative is proposing a new action they may wish to provide more specific details as to how this will occur (if who/how is not readily clear). Similarly, in most debate rounds it is claimed that funding (where the money will come from to implement the plan) will be done through "normal means," however, there are times when you may wish to specify this information (i.e., to preempt claims of "deficit spending," one may choose to specify that funding for government program X will come by eliminating government program Y or increasing revenue through method Z; or if "pay-go" stipulations are the norm in federal action at the time, then specification of the funding mechanism may be an essential element of the discussion).

In addition to a specific plan of action, the affirmative is charged with developing a slightly different form of argument to support the policy resolution. Here, affirmatives must establish harms, inherency, and solvency. Initially, the affirmative must develop arguments concerning what is problematic in the status quo (or "harms"). Much like the evaluative arguments of a value resolution, these issues can be debated as well (as the old axiom goes: "one person's trash is another person's treasure"). After establishing the harms, the affirmative must explain why the current approaches will not solve the problem (inherency). Inherency positions sometimes appears to be a contradictory argument to an affirmative's thesis (after all, if the current decision makers have determined that this is not a policy worth adopting, why should we choose to adopt this policy?); however, it is essential to establish the need for the plan. For example, if you have a headache and you propose to take an aspirin to solve that headache, immediately after taking that aspirin your headache would not disappear. But, the mere existence of the headache would not justify taking another aspirin because in the status quo you have already done so; you must allow time for the previous plan to take effect (otherwise, one could stand at the medicine cabinet taking aspirin after aspirin ultimately resulting in an overdose). Similarly, inherency arguments are a manner for an affirmative to establish that not only is there a problem, but without the passage of the affirmative plan that problem will continue to exist (and arguing that the status quo has a mechanism in place to fix the problem provides an area for the negative to argue). Finally, the affirmative has a duty to explain how their proposal will remedy the problem (solvency); even if the problem exists and the current system will not remedy the problem, the proposed action is not justified unless it remedies that problem. An additional level that many affirmatives choose to add to their affirmative case is the inclusion of "advantages." While any affirmative that "solves" for the "harms" established can be said to achieve the advantage of eliminating those harms, there may be additional benefits to the plan which can be included as additional "advantages" to the case. For example, if debating the topic "Resolved: that the United States should take action to decrease smog in America's largest cities," an affirmative case that decreases automobile and power plant emissions may be able to solve for harms of smog (such as harming the quality of life for those with respiratory problems), but also claim an additional advantage of taking an action that slows global warming.

Symbolic Resolutions. Symbolic resolutions are those that can be interpreted as representing something more impactful than the general wording of the topic. Here, symbolism is in the eye of the beholder. For example, one may look at the topic "Resolved: that Barbie needs a makeover" and choose to debate the merits of applying blush, lip gloss, and eye-liner to the Mattel doll. However, others may see this as a symbolic resolution and interpret it as being whether or not childhood dolls can affect individuals' perceptions of reality (a fact case); others may see the issue as concerning a debate of feminism versus patriarchy (a value case); and others still may view the topic as representing media portrayals of ideal women and their effect upon women's body image, and thus propose a

136 • *IPDA Textbook*

plan to regulate such portrayals (a policy case). Ultimately, affirmative cases for symbolic resolutions are debated in one of the previously discussed styles (fact, value, or policy), depending on the affirmative's interpretation of the resolution.

CLOSING THE AFFIRMATIVE CONSTRUCTIVE

When developing the structure of the case, work to establish an effective closing for your speech. "Persuasive argument neither comes to an abrupt halt nor trails off in a grab-bag of minor points. The art of rhetoric features what is known as peroration—the conclusion of argument, which is meant to *move* the listener to act on what the preceding argument has logically described. . .The trite phrase 'for all the foregoing reasons' is hopelessly feeble. Say something forceful and vivid to sum up your points" (Scalia and Garner 2008, 37–38). If you have capitalized on the effective thematic introduction at the start of your speech, this closing can provide the opportunity to drive that theme home with your judge(s). Effective affirmatives do not just end because they have run out of time, but they end with a closing that synthesizes their main ideas and clearly establishes why they believe the judge(s) should vote to support their advocacy. Furthermore, remember the old communication axiom that you "can not, not communicate," which simply means that you are constantly sending messages through posture, facial expressions, etc. Plan to exude confidence even once your affirmative constructive has come to a close. After closing the speech and waiting for cross-examination to begin—be conscious of the messages that you are sending during those moments of silence. As Scalia and Garner caution, "to rush from the lectern would suggest that you have not thoroughly enjoyed the experience, an impression you don't wish to convey" (174). Be purposeful in your movement—if you are vacating the lectern, pause for a moment after closing the speech, and then purposefully gather your notes and confidently walk away.

FINAL PREPARATIONS FOR YOUR DEBATE

When crafting the case, it's important to only write bulleted points in your notes. Scalia and Garner advise that you "remember the relationship you're trying to establish," and thus if you are reading significant portions of the presentation it can result in the perception that you are not as familiar with the topic as you should be (181–182). Furthermore, bulleted points are more conducive to adapting to the judge's nonverbal feedback (since your complete phrasing/explanation is not written out, but will be developed as you are delivering your message).

Finally, as your preparation time comes to an end, be sure to leave plenty of time to find your competition room. This can not only be a time for you to calmly reflect on the case that you are about to deliver, but is also essential to an effective presentation. "The proper frame of mind for making an oral argument is calm concentration. A last-minute, frenetic rush. . .isn't conducive to this attitude" (Scalia and Garner 2008, 161). Allow for the fact that you will need time to find the building and/or room that you will be competing in and leave with plenty of time to get there so that you can enter the room calm and confident (just like with the nonverbal impressions after closing your speech, your impression management begins the moment that you enter the room).

Chapter 11: The Affirmative Case • **137**

TIPS FOR THE AFFIRMATIVE

1. Use your topic strikes first to eliminate bias, and second for personal preference.
2. Think of the ideal circumstances for your final speech as you craft your first.
3. Attempt to preempt negative arguments in your first speech.
4. Tailor your delivery style to your judge and the feedback you are receiving.
5. Be sure to define the key terms of the resolution.
6. Use a case introduction to establish the tone for the round.
7. Choose the style of advocacy that is appropriate for the resolution type (fact, value, or policy).
8. Remember the basic structure of an affirmative case:
    *   Case introduction
    *   Definitions
    *   Case statement (may occur at the end of the introduction if it is a simple advocacy thesis)
    *   Criterion/Weighing mechanism (may be implicit when debating a policy resolution, or may be included to clarify the foundation of advocacy)
    *   Observations/Contentions
    *   Closing

KEY TERMS

A Burden of Proof: The responsibility of an advocate to prove any claim statement to be true.

Affirmative: The position of the individual who is designated to uphold a resolution.

Agent: A plan element; agent is the requirement to state "who" will be taking action (as directed by the plan of action).

Balance of Probabilities: A standard for determining truth, where an advocacy that is seen to be more likely true than not is accepted (often referred to as "preponderance of evidence").

Case Introduction: The affirmative's introductory statement that sets the tone for the round, establishes relevance of the topic, and/or establishes meaning.

Case Statement: The thesis statement an affirmative offers when debating resolutions of fact or value.

Connotative Definitions: Connotation goes beyond the literal definition of a term to include the emotional association that one may have with a term (a subjective interpretation).

Contention: A grouping of arguments that support a common singular claim to support an advocate's position. Typically, an affirmative case will contain multiple contentions providing a diverse range of backing for their advocacy.

Criterion: A standard for evaluating a value claim.

Denotative Definitions: The literal definition associated with the term (an objective definition).

Enforcement: A plan element; enforcement is an explanation of who and how a plan will be regulated (as directed by the plan of action).

Fact Resolution: A resolution that asserts a factual claim or a relationship.

Fiat: The idea that debaters should assume that an affirmative plan *would* be adopted in the manner the affirmative proposes, so that the debate can focus on whether it *should* be adopted.

Flow: The process of organized note-taking, where an individual can visually see the progression of arguments throughout the course of a debate.

Funding: A plan element; funding is the requirement to state where the money for implementation will come from (as directed by the plan of action).

Harms: A segment of policy cases; this segment explains what problems are present in the status quo (or may be emerging in the near future).

Inherency: A segment of policy cases; this segment explains why the status quo approach will not be able to solve the harms articulated by the affirmative case.

Mandates: A plan element; mandates are the statement of what action will be taken (as directed by the plan of action).

Negative: The position of the individual who is designated to refute a resolution.

Null-Resolution: The hypothesis that makes the resolution untrue; what the negative attempts to prove. For example, with the resolution "Resolved: that we should tax fatty foods" the null-resolution would be "Resolved: that we should *not* tax fatty foods."

Plan: The course of action an affirmative offers when debating a policy resolution; a plan should include the agency, mandates, funding and enforcement.

Policy Resolution: A resolution that requires the affirmative to advocate a specific plan of action.

Preemption: Attempting to refute an argument before that argument has been made (i.e., the affirmative will try to preempt negative arguments during the first affirmative speech).

Preponderance of Evidence: See "Balance of Probabilities" above

Primacy Effect: When information is judged by the standards established by what is first heard on an issue.

Recency Effect: When information is judged by the standards established by what is last heard on an issue.

Resolution: The topic that will be debated during the round.

Right to Define: A privilege granted to the affirmative, where the affirmative has the first option of providing definitions of the terms within the resolution (as long as they do so "reasonably").

Solvency: A segment of policy cases; this segment explains how the affirmative plan will successfully remedy the harms articulated by the affirmative case.

Strike: During the topic selection process, each side (affirmative and negative) gets the opportunity to eliminate two of the five potential topics. Beginning with the negative, each person eliminates one topic (by "striking" the topic) until only one topic remains.

The Burden of Proof: The responsibility of the affirmative to prove the resolution to be true.

Symbolic Resolution: A resolution that contains language to be interpreted by the individuals in the debate.

Topicality: A common label applied to an argument advanced by a negative speaker who claims that the affirmative case does not uphold the resolution.

Value Resolution: A resolution that asks an affirmative to establish a hierarchy of merit between competing concepts either explicitly (i.e., "Resolved that national security is more important than individual liberty") or implicitly (i.e., "Resolved that improving national security would be desirable").

REFERENCES

Bell, B., and E. Loftus, E. 1975. "Vivid Persuasion in the Courtroom." *Journal of Personality Assessment* 49 (6): 659–664. Retrieved from Academic Search Complete database.

Corbett, E. P. J., and R. A. Eberly. 2000. *The Elements of Reasoning*, 2nd ed. Needham Heights, MA: Allyn & Bacon.

Costanza, R., Fisher, B., Ali, S., Beer, C., Bond, L., Boumans, R., Danigelis, N. L., Dickinson, J., Elliott, C., Farley, J., Elliott Gayer, D., MacDonald Glenn, L., Hudspeth, T. R., Mahoney, D. F., McCahill, L., McIntosh, B., Reed, B., Abu Turab Rizvi, S., Rizzo, D. M., Simpatico, T., and R. Snapp. 2008. "An Integrative Approach to Quality of Life Measurement, Research and Policy." In *Surveys and Perspectives Integrating Environment and Society*. (November 11). Retrieved on March 25, 2009 from www.surv-perspect-integr-environ-soc.net/1/11/2008/

Dennis, M. J. and W. K. Ahn. 2001,. "Primacy in Causal Strength Judgments: The Effect of Initial Evidence for Generative Versus Inhibitory Relationships." *Memory & Cognition* 29 (1): 152–164.

Drake, W. 2008. "A Call to Statesmanship." *Journal of the International Public Debate Association* 2 (1): 3–6.

Freeburg, V. O. 1915. "Debating in the College Curriculum." *The English Journal* 4 (9): 577–581.

Hill, B. and R. W. Leeman. 1997. *The Art and Practice of Argumentation and Debate*. Mountain View, CA: Mayfield Publishing Company.

Lopez, F. J., Shanks, D. R., Almaraz, J. and P. Fernandez. 1998. "Effects of Trial Order on Contingency Judgments: A Comparison of Associative and Probabilistic Contrast Accounts." *Journal of Experimental Psychology: Learning, Memory, & Cognition* 24 (3): 672–694.

McBaine, J. 1944. "Burden of Proofs: Degrees of Belief." *California Law Review* 32 (3): 242–280. Retrieved from Academic Search Complete Database.

McElhaney, J. 2008. "Organizing the Case." *ABA Journal* 94 (12): 24–25. Retrieved from Academic Search Complete database.

Mitchell, J. B. (2000). Why should the prosecutor get the last word? American Journal of Criminal Law, 27, 139–216.

Redmayne, M. 1999. "Standards of Proof in Civil Litigation." *The Modern Law Review* 62 (2): 167–195. Retrieved from JSTOR database.

Rokeach, M. 1974. "Change and Stability in American Value Systems, 1968–1971." *The Public Opinion Quarterly* 38 (2): 222–238. Retrieved from JSTOR database.

Scalia, A. and B. Ganer. 2008. *Making Your Case: The Art of Persuading Judges*. St. Paul, MN: Thomson/West.

Smith, G. H. 1995. "How to Define Your Terms." In *Liberalism, Values & Lincoln-Douglas Debate*, 2nd ed. (pp. 5–7). Houston, TX: The Free Enterprise Institute.

Chapter 12

The Negative Case

Christopher M. Duerringer
California State University: Long Beach

THE ROLE OF THE NEGATIVE IN IPDA

Students are sometimes confused about the obligation of the negative. Despite what some may have guessed, the debater arguing against the affirmative is not required to prove the opposite of the debate proposition. Newcomers may find it helpful to conceptualize the role of the negative much as one understands the job of a defense attorney. When a person is accused of murder, the accused's attorney is not required to prove that the accused *did not* commit the crime; the attorney must only prove that there is not enough evidence to conclude that the accused *did* commit it. In much the same way, negative debaters are tasked with the job of convincing an audience that the affirmative has not provided a case sufficient to warrant a decision in favor of the proposition.

It may also help to understand how the negative helps audiences benefit from the debate. Although academic debate may be primarily valued for its use as a pedagogical tool which prepares students to speak elegantly and think critically, it is also a rare island of public discussion in our frequently top-down media culture. Because the debate round poses the potential to provide an engaging educational opportunity, the negative debater performs the important work of testing the advocacy presented in the round. Skilled negative debaters provide audiences the service of rigorously testing all, or at least the most important, of the arguments provided by the affirmative debater in the round. When done well, this ensures that, no matter the outcome of the debate, audience members leave the round better prepared to think about the question at hand and related questions in the future. The fundamental component of this service, which is the negative's primary obligation, is frequently described as the "burden of clash." In addition, the negative provides additional considerations, which may merit the negation of the resolution, by offering the negative case or the "off case."

Contributed by Christopher M. Duerringer. Copyright © Kendall Hunt Publishing Company

THE BURDEN OF CLASH

While the affirmative is required to meet the burden of proof, negative debaters must uphold the burden of clash. Put simply, the burden of clash requires that the negative debater refute every argument offered by the affirmative. This obligation is central to the negative role in the debate round. negative debaters who fail to uphold the burden of lash cannot claim to have won the debate round. Since the fulfillment of this burden is central to the negative's job, we must consider the ways one could clash or refute affirmative arguments.

REFUTATION TECHNIQUES

To begin, we ought to note that the negative debater must not engage in, and would not have time to engage in, each of these strategies when refuting the affirmative case. It is sufficient to employ any of them to demonstrate the weakness of an argument.

Refute parts of the argument. Many debaters have found the Toulmin model an effective method for organizing arguments. Though this model should not be understood to be the only way to organize arguments, it is widely accepted. According to Stephen Toulmin (1958), common arguments are generally composed of at least three and potentially as many as six parts. Any of these parts may be a target for refutation. Let us consider each option in turn.

Refute the claim. An argument's claim is the component that makes a declarative statement which, if proven, lends credence to the proposition being advocated. If, for example, you are attempting to convince your friend to join you at a newly opened Chinese restaurant, you may make the claim, "They've got the best General Tsao's Chicken in town." Of course, if you truly hope to win your friend's approval, you may have to support this claim with credible evidence that proves that the establishment's chicken is, in fact, the best in town. But every good argument centers upon a claim.

Now, how can one refute a claim? To begin, one can point out a lack of a claim. Sometimes affirmative debaters make the mistake of simply reading off reams of evidence without ever explaining what point such evidence proves. So, negative debaters can start by making sure that the affirmative has provided claims for each argument. Furthermore, make sure that each claim is precise and simple. A claim is precise when it is worded in relatively straightforward and clear language. Of course, one could, if she or he were inclined, make many philosophical arguments about the possibility of perspicuity in a system of representation as obtuse as our language. But, at a minimum, we expect the affirmative to make claims in language that makes sense to the people in the room. A claim is simple when it expresses only one thing about a subject. For example, "The Ford Mustang is a boring design," is a simple claim. "The Ford Mustang is boring and unreliable," is not a simple claim because it conveys two separate ideas about the subject being discussed. negative debaters should make sure to test each of these ideas as separate claims.

Refute the evidence. After evaluating an argument's claim, look next at the evidence offered as its support. If the affirmative failed to provide evidence to support the claim, be sure to point this out. Generally, claims provided without evidence are either truisms or unwarranted assumptions. Unless your opponent happens to be an expert in the field in which the proposition is based, she or he ought to provide evidence to support the claims offered. Furthermore, the evidence provided should be credible, topical, and precise.

When we say that evidence is credible, we mean that it is provided by a trustworthy source, that it conforms to accepted standards of scholarship, and that it provides statements which are probably true.

The question of source trustworthiness has to do with both the source's ability to provide good evidence and also the willingness of the source to provide good evidence. Ability can be determined by examining the source's qualifications. For example, a cardiologist is probably able to provide credible testimony on the subject of heart disease because she or he has received considerable training and is considered an expert in the subject area. Willingness is more often determined by examining the source's motive for providing evidence. A source may be said to be credibly willing if she or he does not stand to benefit from a decision on the issue or if she or he stands to suffer if their opinion is accepted.

The question of adherence to scholarly standards has to do with the way in which the evidence was gathered. Regardless of the genre within which the source is operating, there are likely to be standards which govern proper research. It is the duty of the negative to ensure that the evidence provided conforms to those standards in each case. This is especially true in the case of statistics, which often are casually tossed around in debate rounds.

At a minimum, statistics must be based upon a sufficiently large sample, must be based upon a representative sample, and must be applied to related cases. In other words, to be helpful, a statistic must be a representation of a large enough body of data to be generalizable; taking a survey of three people is probably not a reliable way to understand what the average person thinks. It must also be based upon a group of people who are basically like the people we are talking about; a survey of retirees in an assisted living center, for example, will not provide us a picture of how the average American feels. Even statistics which meet these standards must only be used in appropriate situations.

If nothing else, negative debaters ought to subject each piece of evidence to the following three-pronged test: narrative probability, narrative fidelity, and recency. Narrative probability and fidelity, which are derived from Walter Fisher's (1984; 1989) work, deal with the likelihood of the evidence being true. Recency deals with the temporal link between the evidence and the present. Evidence is said to have narrative probability when the statements contained in the evidence seem likely given everything else we know about the world. That is, considering our understanding of life, the evidence must seem likely to have happened. Narrative fidelity exists when the statements that comprise a piece of evidence support each other. If, on the other hand, parts of the evidence seem to contradict each other, then narrative fidelity does not exist. Finally, evidence possesses the quality of recency if it can be shown to be the product of a relatively recent time. All things being equal, the more recently a piece of evidence was authored, the more likely it is to be accurate.

Refute the warrant. After evaluating the claim and evidence, next consider the argument's warrant. According to Toulmin, the warrant is the link between the evidence and the claim being made. It explains why the evidence offered is proof of the claim being advanced. For example, if someone claims that a certain restaurant is the best Chinese restaurant in town, they may support such a claim with the testimony of a restaurant reviewer who agrees. In order to prove the claim, however, they must also show that this evidence is sufficient to prove the claim. In our example, the arguer must prove that the restaurant reviewer's testimony is a reason to believe the claim that the restaurant is the best in town. Therefore, the warrant might be something like, "Generally speaking, this restaurant reviewer is widely approved as an authority on fine dining."

Obviously, the first avenue of refutation here is to point out the lack of a warrant if the affirmative has not provided one. Next, ask yourself whether or not the warrant is arguable.

144 • *IPDA Textbook*

Is the link between the evidence and the argument obvious or is it less clear? If the link between the argument and the evidence is based upon another expert or witness, can you question that witness's authority?

Refute the backing. If your opponent has not provided very strong evidence or warrants, she or he may feel compelled to add backing. In Toulmin's model, backing consists of additional information which serves to lend extra credibility to evidence or warrants. It frequently occurs in the form of information about the source of a piece of evidence or additional proof that a warrant has been found to be valid. If, for example, the affirmative quotes a Dr. Smith, he or she may provide backing which speaks to Dr. Smith's expertise. Put simply, backing is evidence which supports previously mentioned evidence. As such, you should employ all the aforementioned tests of evidence on these additional pieces of information.

Refute the qualifier. Every argument has, whether explicit or implicit, a qualifier which describes the degree of certainty the arguer has in the argument's conclusions or impacts. When we are certain of the conclusions we draw, we often leave the qualifier unstated. For example, "If you hold your breath for ten days, you will die," does not contain an explicit declaration of certitude; the lack of a qualifier may justifiably be interpreted as a perfect level of certainty. However, other arguments are more nuanced. One might also say, "If you adopt a diet consisting primarily of green vegetables and fresh fruit with only rare indulgences of red meat and dairy, you will probably reduce your cholesterol." In this case, the conclusion has been qualified with the word "probably."

For the negative, the most important step is to highlight the qualifier in each argument. How sure is the affirmative of their conclusions? Does the evidence provided actually afford them that degree of certainty? If you can commit them to a lesser degree of certainty, this provides a great opportunity for refutation. Qualifiers are especially important if the debate is to be judged on the basis of a cost-benefit analysis. Weak qualifiers can diminish the power of even the most impressive benefits or advantages offered by the affirmative: when forced to consider benefits which may never arrive at the price of disadvantages which will almost certainly be incurred, many judges will vote negative. Make sure to force the affirmative to enunciate any qualifications on their conclusions and then work to whittle away at that degree of certainty.

Refute the rebuttal or exception. The final part of an argument, according to Toulmin, is the rebuttal or exception. The rebuttal consists of any other conclusion which might otherwise occur aside from the preferred outcome drawn by the arguer. For example, one might say: "If you eat well, exercise, and treat people well, you will live a long life unless you are struck by lightning." In this case, the possibility of an early lightning-related death serves as the rebuttal. The rebuttal is, thus, a condition upon which the argument may not follow to its conclusion. Unseasoned affirmative debaters may often omit this part of the argument entirely, feeling that disclosing the possibility of unintended outcomes will diminish their case. However, there are typically many contingencies which may prevent a conclusion from occurring. Just as with the qualifier, negative debaters would do well to highlight this aspect of the argument. Has the affirmative offered a rebuttal? Have they been forthcoming in assessing the probability of the rebuttal? Are there even more pressing possibilities which the affirmative has neglected? Take this opportunity to highlight the rebuttal and look for as many possible alternate conclusions as possible.

Refute the impacts of the argument. Perhaps, despite your best efforts, you have been unable to locate a problem in the structure of an argument offered. You may, instead, choose to refute the result of the argument. Ziegelmueller and Kay (1997, 280–281) refer to this tactic as "minimizing." The point is not to deny that the argument is valid but, instead, to argue that the argument is not all that important in the larger scheme of things. For example, if you cannot prove that the affirmative is wrong in claiming that their plan will reduce a problem, perhaps you can argue that the reduction will be so small as to be practically irrelevant. Even if you cannot "minimize" the impacts directly, you may be able to diminish them relatively by "maximizing" the costs or disadvantages of the advocacy.

Turn the argument. Another particularly powerful method of refuting an argument is to "turn" it. One turns an argument by admitting that the argument is valid and then subsequently showing how the opponent's argument is actually a good reason to vote for one's own advocacy. For example, the problem of cost is a frequent attack on policy advocacy. However, we might imagine a way to turn the problem of cost like so: perhaps the high cost of a government policy can be explained as a necessarily infrastructural investment which will not only benefit the general public, but which will employ a great number of citizens and stimulate the economy. Assuming the judge and audience are sold on this line of reasoning, the debater can be said to have "turned" the cost argument in her or his favor. Turns are particularly effective for at least two reasons: first, your opponent has already done the legwork in crafting and delivering the argument; second, some debaters may feel a loss of face if they believe that their own arguments are being used against them.

Pit the arguments against each other. Thus far, we have treated arguments as isolated elements of discourse. However, we can also analyze the connections between arguments in the round. As you consider each argument offered by the affirmative, think about whether the arguments actually make sense together. If you can effectively illustrate that two or more arguments are contradictory, the affirmative will likely feel compelled to choose between them. Imagine, for example, that the affirmative has argued that adopting a plan will eliminate a city's homelessness problem and also provide more funds for the local homeless shelter. A skillful debater may point out that these arguments are contradictory; either the plan will eliminate homelessness and make the homeless shelter redundant, or the homeless shelter will be needed and homelessness will continue to persist in the city. Regardless of which argument she or he chooses, they will have failed to uphold the prima facie case.

Refute stock issues. In any given debate, some concerns repeatedly arise. Particularly in questions of policy, stock issues are important. The most common issues investigated include the following: significance, harms, inherency, topicality, and solvency. The following questions should help you address these issues:

- (Significance) Is the problem significant, in terms of breadth or depth, enough to warrant this action?
- (Harm) Has the affirmative precisely described the problem or harm to be addressed?
- (Inherency) Is it impossible for the status quo to solve the problem without adopting the plan?
- (Topicality) Does the plan directly address the problem?
- (Solvency) Has the affirmative shown that the plan will probably significantly improve or cure the problem?

In a policy round, each of these issues is essential to victory for the affirmative. If the affirmative fails to address any of these issues in the first speech, you may point this out to the judge and, upon these grounds, ask for a decision for the negative.

CONSTRUCTING THE OFF CASE

In addition to refuting the affirmative case, negative debaters may, if time allows, also present a case of their own. This case, frequently called the "off" case consists of additional arguments which suggest a vote against the resolution is appropriate. At a minimum, such an "off" case generally consists of definitions, weighing mechanism, and arguments based on a general approach toward negating the resolution.

Even though the affirmative is granted permission to set the bounds of the debate by offering definitions and weighing mechanisms, negative debaters are advised to prepare some of their own in case the affirmative debater neglects this duty or provides ones which constitute a violation of topicality. So, while these definitions may never be used, it is a worthwhile effort to collect them before the round.

After collecting definitions and an appropriate weighing mechanism, it is often helpful to consider your general approach toward negating the resolution. At the opening of this chapter, we noted that negative debaters are not required to prove the opposite of the resolution. If, for example, the resolution states, "The Ford Mustang is the greatest sports car available," the negative is not required to prove that the Mustang is the worst. The negative is not even required to prove that the Mustang is not the greatest sports car available. The negative is only charged with preventing the affirmative from proving that it is. However, one could achieve this task in a number of different ways. Consider these ideas:

- The negative could argue that there is insufficient evidence to judge which sports car is the best.
- The negative could argue that some other car is the greatest sports car available.
- The negative could argue that the Mustang is not a sports car.
- The negative could argue that the Mustang is tied with several other cars for top ranking.

Each of these broad strategies approaches the resolution differently, focuses upon different words in the resolution, and necessarily suggests different arguments. None of these is necessarily a better angle than the others. This example is instructive insofar as it illustrates the variety of trajectories a negative case might follow.

Now, with your broad strategy in hand, it is time to begin creating arguments in support of this claim. Arguments can be fashioned in any number of ways. Though traditional argumentation textbooks, and judges, have preferred rational models like the one provided by Toulmin, performance and personal narrative are increasingly viewed as legitimate methods of argumentation. Within the relatively normative bounds of the IPDA, however, students are advised to construct arguments on the Toulmin model. At a bare minimum, make sure that each argument makes an assertion related to the broad strategy, and be sure to support that assertion with credible evidence. Try to prepare at least three, but not too many to explain fully during the round.

PUTTING THE OFF CASE INTO ACTION

Despite all your preparation, it is unlikely that all of your negative case will be useful during the round. First, you cannot know how the affirmative will approach the resolution. Some of your arguments may be rendered irrelevant depending upon the affirmative's definitions, weighing mechanism, and arguments. While a bit discouraging, this is simply a part of the game. Unless the affirmative has provided definitions or weighing mechanisms which are simply unfair, it is your obligation to provide refutation under these terms. Second, some of the arguments you prepared for your off case may correspond directly to arguments offered by the affirmative. In this case, these arguments should be used as refutation and not as the off case.

As the round begins, remember your obligation to clash. This must be your first priority. Take careful notes of the affirmative's definitions, weighing mechanisms, and arguments. If you have any questions, be sure to indicate these somehow on your flow sheet. For each argument, quickly consider whether some element in your off case might be used as a direct refutation. If so, apply it to the affirmative case and remove it from the off case. Otherwise, use any of the refutation tactics discussed above to formulate an appropriate rebuttal to the arguments. As you refute each argument, remember the importance of organization. Your arguments, however brilliant, will fall on deaf ears if you fail to be logical, concise, and coherent. When refuting an argument, briefly summarize the affirmative's point, provide your rebuttal, and illustrate the net impact this negation has for the affirmative's case. Presuming you are able to rebut each argument in a timely manner, you may use whatever time is remaining to launch your off case. Clashing the affirmative case, however, is always your priority.

FINAL THOUGHTS

Although much of this chapter has been devoted to the nuts and bolts of debate refutation, it is important to remember that debate ought to prepare us for experiences beyond the academy. Debaters leaving the circuit will find that effective interlocutors must do more than apply jargon and technical ability to the case. And even within debate circles, those who can fuse logic with pathos and ethos are far more successful. Remember that effective negation is more than saying the right things; it is engaging the audience, encouraging them to examine the issues at hand, and fostering the kind of critical attitude which is necessary for the evaluation of important propositions.

REFERENCES

Fisher, W. 1984. "Narration as Human Communication Paradigm." *Communication Monographs*, 51: 1–22.

Fisher, Walter R. 1989. "Clarifying the Narrative Paradigm." *Communication Monographs*, 56: 55–58.

Toulmin, S. 1958. *The Uses of Argument*. Cambridge: University of Cambridge Press.

Ziegelmueller, G. W., and J. Kay. 1997. *Argumentation: Inquiry and Advocacy*. Boston: Allyn and Bacon.

Chapter 12 Sidebar

Preparing for Battle: Negative Sidebar

Anthony McMullen

When it comes to preparing the negative case, there is good news and bad news. The good news is that the burden of proving the resolution is on the affirmative. The negative debater has no affirmative duty to disprove the resolution. Because of this heavy burden, however, the affirmative has the right to define the terms of the debate. This leads into the bad news: As long as these terms are reasonable, the negative debater must be prepared to debate on the affirmative's terms. It is conceivable that a negative debater preparing for the resolution "Hybrids are the future" has to speak intelligently on hybrid food seeds when he or she spent the prep time doing research on hybrid cars.

The best preparation for such cases occurs before the tournament even begins. As liberally educated students, debaters are expected to have at least basic knowledge of a wide range of subjects. In his piece "Only Connect . . . : The Goals of Liberal Education," Professor William Cronon (University of Wisconsin-Madison) writes that one of the ten qualities of a liberally educated person is, "They read and they understand." He elaborates:

This too is ridiculously simple to say but very difficult to achieve, since there are so many ways of reading in our world. Educated people can appreciate not only the front page of the *New York Times* but also the arts section, the sports section, the business section, the science section, and the editorials. They can gain insight from not only THE AMERICAN SCHOLAR and the *New York Review of Books* but also from *Scientific American,* the *Economist,* the *National Enquirer, Vogue,* and *Reader's Digest.* They can enjoy John Milton and John Grisham. But skilled readers know how to read far more than just words. They are moved by what they see in a great art museum and what they hear in a concert hall. They recognize extraordinary athletic achievements; they are engaged by classic and contemporary works of theater and cinema; they find in television a valuable window on popular culture. When they wander through a forest or a wetland or a desert, they can identify the wildlife and interpret the lay of the land. They can glance at a farmer's field and tell the difference between soy beans and alfalfa. They recognize fine craftsmanship, whether by a cabinetmaker or an auto mechanic. And they can surf the World Wide Web. All of these are ways in which the eyes and the ears are attuned to the wonders that make up the human and the natural worlds. None of us can possibly master all these forms of "reading," but educated people should be competent in many of them and curious about all of them. Cronon 1998*

Like the liberally educated people they are, debaters must be well-versed in a variety of topics. This comes though exposure to many different areas of the world. At a minimum, debaters can help themselves by paying more attention to the world around them. Serious debaters should spend, at a minimum, 30 minutes a day reading current events. They should not limit themselves to the front-page stories. Instead, they should take a little from every section, from top stories to world affairs to the business section to entertainment.

Debaters should also fight any cognitive dissonance they may feel. Politically liberal debaters should turn on Fox News on occasion, while politically conservative debaters should turn their radios to their local NPR station every once in a while. Ambitious debaters may even consider international news sources like the BBC. By acquiring different perspectives on "hot-button" topics, they will be more equipped if they find themselves debating an issue with limited prep time.

By being more knowledgeable about the world around him or her, the studious debater is more prepared for skewed interpretation of a topic than the debater who does not take the time to learn more about the world. The studious debater likely may not know more about the topic than the affirmative debater (who actually got to use his or her prep time to research the issue at hand). But at least he or she will be better equipped with the tools necessary to gain the victory in the round.

William J. Cronon, "Only Connect . . . : The Goals of Liberal Education," in *The American Scholar* (Autumn 1998), *available at* http://www.williamcronon.net/writing/Cronon_Only_Connect.pdf.

---

*Reprinted from *The American Scholar*, Volume 67, No. 4, Autumn 1998. Copyright © 1998 by the author.

Chapter 13

Cross-Examination

Robert Alexander
Bossier Parish Community College

> It is little wonder that great reliance is reposed in cross-examination as the "greatest engine ever invented for the discovery of truth," albeit one capable of producing light that may illuminate or blind with equal brilliance. (Birzon 1992, 78)

It is the goal of this chapter to ensure that the reader has the ability to utilize cross-examination for illumination. At times, the focus of public debate may appear to be on the development of dueling cases—with the construction of one's case being their primary concern. However, public debate is an extremely interactive event. Perhaps the greatest level of interaction comes via the direct give and take of cross-examination, where many debates are won or lost on these exchanges.

The most important thing to remember, whether asking or answering questions, is that, like all aspects of debate, cross-examination is about adapting to persuade the judge(s). Pride, anger, frustration, and other sundry factors that could emerge should NEVER dictate our actions; we must always remain in control. Through effective control of cross-examination, we can garner approval of our advocacy. Wellman's classic legal text offers an example that illustrates the power of adaptation:

> A story is told about Scarlett by Justice Wightman, who was leaving his court one day and found himself walking in a crowd alongside a countryman, whom he had seen, day by day, serving as a juryman, and to whom he could not help speaking. Liking the look of the man, and finding that this was the first occasion on which he had been at the court, Judge Wightman asked him what he thought of the leading counsel. "Well," said the countryman, "that lawyer Brougham be a wonderful man, he can talk, he can, but I don't think nowt of lawyer Scarlett."—"Indeed!" exclaimed the judge, "you surprise me, for you have given him all the verdicts."—"Oh, there's nowt in that," was the reply, "he be so lucky, you see, he be always on the right side." (1986, 212)

In addition to the direct exploration of issues and advocacy, in public debate, cross-examination offers a unique opportunity for each speaker. It is during cross-examination that the negative first speaks and thus influences the first impressions of the judge(s). For the affirmative, cross-examination provides the opportunity to combat the negative

---

Contributed by Robert E. "Bob" Alexander. Copyright © Kendall Hunt Publishing Company

time disparity (in individual debates the second affirmative speech is limited to a much shorter duration than the negative's speech which is being answered and in team debate you're establishing a foundation toward the similar time disparity in the First Affirmatives Rebuttal (1AR); through the effective establishment of a foundation in cross-examination, an affirmative can decrease the amount of explanation required in developing his or her arguments in the following affirmative speeches.

It is a common theme that preparation is an essential element of cross-examination (Smith 2001; Easton 2006; Lennard 2001; Valdespino 2004). This preparation includes pre-tournament practice at asking and answering different types of questions, with different types of questioners/respondents. Effective cross is a learned skill, and practice is essential. However, preparation is not limited to pre-tournament activities. As a competitor, one should spend a portion of his or her pre-round preparation time developing potential questions and lines of questioning. As Smith notes ". . .you will lose one of your best opportunities to advance your case (and damage the other party's) if you haven't structured your cross-examination properly from the start" (2001, 22). Of course, because of the fluid nature of debate, one must not limit themselves to pre-round preparation. As Easton notes "careful planning, though necessary, is not sufficient to ensure success. . .listen carefully. . .and make quick, but nonetheless carefully considered, judgments about how to react" (2006, 317). These changes should include additions/adaptations to lines of questioning based on information introduced during your opponent's speech, as well as the information they have provided during the cross-examination, and, perhaps most importantly, to the feedback you and your opponent are receiving from the judge.

GENERAL TIPS

It is important for both questioners and respondents to consider the psychology of judges and the cues that resonate with them. Because of the general populace nature of IPDA judging pools, much of the research into juries can be effectively cross-applied to this genre. For example, Cramer noted that jurors equate professionalism with the perceived level of preparation and they have an expectation that lawyers (or debaters in our case) will speak at appropriate levels, avoiding slang, jargon, and extreme informality (1979).

It is safe to assume that most would expect different stylistic choices for a lawyer questioning a soft-spoken elderly mother as opposed to an alpha personality corporate executive. Issues such as demeanor, attitude, aggressiveness, firmness, and harshness all become variables that are adjusted for this situation (Starr and Foster 2001, 154). While this initial distinction is often clear, there are other concerns to consider when establishing the appropriate level of assertiveness in cross-examination.

The eyes have it: non-verbal considerations. Brodsky noted that, because eye contact is associated with increased credibility, trial advocacy instructors often teach law students ways to keep witnesses from making eye contact with jurors by blocking and/or attempting to draw eye contact in a different direction (1997, 143). For debaters, this illustrates a key concept: focus your eyes on the judge(s). It's often tempting to look at the person who you are questioning or being questioned by, but debaters should remember that the purpose is to convince the adjudicators and thus focus their eye contact accordingly. This focus upon the judge(s) does not necessitate exclusive focus upon them as this extreme

Chapter 13: Cross-Examination • **153**

focus could result in a counterproductive appearance of insincerity. Instead, for example, respondents should briefly visually acknowledge the questioner when beginning to answer a question, and then turn to the judge(s), occasionally making eye contact with others in the room—while remembering to focus a majority of the time on the judge(s) (Brodsky 1997, 144–145).

"When something terrible happens, the most important thing for you to do is to avoid showing that something terrible just happened" (Easton 2006, 318). As important as what we say, is how we say it. For example, studies have shown that audience perceptions of truthfulness during cross-examination are nearly identical when audiences are shown the responses with video only (no audio) and when audiences are shown video and audio together (Kerr and Bray 1982, 171). In other words, as advocates, we must express our passion not just with our voices, but with our bodies as well; and, when responding to questions, we must remain poised and nonverbally assertive. Additionally, some characteristics often associated with communication apprehension are often interpreted as deception cues (and the reverse is interpreted as credibility enhancers), such as excessive gestures (as opposed to purposeful gestures), shifting posture, blinking and/or shaking (as opposed to moderate relaxation), slower than usual rate of delivery when responding (as opposed to a slightly faster rate), and increased disfluencies (as opposed to clarity, more intonation, and pitch variety) (Kerr and Bray 1982, 172–177). Because many of these deception cue behaviors can be caused by anxiety, one can address these concerns through implementation of standard methods for curbing communication apprehension (positive visualization, muscle tension, practice, etc.). Ultimately, our aim should be to ensure that our nonverbal messages are conveying our intended messages.

ASKING THE RIGHT QUESTIONS

The Cordial Questioner.
Scarlett would take those he had to examine, as it were by the hand, made them his friends, entered into familiar conversation with them, encouraged them to tell him what would best answer his purpose, and thus secured a victory without appearing to commence a conflict (Wellman 1986, 211–212).

It is easy to fall into a trap of viewing cross-examination as an extreme adversarial interaction, in which the questioner focuses his or her will upon the respondent. After all, popular television courtroom dramas frequently focus upon the browbeating attorney who accuses and shouts at witnesses ultimately gaining the confession or information necessary to win the case. However, in most circumstances, this form of cross-examination is ultimately counterproductive.

Initially, let us evaluate the benefits of cordial cross-examination from the point of view of the respondent. During the cross-examination period, respondents are faced with the uncertainty of subject areas or questions to be raised coupled with the concern that giving the "wrong-answer" could ultimately destroy their case. These concerns alone are enough to generate a sense of anxiety. When you combine the aforementioned concerns with a hostile examiner, the propensity for generating overly defensive responses dramatically increases. On the contrary, a cordial questioner can help to put the respondent at ease, which ultimately can aid the questioner in getting the answers that he or she wants

154 • *IPDA Textbook*

(Wellman 1986, 10–11; Matlon 1988, 225). As the old axiom goes: "You can attract more flies with honey."

> By their shouting, browbeating style they often confuse the wits of the witness, it is true; but they fail to discredit him with the jury. On the contrary, they elicit sympathy for the witness they are attacking, and little realize that their "vigorous cross-examination," at the end of which they sit down with evident self-satisfaction, has only served to close effectually the mind of at least one fair-minded juryman against their side of the case. . . (Wellman 1986, 10–11)

Beyond relaxing your opponent, a cordial style offers the opportunity to appeal to the judge(s). Studies have shown that juries (or judges in our case) are more apt to empathize with the person being attacked in cross-examination (Matlon 1988, 243; Starr and Foster 2001, 158). These attacks are not just hitting your opponent, but the judge can often see himself or herself being victimized by these attacks as well (clearly not the best way to gain favor). In a study of simulated juries, Gibbs et al. found that authority and power were associated with persuasiveness (meaning that questioners should maintain control, but through cordial means), but that likeability strongly correlated with persuasiveness. The study concluded that, in general, nonhostile questions were more effective than hostile questions when all other variables are equal (1989). In short, it is your opportunity to ask questions, and you should remain in command; but, if one can maintain this power balanced with cordiality, they will achieve the highest level of effectiveness.

> Next comes the Lowest Common Denominator. This landmine typically goes off when you let Mongo conduct the cross-examination. You know Mongo—your inner beast, the one in charge of fighting, feeding, and fleeing. He also has no sense of humor and when aroused, no sense of proportion.. . .When Mongo tries to make a big deal over something that really doesn't matter, everyone thinks, "Is that the best you can do?" And that thought pulls the rest of your cross-examination down with it (McElhaney 2000, 69).

Part of the success of the cordial questioner is the suppression of "Mongo" (not overdramatizing issues). Another tendency that often arises among inexperienced questioners is the desire to utilize the silver-bullet question that forces the opposition to admit that their advocacy is 100 percent wrong (think courtroom TV drama: "After all, you did kill the victim didn't you? Yes, yes, I did it, I'm sorry!"). In the real world, the response to such questions is seldom, if ever, the one desired by this form of inquiry. Here too is an example where less can be more. When levying the killer question, pragmatically (assuming one does not get that one-in-a-million confession), one of two scenarios arises: the question immunizes the opposition against the questioner's strongest line of argument or the questioner unwittingly falls into a trap laid by the respondent.

Immunization occurs when the questioner allows his or her main arguments to be answered before he or she has the chance to develop them. Matlon describes this concept as "inoculation by two-sided argument." Matlon explains that ". . .subjects who (initially) hear two-sided arguments are less persuaded. . .than those who initially hear a one-sided argument" (1988, 230). In other words, by introducing the issue directly during cross-examination, you give your opponent a chance to raise doubts and thus significantly increase your own burden of proof. On the contrary, first raising your central theme during your speech affords you the opportunity to fully develop your argument and to let that argument resonate with the judge(s) before your opposition must mount the uphill charge to refute your claims. In short, you're better off not directly introducing your central theme during cross.

Beyond the potential for neutralization established in the previous paragraph, levying the killer question could place the questioner into a well-laid trap. McElhaney (2000) uses the metaphor of a mousetrap and encourages questioners not to be lured by the cheese. McElhaney explains that often that "too good to be true" hole in your opposition's case was intentionally presented in that fashion to encourage you to focus your questions in this area (and away from potentially weaker areas). Once questioned, the response is clear, justified, and irrefutable—and now this area, which you have established by your questioning as an area of prominence, has been succinctly turned against you. Once you've seen the trap—it's too late (2000, 68). When reading this, one may think "with this possibility of a trap is there any area that I can question?" The author's advocacy is not that one should avoid questioning areas that appear weak, but that you should tread lightly (so as to avoid springing the trap). If questions (but not the "killer questions" that inherently establish prominence) are pursued in a cautious manner, you can get all the cheese that has been left unguarded while backing away from the baited traps. In general, the advice is not to fall into the common mistake of trying to do too much. "You simply have to recognize there are limitations to what you can do on cross; there are only certain things you can accomplish. . .it only takes one line of cross to destroy your entire cross-examination impact (Starr and Foster 2001, 161)." On another level, one should consider how to react when one receives an unanticipated admission. Wilcox (2010) noted that occasionally you may receive a gift in the form of an admission of weakness during cross-examination; when facing this situation, skilled questioners will switch to another line of questioning or perhaps end the cross-examination at that time (as a failure to do so may give the respondent the opportunity to explain their way out of the answer).

Additionally, there is an often expressed notion that one should maintain control of cross by "cutting off" a respondent who is providing an undesirable answer. While this may be necessary from a pragmatic standpoint (because of the time constraints of the cross-examination period in academic debate), it should by no means be the rule. Not only does this tactic risk violating the cordial questioner practice, but it also risks highlighting an answer that otherwise could have been buried within the cross-examination. As McElhaney notes "if you think about it, trying to cut off the witness draws a lot of attention to the answer you do not like" (1994, 96).

Questioning for Clarification. Another purpose of cross-examination is to clarify issues. Sometimes you may be seeking honest clarification for yourself (perhaps the speech was difficult to flow or you simply may want to ensure that you have not missed any of the main points). At other times you may be seeking clarification for the judge (either to ensure that they have the same arguments on their flow or to pin down the respondent's advocacy to protect against any shifts that could be made later in the debate). The first maxim for questioning to clarify is to avoid long-winded summarizations of your own advocacy. Inexperienced debaters often feel the need to restate much of their initial argument followed by an "isn't that right" style of question. Not only does this eat up much of your question time, but it invites an equally long response that can exhaust whatever time remains. Simply put, ask short questions with a goal of inviting short answers.

Setting the Trap.
Much depends upon the sequence in which one conducts the cross-examination...You should never hazard the important question until you have laid the foundation for it. . . (Wellman 1986, 115)

The literature concerning cross-examination consistently explains the potential pitfalls of open-ended questions, and generally suggests that one should primarily ask closed-ended (i.e. "yes" or "no") questions in order to maintain control (Matlon 1988; Easton 2006). However, the most effective use of closed- and open-ended questions can be when the two are sequenced so that the closed-ended questions trap one's opponent and then the open-ended questions are used to emphasize the dilemma. For example, witness the following line of questioning:

Q: "Your plan calls for a $.50 raise in the minimum wage to help address cost of living, is that correct?"
A: "Yes."
Q: "If this is desirable, then would a $1 increase be desirable?"
A: "Well, yes, I guess."
Q: "What about a $2 increase?"
A: "Yes, that would be good too."
Q: "How about a $10 increase?"
A: "No."
Q: "Why not?"

In this example, the trap is sprung and with the open-ended "why not" question, the respondent is placed into a position where he or she will be explaining that at some level a minimum wage increase is no longer desirable. Accordingly, the questioner's burden will be decreased when his or her speech begins (he or she can reference the respondent's admission from cross-examination, and now no longer has the burden to prove that increasing the minimum wage could be a bad idea, but just that the level at which his or her opponent is suggesting an increase is a bad idea).

Of course, the answer given to your open-ended question may not always be the one you anticipated (undoubtedly, you have seen politicians and/or debaters who are very skilled at avoiding questions). The general idea is to lay the foundation so that the answer given is "the only answer that can rationally be given" (Birzon 1992, 78). If your opponent chooses to answer the question in an irrational manner, do not be dismayed. Recall the earlier advice about adaptation (this is for the judge(s) benefit—not the self-satisfaction of the questioner). If the foundation has been properly laid, the judge(s) will be following along with you, and they will have arrived at the rational answer on their own. Accordingly, with an appropriate reference to the line of questioning during your next speech, you can capitalize upon this rational answer (even though it may not have been explicitly given during the cross-examination). Ultimately, this type of questioning contradicts the maxim of "don't ask a question you don't know the answer to," but it is with a cautious caveat. That stipulation is "analogous to 'the fork' in chess—that's when one piece of yours threatens two of your opponent's. He can only save one by sacrificing the other. When you've got the witness in that situation, you don't care what he says. Either way, you're ahead" (McElhaney 1994, 96).

In almost every trial there are circumstances which at first may appear light, valueless, even disconnected, but which, if skillfully handled, become united together and at last form wedges which drive conviction into the mind. This is obviously the business of the cross-examiner (Wellman 1986, 169).

Wellman's timeless maxim illustrates another effective method to trap the opponent: sometimes cross-examination involves careful misdirection in order to bait the trap. One option is to capitalize on an opponent's desire to be proven right (McElhaney 1999, 78–79). For example, one may seek guised "clarification" as follows:

Q – So just to clarify, your first response to my Johnson evidence was that it should not be considered because the evidence was conclusionary. Is that right?
A – Yes, it's flawed because it only provides assertions and not reasons.

When done effectively, the questioner can use his or her next speech then to explain how the respondent's answers also indict his or her own evidence. At other times, the misdirection can occur at a substantive level. For example, assume your opponent's advocacy was that the US should abandon the war on terror, because the war cannot be won; you may choose to address an issue that shares a common foundation:

Q – Should we continue prosecuting murder?
A – Yes.
Q – Why?

During application in the following speech, you could then reference this line of questioning and explain that it is analogous: "While we cannot stop all murder, to stop prosecuting would both send the wrong message as well as likely exacerbate the problem, similar to the war on terror. Accordingly, just because we cannot achieve a conventional 'victory' is not sufficient reason to abandon the efforts."

Dealing with different types of respondents. Cross-examination can often seem to be a frustrating endeavor, especially when dealing with difficult respondents. However, as a questioner one should come to expect these challenges (because of the inherent adversarial nature of debate) and welcome them (because the "difficult" respondent can be a blessing in disguise). Regardless of the type of respondent, the most important aspect to remember is that through cross you are given the opportunity to create "your side of the story" and to that extent your credibility is key (McElhaney 1997, 82). To that extent, maintaining a controlled and balanced demeanor helps to enhance one's case (especially when contrasted by the difficult respondent). For example, McElhaney notes that when dealing with the evasive witness, if you lose your self-control and begin to argue with the respondent, you not only lose the opportunity to demonstrate that you are the better source of information, but also risk justifying what your opponent says (and having your advocacy lost in the shuffle) (McElhaney 1997, 82). Furthermore, one should not allow previous competitions with a respondent to force them into a demeanor that alienates the judge. For example, perhaps you are facing a debater who has a tendency to become evasive—you should not then initiate your cross-examination immediately in an overly constrictive mode as doing so could establish sympathy for your opponent from your judge(s). "You can find a way to expose his antagonistic side, but do so politely. If you treat this witness with hostility or contempt, the jurors won't feel angry at him, they'll feel sorry for him" (Wilcox 2009, 6).

Before determining the type of respondent you are facing, the first step is determining the way in which you plan to treat the respondent. Based upon your opponent's speech, you should determine if your effort would better be served through tearing down your

158 • IPDA Textbook

opponent's advocacy through cross (destructive mode) or ignoring parts of their case and instead seeking confirmation of your points (constructive mode) (Starr and Foster 2001, 153). This choice will guide your goal(s) and thus your line(s) of questioning.

Born a rambling man. The first type of respondent is the one who insists on turning answers into monologues. The first line for addressing this issue is to preempt rambling answers through the type of questions asked. McElhaney suggests that one ask "short, simple statements of fact. . .(that) invite not comment but 'yes' or 'no'" (1997, 82). These types of questions result in one of two outcomes—either the respondent complies (and your goal of preempting a monologue has been achieved) or the opponent launches into a story in spite of your effort. In the event that your opponent chooses to respond with a narrative, at first gently request a more direct response to the question (for multiple offenses, a strategy of constriction will be discussed later in this segment). In general, your poised request will serve to illustrate the respondent's evasiveness, which can serve as a plus with your judge(s).

At other times you may be faced with the respondent who distorts evidence, argument, and/or analysis. Here, the first step (before directly asking questions on the areas of importance you plan to address) is to clearly illustrate to the judge this respondent's penchant for distortion. Begin by asking a question to which the answer should be clear to the judge and simply allow the respondent's tendency for twisting the facts to expose itself. Now that your opponent's credibility has been compromised, you can move into the murkier waters with the assurance that the judge has at least concluded that previous answers have been distorted; and, with your artful handling, he or she will reach a similar conclusion for these issues as well (Starr and Foster 2001).

Whether the rambler or the twister, once a respondent shows a pattern of outrageous statements, they invite a more constricting cross-examination (Starr and Foster 2001, 159). Questions that may have previously been perceived as unfair or too narrow can now be asked (as you will have laid the groundwork for their necessity through the handling of your initial questions). Of course, depending on the nonverbal implications (earlier discussions of judge feedback, assertiveness, etc.) you should evaluate the proper tone for these questions.

All the right answers, just not to your questions.

Then comes the nonresponsive answer, which is usually argumentative as well. That's when Mongo taps you on the shoulder and offers to kill the witness. Tell Mongo to sit back and watch. You are going to have some fun (McElhaney 1997, 83).

The nonresponsive "respondent" (one who willingly gives answers, but not to the questions you're asking) can occasionally engage questioners in an exasperating dance—you step forward with a question and they step away with an answer. The first key to remember is that (assuming your question was clear) they have specifically chosen not to answer your question. In this circumstance, you are likely on to something, so do not back away now. Here too is an opportunity to demonstrate your poise and control while illustrating your opponent's evasiveness. For example:

Q – You're advocating that we pull all troops out of the Middle East by the end of the year, is that correct?

A – Violence is increasing and this is clearly a war we cannot win.

Q – I'm sorry, what I was asking was if you're advocating an end of the year withdrawal. Are you?

A – The region is spiraling toward internal war.

Q – Is there a reason why you will not answer my question about your end of the year deadline for withdrawal?

For this example, note a couple of things. First, the questioner restates the question three times so that it is prominent in the judge's mind. Second, the questioner is politely seeking his or her answer. Let the respondent squirm, but ensure that it is the respondent's behavior that is highlighted and not an overaggressive response of the questioner. In sum, the first goal for this type of respondent is to not move on to additional lines of questioning until you have received an answer to your question (Lennard 2001). The second goal is to illustrate the respondent's lack of responsiveness.

I Completely Disagree – The Reactionary Denier. There are a host of other types of respondents that one may encounter. At times, one may encounter the reactionary denier—the individual who instinctively negates whatever assertions are implicit within the questioner's probe. The respondent who repeatedly engages in knee-jerk denial of all questions will diminish his or her credibility as it becomes obvious that they are not truly evaluating and responding to questions, but simply reacting with opposition to the inquiries (Brodsky 1997, 130–131). An additional strategy for dealing with these types of respondents is to use their own tendency against them. For example, were a negative questioning an automatic denier style of affirmative speaker who was charged with defending the resolution "The minimum wage should be increased," the negative may offer a guised question such as "Wouldn't increasing the take-home pay for entry-level workers be a better solution?" If the exchange is handled skillfully, the questioner may be able to trap this reactionary respondent into explaining why his or her own advocacy is flawed—and later use the respondent's own words against him or her.

GENERAL TIPS

Reiteration. Replication. Reverberation. The first tip for wording choices is the simple reminder that through repetition of key ideas, we increase the odds that a judge will remember these segments. While we often consider this tool during speech making, frequently debaters fail to take advantage of the same tool during cross. One way that repetition can be worked into cross is through the loop-back question. "A question that includes the prior answer. . .is a way of emphasizing favorable and important witness information" (Matlon 1988, 227–226). The caveat to this advice is that "key words in vital answers should be used in subsequent questions. . .however, repeating all or some part of every answer, regardless of its importance, minimizes the effectiveness of an examination" (Matlon 1988, 246).

Another tip on wording involves the language choice. Usage of definite articles and strong verbs can enhance the level of judge expectation regarding answers. Studies have shown that implicative questions using definite articles ("could X be *the* cause") create twice the level of expected affirmation as contrasted with indefinite articles ("could X be *a* cause") (Matlon 1988, 228). Similar studies have shown that employing stronger verbiage influences mental image as well. For example, one group "was asked to estimate the speed of one vehicle.

160 • *IPDA Textbook*

Those who were asked, 'How fast was the yellow car going when it *smashed* into the other car?' averaged 40.8 miles per hour; those who were asked, 'How fast was the yellow car going when it *hit* the other car?' averaged 34 miles per hour" (Matlon 1988, 228). In other words, employing these wording techniques can subtly enhance the judge's expectation of a given response and thus help to implicitly sway them to your side (your opponent's answer is important with consideration of the previous concerns addressed in this chapter; but, all things equal, this benefit accrues regardless of the answer provided by your opponent).

Giving the Right Answers.

"When the time is right to disagree with cross-examination questions, do so with strength, clarity, and conviction" (Brodsky 1997, 131).

When answering a question, let the judge(s) know where you stand on the issue. You will need to demonstrate confidence in your answers and avoid being intimidated by the questioner. Part of that confidence includes a willingness to admit when you do not know the answer. Respondents sometimes fear that this type of admission could be a fatal mistake; however, it is preferable to the hazards associated with making up the answer. As Boyce noted, ". . .the penalty for not having an answer at your fingertips is less severe than the penalty for trying to fake it, getting caught, and giving the court an opportunity to bat you around like a cat playing with a ball of yarn" (Scalia and Ganer 2008, 193).

When answering, be sure to bring up the high points from your first speech. It is important to emphasize what you have said and remind the judge(s) of what you are advocating. This advocacy requires direct confrontation of the questions being asked; even a question that threatens a vulnerability in your advocacy provides an opportunity (you have the chance to sell your side of the story before the counterargument is fully expressed). "Don't run away from difficulties. Acknowledge and neutralize them" (Scalia and Ganer 2008, 199). That being said, when questions themselves are faulty, the respondent should point out the flaw in a question rather than simply providing what they feel could be a justifiable answer. For example, sometimes you may be placed into a false dilemma (a forced "either-or" situation where other choices exist); when faced with the false dilemma, a skilled respondent will point out that the issue is not as simple as a "yes or no" or "choice A or B" and then highlight the complexity and the other options that exist. Additionally, a questioner may pose a hypothetical scenario –before answering a hypothetical scenario, a skilled respondent should point out the hypothetical nature and discount the value of the speculative question versus the concrete analysis of scenarios that have actually occurred. Other times, you may be faced with questions that are tautological in nature (a question that uses circular logic), the "non-question" (where a questioner seeks to make statements rather than providing a direct question), or a host of other potential flaws; regardless of the flaw, it is best to point out the flaws in the question before providing any type of answer, so that one's answers are not easily misconstrued.

CLOSING

The cross-examination period in an academic debate is an extremely short period of time; it necessitates proper planning and strategy as well as a limited focus on the most vital areas. The most important aspect to remember about each and every one of the maxims espoused in this chapter is that these "rules" are by no means absolute. When considering the cross-examination period and the "rules" associated with it, you should engage in a cost-benefit calculation. "Janis Joplin used to sing, 'Freedom's just another word for nothing left to lose.' When you've got nothing to lose, break the rules and risk the home run" (McElhaney 1994, 95). Put another way, do not allow yourself to develop a one-size-fits-all approach to cross; "the experienced examiner, like a baseball pitcher, relies upon a change of pace to suit the varying conditions in the game" (Matlon 1988, 242).

SUGGESTED ACTIVITIES FOR FURTHER PRACTICE

After having discussed the elements of cross-examination, here is an exercise that can be done to help debaters internalize the principles of cross-examination. Take a pro/con brief from a website like IDEA's debatabase (http://www.idebate.org/debatabase/topic_index. php) and assign the debater(s) to be either affirmative or negative on a given topic. If they are assigned to be affirmative, have them first read through the arguments that are listed for the affirmative and assume that these are the justifications that they decided upon during preparation time—now craft a series of questions based upon anticipated negative responses; then allow the debater(s) assigned to be affirmative to read arguments listed for the negative and assume that those were the responses provided during the negative constructive, and determine additional lines of cross-examination based upon these responses. Similarly, for the negative, have them first read the negative arguments and construct set-up lines of cross-examination; and then read through the affirmative arguments with the assumption that these were the arguments presented by the affirmative constructive, and then construct additional lines of cross-examination based upon these questions.

When first engaging in this exercise, allow 10 to 15 minutes for preparation of these lines of cross-examination (while this is much more time than debaters will spend during actual preparation, it helps to illustrate the value of forethought and develops better questions). During additional practice sessions, limit preparation to a shorter period of time, so that it generates a more realistic simulation of an actual debate. If you have multiple competitors, having them prepare these lines of cross-examination in small groups can aid in understanding for each competitor by integrating an aspect of peer-teaching and learning as well.

Once the questions have been generated, have the competitors engage in a cross-examination. If you have multiple students present, you may choose to have them engage in a cyclical cross-examination (where one questioner will ask questions until he or she has run out of questions, and then they will yield the floor to the next questioner, and this process will continue until all questions have been asked—meaning that some may think of new questions once they have yielded the floor, and are free to get back in line to ask those questions once others have completed their turn). Similarly, the respondents should be rotated, either every couple of minutes or every few questions. Once the negative has completed their questioning, the affirmative then should follow the same process in the role of questioner. Similar to preparation time, the first time that you do this exercise, do not impose a time limit; instead, encourage the full exploration of potential lines of questioning, but in future exercises, begin limiting the competitors to the amount of time that they will actually have in a debate (to simulate a real debate round).

General areas to remind the competitors of during the preparation phase:

- Negatives – Remember to set up the arguments that you are going to make.
- Affirmatives – Remember to re-establish the validity of your initial points.
- Both sides – Develop a closed-ended trap coupled with an open-ended follow-up.
- Both sides – Develop questions to pin down the opponent's advocacy.
- Both sides – Develop a misdirection trap to question the underlying assumptions.

KEY TERMS

Constructive mode: Seeking affirmation of one's own points during cross-examination.

Destructive mode: Attempting to tear down your opponent's advocacy during cross-examination.

Immunization: When a questioner allows his or her main arguments to be answered before he or she has the chance to develop them.

Line of questioning: A series of questions focused on a single subject area and/or with the goal of receiving a specific answer from a respondent.

Loop-back question: A question that includes a prior answer of the respondent; used as a method to emphasize favorable and important information.

Sequencing: Establishing questions in a purposeful pattern to meet the goals of the questioner.

Trap: A line of questioning that backs a respondent into a position where he or she is left with only one logical answer; or, a strong area of a respondent's advocacy that is disguised as an apparent area of weakness with the goal of having the questioner establish this as an area of prominence for the judge and/or taking focus away from weaker areas.

REFERENCES

Birzon, P. I. 1992. "The Perfect Question: Setting the Trap in Cross-Examination." *ABA Journal* 78 (7): 78.

Brodsky, S. L. 1997. *Testifying in Court: Guidelines and Maxims for the Expert Witness.* Washington, DC: American Psychological Association.

Cramer, M. M. 1979. "A View from the Jury Box." *Litigation* 28 (1): 3–4, 65–66.

Easton, S. D. 2006. "Toto, I Have a Feeling We're not in Kansas Anymore: Using the Wizard of Oz to Introduce Students to the Skills of Witness Examination. *Clinical Law Review* 12: 283.

Gibbs, M., Sigal, J., Adams, B., and B. Grossman. 1989. "Cross-Examination of the Expert Witness: Do Hostile Tactics Affect Impressions of a Simulated Jury?" *Behavioral Sciences & the Law* 7 (2): 275–281.

Kerr, N. L. and R. M. Bray (Eds.). 1982. *The Psychology of the Courtroom.* New York: Academic Press.

Lennard, B. 2001. "Practice Pointers on Cross-Examining the Accused in a Court-Martial." *Reporter* 28 (1): 3.

Matlon, R. J. 1988. *Communication in the Legal Process.* New York: Holt, Rinehart and Winston, Inc.

McElhaney, J. W. 2000. "The Cross-Exam Minefield: Recognize the Traps, then Step Lightly to Avoid Them." *ABA Journal* 86 (12): 68–69.

McElhaney, J. W. 1999. "Misdirect, then Pounce: Don't Always Let Witnesses Know Where You Are Taking Them." *ABA Journal* 85 (8): 78–79.

McElhaney, J. W. 1997. "Evasive Witnesses: Use Cross-Examination to Tell Your Side of the Case. *ABA Journal* 83 (10): 82–83.

McElhaney, J. W. 1994. "Breaking the Rules of Cross: Fast Thinking Will Lift Inquiry beyond Mediocrity." *ABA Journal* 80 (4): 95–96.

Nelson, E. L. 2003. "Testimonial Minefield: An Overview of Interrogation Techniques Utilized by Attorneys during Adversarial Questioning and Cross-Examination." *Issues in Child Abuse Accusations* 13 (2): 30–44.

Scalia, A. and B. Ganer. 2008. *Making Your Case: The Art of Persuading Judges.* St. Paul, MN: Thomson/West.

Smith, M. 2001. "The Best Case Scenario." *People Management* (October 11): 21–22.

Starr, V., and J. Foster. 2001. "Making Out, Not Messing Up, on Cross-Examination of a Key Witness." *Trial Lawyer* 24 (3): 153.

Taylor, K. P., Buchanan, R. W., and D. U. Stawn. 1984. *Communication Strategies for Trial Attorneys.* Glenview, IL: Scott, Foresman and Company.

Valdespino, J. M. 2004. "Cross-Examination: The Rules of the Game." *American Journal of Family Law* 18 (2): 87–92.

Wellman, F. L. 1986. *The Art of Cross Examination.* Washington DC: American Psychological Association.

Wilcox, E. 2009. *The Ten Critical Mistakes that Trial Lawyers Make (And How to Avoid Them!).* Orlando, FL: Trial Theater, LLC.

Wilcox, E. 2010. "Are You Asking Too Many Questions during Cross-Examination?: In *Trial Theater: Archive for Cross Examination.* (March 12). Retrieved April 14, 2010, from http://www.trialtheater. com/wordpress/category/cross-examination/

Chapter 13 Sidebar

Whose Cross-Examination Is This Anyway?

Anthony McMullen

University of Central Arkansas

In any IPDA debate, both debaters have 13 minutes to make their point. For 11 of the 13 minutes (the constructive and rebuttal speeches), the debater has the full attention of the judge. For two of those minutes, however, the debater has to share the stage with his or her opponent and engage in cross-examination. When this time is used effectively, a debater can use concessions from his or her opponent to win the case. When used ineffectively, however, a debater allows his or her opponent additional time to bolster his or her case.

Sometimes, a debater will give up control of the cross-examination by asking open-ended questions without considering the scope of the response. For example, when a debater wishes to clarify an opponent's points, he or she may ask, "Can you repeat your first point again?" Anyone asked this question should jump for joy, as it allows him or her to repeat part of his or her entire case (maybe not a full recitation, but still invaluable time to present before the judge). Debaters should pay sufficient attention to his or her opponent's speech so that a clarification question is unnecessary. Inevitably, however, the clarification question must be asked. In those cases, the questions should be narrowly tailored to get the information necessary for the clarification.

Inexperienced debaters may feel compelled to ask questions. Therefore, to show that they can ask questions, some will simply ask their opponent to restate their points ("give the tag lines") and sit down. While this is not as bad as the situation previously described (and may sometimes be necessary to properly ensure that every adverse point is addressed), it is yet another example of giving away control of the cross-examination. True, judges award speakers points, in part, based on the effective use of cross-examination. But an ineffective cross-examination can be worse than no cross-examination at all.

Finally, some cross-examinations simply devolve into the debaters going back and forth with their own statements. Not only is that the antithesis of a cross-examination, it is the type of behavior that supporters of this activity seek to avoid. In its worst form, the debater starts answering questions from his or her opponent, ultimately shifting the cross-examination from one debater to another and giving that person extra time to make his or her point.

Many of the techniques described in the text are designed to allow the questioner to control his or her opponent to the extent possible. These techniques are very effective when followed. At the end of the day, the debater must realize that his or her cross-examination period does not belong to the opponent. It is an additional two minutes that, if used properly, can spell the difference between persuading the judge and losing the debate.

Contributed by Anthony L. McMullen. Copyright © Kendall Hunt Publishing Company

CPSIA information can be obtained
at www.ICGtesting.com
Printed in the USA
FFHW011545090819
54163843-59867FF